CW01498309

ABOUT THE AUTHOR

Andrew Macalpine worked for thirty five years as a teacher and headteacher in some of London's most disadvantaged secondary schools. He went from grappling with the challenges of a tough boys' school in Somers Town at the start of his career to taking responsibility for the opening of a new secondary school in Barnet, before ending his career as an adviser to the government on improvements to secondary education in London. His book isn't about good management – the ninety per cent that goes right. It's about the ten per cent that goes wrong.

its been great being teached by you

Andrew Macalpine

Copyright © 2025 Andrew Macalpine

The moral right of the author has been asserted.

Apart from any fair dealing for the purposes of research or private study,
or criticism or review, as permitted under the Copyright, Designs and Patents
Act 1988, this publication may only be reproduced, stored or transmitted, in
any form or by any means, with the prior permission in writing of the
publishers, or in the case of reprographic reproduction in accordance with
the terms of licences issued by the Copyright Licensing Agency. Enquiries
concerning reproduction outside those terms should be sent to the publishers.

This is a work of fiction. Names, characters, businesses, places, events
and incidents are either the products of the author's imagination
or used in a fictitious manner. Any resemblance to actual persons,
living or dead, or actual events is purely coincidental.

Troubador
Unit E2 Airfield Business Park,
Harrison Road, Market Harborough,
Leicestershire. LE16 7UL
Tel: 0116 2792299
Email: books@troubador.co.uk
Web: www.troubador.co.uk

The manufacturer's authorised representative in the EU for product safety
is Authorised Rep Compliance Ltd,
71 Lower Baggot Street, Dublin D02 P593 Ireland
(www.arccompliance.com)

ISBN 9781836285076

British Library Cataloguing in Publication Data.
A catalogue record for this book is available from the British Library.

Printed and bound in Great Britain by 4edge Limited
Typeset in 11pt Minion Pro by Troubador Publishing Ltd, Leicester, UK

Dedication

This book is dedicated to all the amazing teachers I worked with and to the students they taught.

ACKNOWLEDGEMENTS

I have benefitted hugely from advice and help from many friends – some of them writers themselves. My wife has been my sternest and most valuable critic. Her ticks and crosses have encouraged the elimination of passages of little merit and the retention of pieces that, hopefully, readers will enjoy.

CONTENTS

INTRODUCTION

'Do you like Harold Wilson? Yes or no?' My father's angry face and belligerence were bolstered by the usual pre-prandial double gin and tonics. He had slightly gingery hair and freckles – neither of which I inherited and both of which had skipped at least a generation. He was always well dressed: creased trousers, shirt, and tie; slim build (he was, like everyone else, still a smoker) and medium height. This must have been around 1964 – Harold Wilson's first spell as Labour Prime Minister. I tried to point out that it was not a Yes/No answer, although I had just voted Labour in my first general election. However, I was not about to inflame further what was already a typically fiery exchange by admitting that. His question might have seemed Tory-inspired, but I don't think my father was ever quite sure where he stood, despite a wealthy, privileged background.

My progress from public schoolboy to inner-city school teacher was a slow burn. Detached house in St John's Wood, annual ski trip to St Moritz, the Golf Club. In the eyes of my parents, I was destined for some gentlemanly career – maybe 'something in the City. The *Telegraph* and *Express* were delivered every day.

I found it hard to rebel at home – but made up for it at school, where I was frequently in trouble. Maybe that stood me in good stead later, when I started teaching in a rough inner-city boys' school in Somers Town in north London. Despite our polar backgrounds, I could empathise with the kids.

Following school, I had the luxury of a gap year in Paris, at the Sorbonne. If not a political one, this was a cultural awakening: plays, films, Sartre. Irritatingly, I'm, sure, I returned 'Frenchified' – extolling the virtues of everything Gallic.

Cambridge University followed and a *political* awakening when I realised the *Telegraph* 'news' items had a right-wing bias – reflecting the views of one of my first-year flatmates who bought the paper most days. Once I left university I turned to the *Guardian*.

I attended debates at the Student Union and marvelled at the erudition and confidence of fellow undergraduate speakers. However, unlike them, I certainly didn't consider myself 'born to rule' – as must many of those who went on to do just that. I was put off by the formality: plummy voices, wing collars, and gowns. My own undergraduate gown (theoretically compulsory) spent much of its time gathering dust, although I was under no illusions that such a tiny rebellion would change the world.

Leaving the rarefied university atmosphere, I had to find a job – definitely not 'something in the City', with the Cambridge Union's wing collars being replaced by pinstripe suits, silk handkerchiefs, and cufflinks. Instead, I lighted upon publishing – still a gentlemanly occupation in those days but, by no means my parents' first choice.

At Harraps, I had the grand title of 'Education Overseas Manager' – managing a staff of one: my secretary. The highlight – and a real eye-opener – was a three-month tour of West Africa. I had the extremely dubious task of persuading West African academics to give their names to English textbooks which, of course, they hadn't written. The textbooks themselves didn't change. There was merely an African name added under the UK author on the front cover. For biology practicals, students still had to cut up imported dogfish. Then there was 'Ode to a Daffodil' – of which there were none in West Africa. The whole approach was, I felt, patronising – if not downright insulting.

It also made me think about the recipients – the children – who were being offered the same diet as their counterparts in the UK with no recognition of, or concession to, huge cultural differences.

By the time I left publishing, I was reading books like Chinua Achebe's *Things Fall Apart* and John Griffin's *Black Like Me*. I heard a Mandela speech over loudspeakers in Trafalgar Square and was well on my way to a new stage of personal development. Then two things happened almost simultaneously. I was offered the opportunity of opening a publishing house with a friend in Lagos, focusing on books written *by* Nigerian writers *for* Nigerians.

And – a lightbulb moment!

I realised that publishing school books was a step removed from actual teaching and that that was what I wanted to do. Engaging with West African teachers and their students had been inspiring and eye-opening. Teaching seemed 'useful' – frontline – in a way that publishing wasn't. Of course, the Lagos job would, I'm sure, have made a positive contribution to Nigerian education, but, for me, everything pointed to teaching. The die was cast.

I decided to start by focusing on immigrants and looked for a course teaching English as a second language. Only four universities in the country offered such a course. One was London, which I applied to. Halfway through my interview, the head of department told me, 'Mr Macalpine, I can't see why we should offer you a place.' I was then, and remained so for many years, a rubbish interviewee: diffident, nervous, and never quite able to let myself go. I needed prodding into action. The comment must have spurred me on though as I got a letter two days later offering me a place. By that time, however, I had turned *them* down and had been accepted by the Leeds School of English.

The 'taught' part of the course was brilliant, but my first teaching practice in a cold, grey part of Bradford was an eye-opener – the leavers' class in a junior school, one-third Indian and two-thirds Pakistani. In a BBC North documentary *East to West*, produced two years before I started my teaching practice, Riffat Akram and his mum (recent arrivals from Pakistan) were quoted as describing Bradford as 'foggy, smog, drizzle – horrible, cold, dull and dark'!

There was little I could do about the weather. However, I did start to feel I could make a difference through their education and was now certain I had set off down a career path I believed in.

My first permanent teaching post was in Somers Town, a rundown area of north London. It was a state secondary, as were all the schools I worked in. As the crow flies, it wasn't far from my family home in St John's Wood – but light years away otherwise and, as with publishing, I had a fine title for the post: Head of English as a Second Language Department. This time it was a staff of three – myself and two part-timers. The students – immigrant and UK-born – were easy to engage with and responsive. I was on my way.

The subsequent thirty five year journey, from facing the challenges of Somers Town to advising London's headteachers, was a huge privilege and one that I have never, even for a moment, regretted. The stories that follow are certainly not a blueprint for successful teaching, or managing schools. They just chart my erratic journey through anecdotes – anecdotes that tend to focus on the ten per cent that goes wrong, and not the ninety per cent that goes right. It would be unforgivably remiss of me if I didn't acknowledge the amazing teachers and students who are responsible for that ninety per cent. It would also fail to reflect my own overwhelmingly positive experiences in education over thirty years.

Readers are invited to dip into the book at any point as each anecdote can be read as a separate piece.

WHEN AND WHERE

1966–1967: Teaching Practices in Bradford and Madrid.

1967–1971: Somers Town – London Borough of Camden. Secondary. All boys. 1,000 on roll. Head of English as a Second Language.

1971–1976: Peckham – London Borough of Southwark. Secondary. Mixed. 900 on roll. Split site. Head of English.

1976–1983: Isle of Dogs – London Borough of Tower Hamlets. Secondary. Mixed. 800 on roll. Deputy Head.

1983: Headship Applications.

1984–1989: Hornchurch – London Borough of Havering. Secondary. Mixed. 1,100 on roll. Headteacher.

1990–1992: London Borough of Havering. Inspector for Secondary Education.

1992–1999: London Borough of Barnet. 'Fresh Start'. Opened 1992. Mixed. 150 rising to 750. Headteacher

ONE

FIRST STEPS – TEACHING PRACTICES IN BRADFORD AND MADRID

BRADFORD

Armed with education theory of varying degrees of usefulness, e.g., the difference in phonetics between the labio-dental and the bilabial (interesting but useless) and the order in which children learn – listening, speaking, reading, writing (simple but useful), I started my first teaching practice in a Bradford junior school in the autumn term of 1966.

It was a strange place. Most of the staff seemed to have been at the school forever and had long since lost any enthusiasm they might have had. They were a depressing bunch. The head, Mr Pickles, was in his third decade there. His priorities were God, hymns, and P.E.!

I was under the not-very-watchful eye of my tutor, Mrs Raji. I think she was happy with my progress but really more interested in taking a back seat – literally and metaphorically. Her main contribution was the infliction of her favourite *Hansel and Gretel* film. As far as the children were concerned, it was much too long and mostly incomprehensible. Five minutes in, and nearly all of them had switched off.

The class consisted of seven Indians and thirteen Pakistanis aged eleven to thirteen. Mixed sex as well as mixed age. They were all local 'Bradfordians' living about a mile southwest of the centre of the city. Partition had taken place twenty years previously (1947), but there were still tensions between the two Asian communities – tensions which have carried on to this day. To my relief, they didn't surface in the class.

My role was to teach the children English, which made it doubly difficult because of the gap between those who had a few words and phrases and those who had none. There were many successes. My favourite was the thrill Aseem got when he realised he could make a sentence – the first of which was 'Batman likes to fight in the morning'!

Activities were varied:

Story time. *The Princess and the Bean.* Why 'bean' was substituted for 'pea' escapes me. The girls liked the story. The boys wanted something more 'manly'.

Swimming. I quoted above a Pakistani mother and son's reactions on their arrival in Bradford just before I started teaching practice – 'foggy, smog, drizzle, cold, dull and dark.' There was much of that when I took my class on their weekly trip to the local baths. It was the era of drip-dry shirts. None of them had coats. A few had tatty jumpers. The boys wore cheap thin trousers. I was shamefully cosy in my expensive overcoat. One time, on the way, my attention was taken by a pretty woman. When I turned back, four of the boys were looking at me mischievously.

'Woman. Woman, Sir.' I kept my eyes on the children after that!

No one in the class could swim, although they all took to it enthusiastically.

An important part of the weekly trip was the **Road Drill**. Look right. Look left. Look right again. Hardly any of them knew. They were shocked to be told a girl had been knocked down and killed just round the corner from the school.

Maths. I only understood my own lesson halfway through! A reflection of the struggle I'd had with the 'O' level. As far as the children were concerned, the universal language of numbers was much less intimidating than English.

P.E. The boys loved it but were very difficult to control. The girls did their best to get out of it, and, as in 2025, they would almost certainly have benefitted from single-sex lessons.

Measuring. My idea of measuring the playground was definitely a bridge too far and as much a sign of my naivety as my enthusiasm. Based on a rough plan and, in the absence of tape measures, I issued them with skipping ropes, all the same length. Terrifying chaos ensued with the 'equipment' being used for skipping, tripping, or just swirling around. Eventually, and amazingly, they actually got down to the task itself. Not only that, but they subsequently produced drawings with measurements. Never underestimate your pupils!

Mime and movement. This was the next most chaotic activity after the playground measuring. I chose some Rossini to get them to dance to. What was I thinking? Clearly, like Mrs Raji's *Hansel and Gretel*, it was not about their own cultural backgrounds. Worse, I took the lead myself. The result was bedlam! Bizarrely there were half a dozen girls who remembered an English country dance from the summer term before I arrived.

Geography. A lesson based on what maps the school had. They were tatty and out of date, with India being shown pre-partition. Definitely not useable! I had to go and buy my own.

Learning control – mine! This reminds me of Rudyard Kipling's poem 'If', which starts 'If you can keep your head...' I lost my temper once – with Geeta, who consistently refused to stop talking. My intemperate shout made her cry. That was a crucial lesson, and over the next thirty years I made sure any inward seething (of which there was a fair amount) stopped at irritability.

MADRID

This was chalk and cheese. A showpiece secondary school in Madrid was built in honour of General Franco, who would still have eight years left in power before dying in 1975. It was a state school but had the feel of a private such was its prestige. I had a class of the most able, and it could well have been tricky, given they were aware of their status and already had some English. However, the arrogance I was to experience when I was given a top set in my Peckham school (see below) didn't materialise, and they were very receptive. By now, I had accumulated a range of teaching aids that I never had in Bradford. The main ones were a flannelgraph (they're still widely used in 2025 and a tape recorder that actually worked. I was only expected to turn up for the class I was due to teach and sat in a waiting room until a buzzer went. I could just as well have been in an office waiting to be interviewed. It was an eerie place. During breaks, there was no sight or sound of staff or students.

What did I learn? At first hand, how appallingly wide the social spectrum is. How schools and teachers are in a position to make a difference. How bright, funny, and stimulating children can be, and the challenges they present when they're none of those things. Above all that, I had found what I wanted to do. And, as if to tie me down, they gave me a distinction for my teaching practice!

TWO

SOMERS TOWN

INTRODUCTION

Somers Town is sandwiched between King's Cross and Euston stations. There is a history of violence in the area that goes back to the nineteenth century. In 1830, the first on-duty fatality for the newly founded Metropolitan Police occurred when PC Joseph Grantham was kicked to death while trying to break up a street fight in Smiths Place, Somers Town. Scroll forward 160 years to the 1990s when the area experienced ethnic tensions between Whites and Bengalis, climaxing in the murder of Richard Everitt. Throughout the past two hundred years, this violence has gone alongside considerable poverty.

Even the twenty-first century has left Somers Town behind. A 2017 study identified it as the most deprived ward in Camden, with 45.9 per cent of children living in poverty. The pizzazz and optimism that have transformed the area around King's Cross and St Pancras, with its magnificent steel and glass buildings and upmarket eateries, has barely been felt north in Somers Town. Much of the area is still not covered by any specific planning and development policies. By the time we get to 2019, it's postcode wars. Stray into or out of NW1 at your peril.

When I started teaching there, nearly 150 years after PC Grantham's murder, I found an area of rough and rundown estates untouched by any gentrification that might have been taking place elsewhere. The area was described by one contemporary writer as '…an urban landscape so desolate and wasted that it became… one of the Kray brothers' favoured places for beating up and maiming their victims…' It didn't quite feel like that in the school, but there were tensions between staff and students, with corporal punishment seen as the norm and the only way to keep a lid on things.

In addition to the white English, there was a heady mix of nationalities – Greeks, Turks, Indians, Pakistanis, Bangladeshis, and Chinese. Many of them came with little or no English (reminding me of the Indians and Pakistanis I taught on that first teaching practice in Bradford), and there were ongoing tensions between communities, particularly between Bangladeshis and whites.

I was naively unaware of where I was coming to when I chose Somers Town. If I had my time over again, would I have chosen differently? Certainly not! It was a tough place to work, but, despite our hugely differing backgrounds, that sense of engagement with the kids convinced me that school teaching was what I wanted to do. The experience also left me confident that, going forward, nothing would faze me.

APPLICATION AND APPOINTMENT

The Somers Town school was my first application – and my first appointment. Not as grand as it sounds – there were no other candidates! At that time, applicants for posts in ILEA (Inner London Education Authority) schools applied to 'the pool'. Those who were successful could be sent anywhere in London – on a much smaller scale shades of the Foreign Office. Maybe teaching in an inner-city school in the 1960s was not that far removed from overseas appointments with their danger zones. If my parents had ever ventured through the squeaky and damaged swing doors of the Somers Town school, they would not have wanted to stay longer. However, rather than subject myself to the vagaries of the pool, I had chosen a specific school – and this was it.

The post was half head of English as a second language – teaching, mainly, recently arrived immigrants to the UK – and half 'straightforward' English teacher. I was interviewed by the head, the head of English, and an inspector. We were in a small office – off the main one. Even with the door closed, the clackety-clack of typewriters penetrated. The head, Philip Edwards, had only recently been appointed, having moved to London from Swindon – a couple of hours up the newly opened M4 – in reality to a different planet. He was a kindly man, hopelessly out of his depth in the wilds of central London. I think he was taken with the idea of a Cambridge English graduate coming onto the books.

'So how did you find Cambridge? Was it picnics on the Backs, punting on the Cam?'

The head of English, Gerald, was a little more challenging. He was tall, with thinning hair and blue eyes. He was wearing the tweed sports jacket that I came to know well – as I never saw him in anything else.

'What are your favourite novels?'

'At what stage would you introduce students to poetry?'

It was all very polite and fairly perfunctory, given there was no one else in the frame. The end of the interview was signalled in the usual way:

'Mr Macalpine. Is there anything you'd like to ask us?'

I declined the offer, and Gerald got up and asked me to wait outside – 'outside' being a corner of the main office.

A friendly typist got up and came over to me. 'Would you like a cup of tea?'

'I'm fine, thank you,' I replied. There was no surface nearby, and I thought balancing a cup of tea might be a challenge too far.

After about fifteen minutes, the inspector – short, wiry, dark-haired, fortyish – who had said nothing during the interview, came out and asked me back into the room. I sat down again in the hot seat.

'Mr Macalpine. We'd like to offer you the post.' Always a nice ring to those words – unless, of course, you'd decided halfway through the interview that you didn't want the job.

I accepted, and then it was congratulatory handshakes all around. Gerald took me out through the school office and into the corridor, and we arranged a preliminary visit. Meanwhile, the inspector had been hovering.

'Which way you going?' he asked as we walked back to the entrance.

'I'll probably get the tube,' I replied.

'I get the bus, so we'll part ways here.' I subsequently discovered that he only ever travelled by bus – cutting down considerably the number of visits he needed to make in a day.

By now, we were at the entrance and about to part ways. The inspector smiled warmly, although his words conveyed a warning.

'Andrew, I'm sure you're going to do well, but I have to tell you this will be a baptism of fire. Anyway, good luck.'

With that, we shook hands, and he was gone. I never saw him again, although his words rang in my ears. No doubt he was happy to get away. Early on in my time at the school, a colleague neatly summed up the prevailing culture.

'It's like this. The staff hit the boys, and the boys hit each other.' As I discovered, a pretty accurate summary.

GETTING GOING

Having survived the interview, it was time for introductions – to students and teachers. Gerald suggested a tour of the English department during class time. Their area was all down one side of a long, gloomy, low-ceilinged corridor. Having just got the job, I was far from gloomy. Even the sight of Mr Markham in the first classroom I was taken into couldn't dull my excitement. His stained trousers (not entirely in the right places) and creased chalk-marked jacket brought to mind the phrase 'If you can, do. If you can't, teach.' Ground down by an ill-chosen career – but there might not have been many alternatives.

We moved down the corridor and came to a sixth-form classroom.

As elsewhere, I was introduced as:

'Mr Macalpine, our new English teacher.'

Cue stage whisper from the back of the classroom.

'Who's the new boy then?' Enthusiasm was slightly punctured, although it wasn't too long before I looked back wistfully at this reference to my youthful looks. At the same time, it felt like a challenge laid down: man or mouse? I should have stood taller and puffed out my chest.

My first day was memorable for the traditional introductory lunch with the school's feared senior master, Mr Stephens. Although slight in build, his dark Brylcreem hair and narrow eyes gave him a sinister appearance, and us five newbies sitting round the table were wary of him. We had already been given hints of his violent approach to students and, as if to confirm it, he had a set-piece story designed to indicate his ability to deal with miscreants. Subsequently, I gathered that while the boy and the offence changed every time he told the story, the climax didn't.

'So I threw the boy through the door. Yes, through it. Made a lot of noise and a horrible mess, but he was as good as gold after that.' It was a climax always greeted with stunned silence.

The story seemed like a crazy sadistic fantasy, but I had no intention of voicing a reaction. I'd already decided (sod any moral issues) that I needed Mr Stephens on my side.

However, a brave (or foolish) voice broke the silence.

'*Through* the door? A closed door?'

Answer in the affirmative. And, of course, ample grounds for an assault charge.

I used to have an image of where Mr Stephens was at any one time. The boys obviously carried the same one. His voice outside the classroom door meant off-task chat stopped; heads went down to their writing or reading. This was a general rule relating to those with any authority. For example, the deputy head, Wathen, would often hover outside a classroom door if he sensed control was not absolute. A frequent occurrence in my case. He would wait a moment, assess the situation, and then burst in to berate the entire class.

'Boy, what are you doing? Show me your work. And you, stop staring out of the window.'

There was pin-drop silence for the minute or two he held forth whilst I stood to one side, marvelling at how different the class now looked – well-behaved and studious. It was a tough call – discipline v. pedagogy, but I really didn't want Mt Wathen to stay forever. The class might have been quiet, but meaningful engagement would have been nil. However, I would have paid him to do a lot more 'hovering' outside the classroom door. That wasn't going to happen, and, sadly, there was a price to pay for his intervention, for as soon as he departed, the gulf between his control and my own emerged – starkly. The hum of idle off-task chatter would be resumed, interlaced with, depending on the class, idle off-task questions:

'Sir, have you taught before?'

'Sir, are you married?'

'What's she like?'

'Sir, where do you live? I bet it's nice.'

'Sir, do you think you'll stay?' That question pinpointed the underlying anxiety the kids had about teachers' stickability. However, their needs and their humour had already made their mark on me.

'Of course, I'm staying. I've only just arrived.'

However, without closing down their curiosity, I tried to bring them back to the lesson plan I had prepared. Even, on occasions, successfully!

One particular question sticks in my mind – and in my gullet.

'Sir, what does 'guttersnipe' mean?' A 'colleague' had finally snapped, finding his class just too much to cope with. He *didn't* stay.

There was much that certainly wouldn't be tolerated in 2022. For example, a subject report included the following 'Produces more rubbish than the average dustbin.' You won't find those words in the bank of statements and phrases that teachers often turn to now.

My first full teaching day started with the registration and form period. These were twenty-minute sessions at the beginning of the morning and then ten minutes at the beginning of the afternoon. One wag on the staff referred to them as periods of 'unarmed combat'. They were too long for the school admin, which was supposed to fill them – times, rules, parents' evenings, exams, events, etc. and too short for any meaningful activity.

In most schools, these sessions took place in year groups, i.e., all pupils of the same age. The Somers Town school, along with many others, was trying out 'vertical grouping' – naively designed to mimic the family unit. It had one serious defect. It mixed the naughtiest of the youngest students (eleven-year-olds) with the fourteen- and fifteen-year-olds – many of whom had long since given up on school and for whom life was always on the edge of criminality. In many ways, it was a perfect 'school for scoundrels'. I could understand the theory. In practice, there was little I could do to stop the Artful Dodgers from consorting with the Fagins. The ten minutes at the beginning of the afternoon didn't work either. Many students 'bunked off' after they had been registered and were not seen until the following day. At least they weren't yet into the twenty-first century phenomenon of County Lines, with many secondary school students disappearing after lunch having been drawn into drug running by criminal gangs. An afternoon of science with Ms Jones followed by French with Mr Leclair was never going to compete with the money available to those coerced by gang masters.

Vertical grouping didn't last long. It didn't work and was soon jettisoned.

Less than a week into the first term, I was approached at the end of morning registration by a fourth-year boy in my vertically grouped form:

'Sir?'

'What is it, Mark?' A couple of days earlier, I might not even have been sure of his name. My twenty-seven teaching periods a week generated over two hundred names. At least I had learnt those of everyone in my form.

'Can you help me with this?'

'What is it?'

Mark produced a crumpled piece of paper. 'It's a reference request for a paper round.'

'Mark, you know I've only been here since Monday. I don't really know you.'

'You know me as well as anyone else, Sir.'

Any sense of pride – quite obviously completely misplaced – that I had established a positive relationship with Mark was quickly overtaken by my shock at finding a student who'd been in the school for three years feeling so anonymous.

Going back to 'man or mouse', it wasn't long before I had a chance to show how manly I was – and to throw off the 'new boy' tag.

'Do you play rugby?'

I was being accosted by bearded, macho man Gavin – head of P.E. – a Welshman as wide as he was tall. I guessed ex-front row forward. He spent all of every day in his Wales-emblazoned tracksuit.

'We're playing the boys after school on Thursday.'

Danger signals flashed through my brain. I hadn't played rugby for some nine years, and my time had mostly been spent shivering on the wing – well out of harm's way and nowhere near the scrum. But 'man or mouse'? What came out of my mouth was:

'OK, as long as I'm not in the scrum or full back.' Scrum was out of the question, and although I had never played there, I knew full back was potentially a lonely and vulnerable position – as I was to discover.

I assumed (ass – you – me) Gavin had taken on board my 'terms'.

Thursday arrived, and thirty of us took to the field, and I still didn't know what position I was going to be playing in.

'Where do you want me, Gavin?'

'You OK with full back?' Gavin was not a great listener. He'd either forgotten or not taken it in at all. I wasn't OK. It was too late to make a fuss.

For the first five minutes, 'lonely' summed it up. I was on patrol with nothing to do. Five minutes in, however, one of their players kicked a high ball in my direction. I managed to keep an eye on it but not on the marauding sixth formers following up. Simultaneously, as I caught the ball, I was buried under some seventy or eighty stones of testosterone-fuelled seventeen-year-olds.

Was it something I'd said? My posh accent?

I emerged from the pile of bodies, conscious of a burning pain in my ribs. A couple of knowing staff diagnosed 'cracked rib'. I trudged off, having failed to convert 'new boy' into 'new man'.

Gavin, of course, never asked me again – or, indeed, about my rib. And that was my last game of rugby.

Somers Town's violence was not confined to rugby. There were elements of the Wild West, viz. the ambush early on in my time there of Mr Jawal – an Indian supply teacher. He was in his fifties, with greying hair, a gentle manner, and always in the same dark suit. On a daily basis, his role was to pick up classes where the regular teacher hadn't turned up. Sometimes it fell to permanent staff like myself to fill a gap. We avoided the role like the plague – classes we didn't know and subjects we weren't familiar with. Anyway, I was returning to the school one foggy winter's night for a parents' evening, lampposts shedding feeble yellow light on the street. I was thinking ahead to the parents of naughty or underachieving children who I particularly wanted to see but who were the least likely to turn up, when I realised I was following Mr Jawal's rather battered Toyota as it approached the school. He wasn't a form teacher and under no obligation to attend – just a measure of his commitment which went well beyond that of a supply teacher. Suddenly his car stopped between two lampposts – accompanied by a graunching noise. It didn't sound good, and I got out to see what the problem was. As I did, I saw a group of boys running off. By this time, Mr Jawal was out of his car, looking as crumpled as his suit.

'I heard a horrible noise and saw these boys.' His hands were shaking, and his voice was trembling. Together we walked round to the front of the car to see what the trouble was. It didn't take forensics to spot that a rope slung between the two lampposts had tangled itself around his front bumper, almost detaching his number plate. We untangled together while I tried to reassure a very upset Mr Jawal. I could see how shocked and threatened he felt; although I knew what we'd witnessed was more sophisticated mischief than murderous intent.

'They're bastards aren't they?' I had never heard Mr Jawal talk like this, and I suggested he skip the parents' evening and make his way back home. Stoically he decided to drive on to school. He was a very loveable man.

Despite sizeable immigrant numbers, Somers Town was still essentially white working class. This was the start of my teaching career, and I knew that my background might be an issue. In the classroom, it was my voice that needed attention. Bernard Shaw's brilliant observation that 'it is impossible for an Englishman to open his mouth without making some other Englishman hate or despise him' certainly held good in the sixties – and there's still an element of it in the twenty-first century. When we hear a certain type of accent, we'll automatically pin a label on the person speaking and file them away into what we perceive to be their social status or category. In fact, scientists have now learnt that visual cues actually come second when people are categorising others. What comes first? The way they sound.

I never had an upper-class drawl, but my long vowels and final consonants were far removed from the glottal stops of many of those I was teaching. When using words like 'bait, late, deep, street, complete, week', my natural tendency was to pronounce the final consonant. Those born and brought up in the areas I was to teach in didn't. The glottal stop was the norm.

The other aspect of Cockney or Estuary English (as Cockney has, to an extent, morphed into in the London area) is the sound, or non-sound, of the letter 'h'. Writers on class, such as Shaw and Orwell, have made a clear link between dropped aitches and the working class. And another commentator pointed out 'they don't drop their aitches, they drop ours.'

I didn't abandon my final consonants or drop my aitches – just tried to weaken them a little! I'm sure that to many readers, this just sounds fake. The truth is that I didn't want my outward appearance and speech to get in the way of my relationship with students. I liked to think that what came across more strongly than anything else was my respect for them and my determination to show them that learning could be exciting and rewarding. If that hadn't been the case, I wouldn't have enjoyed being a teacher and wouldn't have lasted in any of the three inner-city schools I chose to work in. However, although no student ever said it, I have no doubt they still saw me as 'posh'.

Although 'look' came second to 'sound', clothes were important. Jacob Rees-Mogg's waistcoats certainly wouldn't have worked in those London schools. Senior staff tended to wear suits – but not three-piece ones. Sports jackets were common amongst the men although, at the same time, 1970s teachers working in secondary moderns and the newly established comprehensives had a reputation for scruffiness which did little for their public image. Women tended to wear cardigans over their tops and skirts below the knee. Dress wasn't such an issue for them. However, on our many protest marches (e.g., pay, conditions, class size, lunchtime supervision), the men were commonly in jeans and bearded, and alongside the scruffy look went a reputation, in company with many other groups of workers, for being 'bolshie'. To the point where, in 1968, Labour's employment minister, Barbara Castle, wrote a paper called 'In Place of Strife'. It was an attempt to pull the rug out from under the Tories by legislating to prevent unofficial strikes. It took a further six years to become law. So… on marches, I would abandon my neutral attire and wear a suit in an attempt to give our 'profession' status. I decided that, as with my voice, the ends justified the means.

MY YEAR 7 CLASS AND 3B'S 'NEWSPAPER'

After the vertical grouping I encountered when I first arrived, it was a joy to have my own Year 7 class at the beginning of my second year.

'Delightfully pristine' might not have been the most accurate description of the children I was taking on, for there were already some who had made their mark – literally and metaphorically – at primary school. However, I loved them and felt privileged to be with them as they started their secondary school career.

I had joined the NUT (National Union of Teachers) almost immediately after my appointment, and at the end of this second year I found myself caught up in strike action. The union had been consistent in campaigning for better pay and conditions. Although I forgot the details, I was aware that the parents of my Year 7 class would need more than a leaflet if they were to understand why their children were being sent home. I tried to put myself in their shoes – and found I couldn't. I decided the only thing for it was face-to-face explanations – so I arranged to visit all of them in their homes. How reassured they were, I never knew, but they were certainly welcoming. Most of the families lived in council blocks. Some two-storey flats. A tiny minority in houses. The pressures on parents were considerable – jobs, pay, living conditions – as far removed as possible from my own privileged background. Many of their children were constantly falling between what safety nets there were – and certainly, when they were in trouble, between school and the police. Of the twenty-four boys in my first 'same age' form group, a quarter of them (or their sibling) was, at some time or another, in trouble with the law. These were eleven-year-olds just starting secondary school! Early on in my time in Somers Town, I wrote to the local chief inspector at Tottenham Court Road Police Station, suggesting we should try to regularise our frequent contact. His reply was extremely positive, recognising, as he did, the need.

I made a note of all these visits, and I can still recall many of the children's faces – even fifty years on. Apart from those heading towards a criminal record (one brother actually in prison), there were others who pulled one up short. My contemporaneous notes:

'Paul. Paul wets his bed. Mum would like to send him to school with a placard on his back saying "I wet my bed."'

'John. One of a family of nine children living in three bedrooms. Dad gave me a pen portrait of each sibling including their hobbies. Not surprisingly, many of them were stereotypical, with daughters enjoying sewing, ice skating, tennis, reading, and playing with dolls. The sons' hobbies included playing with soldiers, fighting, and being a nuisance!'

'Philip. Philip suffered prolonged absence in his second year after being struck by a cricket ball hit by Gavin (the head of P.E. I introduced above). Apparently, he seemed fairly unconcerned. Gavin that is. No surprise there!'

I came away from these visits much better able to understand the children and their backgrounds – and I like to think it helped me to engage with them more empathetically.

Sadly, in my time in education, I never had the opportunity to repeat such visits – a combination of safeguarding issues, promotions, and accompanying lack of time. However, we did have freedom over what to teach and how to teach it – the National Curriculum straitjacket not being introduced until 1988. I had found my feet sufficiently to move away from stultifying textbooks, traditional poems, and storybooks to stuff that was more contemporary. This included setting up a class newspaper. With a little prompting from me, they responded enthusiastically, and once a week (and quite often after school) we established a newsroom. Printing was courtesy of the Banda spirit duplicating machine, which gave off its distinctive fumes – remembered years on by all who used them, although not quite sufficient to subdue undesirable staff or students. The paper was called the '3B Times'. The children wrote poetry and short stories for it. There was a puzzle page, and roving reporters conducted interviews. One of these was with the previous head, Mr Allsop, on his return to school for some function.

Anthony Joseph, interviewer: 'What does it feel like being retired?'

Mr Allsop: 'Marvellous! I've even forgotten how to cane boys!'

'2001: A SPACE ODYSSEY' OR THE TEACHER LEARNS A LESSON

Nineteen seventy-one and I had arranged a special treat for my form of thirty fourteen-year-old boys. Most of them unused to treats. My choice was a trip to the cinema, and I chose a relatively recently released film – '2001: A Space Odyssey'.

All kids love sci-fi, don't they? 2001: A Space Odyssey had been released to massive fanfare in 1968. Maybe that was my first mistake. Three years is an eon in the life of a fourteen-year-old. Hundreds of blockbuster films had been released since then, including *A Clockwork Orange* and *Diamonds are Forever*. To be fair to myself (hugely generous might be a better description), between 1968 and 1971, we had the first Moon walk – 'One giant leap for mankind' and all the excitement that had generated. However, fourteen-year-olds live for the moment and that moment had passed.

Having failed to look up the reviews (see below) and armed only with an inflated sense of laying on a real treat, we left school for the bus stop. The concept of a private girls' school crocodile formation certainly hadn't caught on, but with much cajoling we reached the stop. With a background of pushing, shoving and generally messing about, there were the usual comments from those in the queue.

'Rather you than me, mate.' Cloth cap, fag hanging out of his mouth.

'I don't envy you with that lot.' Woman with hair under a scarf. Baby in a pram.

'You should get a medal.' Kindly looking, elderly lady.

'They need a police escort – not a teacher.' Tall, military-looking gent who would quite probably have instilled more order than I was mustering. I was tending to agree with them but knew it was all going to be worth it once the class settled to watch a classic film.

A mercifully brief wait cut the comments and the advice short, and we boarded. Cue manic tumbling up to the top deck. The noise from above continued as I took possession of thirty-one tickets.

'They'll need to sit down, or this bus ain't going nowhere.' The big, burly conductor clearly meant business, and I made my way up to the top deck and passed on the threat. It seemed to work.

No… I hadn't read the reviews, but at least I had researched the bus stop – right outside the Odeon. Renewed tumbling – down the stairs this time and out onto the pavement accompanied by shouting and laughing. Fortunately, there was hardly anyone about, so I was spared more comments and advice.

I organised a vague line and in we went. More prolonged ticket buying while trying to keep at least one eye on what 3H might be doing to the foyer. I was hoping none of them had spotted the stairs going up to the circle. One had, but I was able to nip the escape in the bud.

'Michael, we're not going upstairs. Please come down now.' Fortunately, he acquiesced and joined his mates in the foyer.

Although I'd had special dispensation from the head to take them to an afternoon session when it was likely that there'd be few other people around, the Odeon, displaying shrewd business sense but no concern for order, had opened their kiosk. Before I could stop it, an unseemly scrum formed round the front, and sweets and ice creams were being sold. Not for the first time did I regret not taking up the kind offer from a supply teacher to come with me. Oh well.

'Boys, there will be an interval. You can come back then.'

I approached the lady behind the glass.

'I'd be really grateful if you could stop serving now. They can come back in the interval.'

This seemed to work, and despite moans and grumbles – 'She was just about to serve me', 'Can't I get a drink?', etc. – we got in as *2001* was about to start.

I shepherded my charges to the row suggested by the manager. There was good news – and bad. The good news was that there was no one else in the cinema. The bad news was when I came face-to-face with the realisation that no matter where I sat, I could only deal with a tiny minority of miscreants (of which there was a number in 3H) because of the way they were strung out along the row. No other formation seemed remotely feasible, and the row seemed a mile long. After animated discussions – 'I'm not sitting next to him', 'Oi, Pratish, come over here' – and the odd climbing into the row from the back, they more or less settled down.

Where to sit? Maybe the middle while words and possibly more solid items flew across me. I could sit at one end – or the other – but with no influence on the furthest child. In my naivety, I was hoping this would indicate trust. It had little effect, and I decided to sit in the row behind. It meant I could patrol up and down – a bit like a sheepdog.

I may have researched the bus stop. What I hadn't taken on board was the film's length. Two hours forty-five minutes! No dialogue for the first thirty while this spaceship made its unbearably lengthy trek across the screen. Paint drying would have run it close. I say 'no dialogue' – no dialogue on screen anyway. The film was so long that there was an intermission. Cue a rush of questions:

'Can I go to the loo?'

'Can we get something to eat?'

'Alright, but you've got ten minutes. No more.'

Nine minutes later, a smattering of returning boys. I was torn between making sure those returning weren't using the aisles as a racetrack and getting those still outside away from sweets, drinks – and toilets. I would probably have been more effective with recalcitrant sheep.

Fortunately, the second half contained a modicum of action which occasionally distracted 3H from previously mentioned pursuits. Nevertheless, I had to continue patrolling, given there were a number of boys who'd decided long ago that this was a film they could live without.

Eventually, after what seemed like a never-ending nightmare, the credits rolled – rather a couple of hours too late than 'not a moment too soon'. Without waiting for the names of the stand-by plasterer, the wardrobe assistant, the assistant hairdressers, etc., I rounded up my charges. To my relief, the energy expended over the previous few hours seemed to have had a calming effect, and the journey back to school was relatively uneventful. There were the odd comments:

'A bit long, Sir.'

'Sir, can we see something a bit shorter next time?' Next time???

'Great sound effects.' That was the class geek.

There were even a couple of thank yous.

I wasn't going to give up, and there was a 'next time', but I made sure to read the reviews first…

Here's a selection from 'Rotten Tomatoes':

'For anybody to dismiss *2001: A Space Odyssey* as 'boring' they must have no interest in science, technology, philosophy, history or the art of film-making.' 3H's interest in any of the above was fairly limited.

'There are two schools of thought about *2001: A Space Odyssey*. One is that it is the greatest science-fiction epic ever made. The other… it is as absorbing as watching paint dry…' 3H certainly hadn't been brought to watch paint dry as testified by their farting competitions, play-fighting, shouted conversations across four or five seats, sweet wrapper throwing, and never-ending visits to the toilet.

'The film is a poetical contemplation of most exciting eternal questions.' Damn! I'd forgotten to cover this with 3H.

'I'm always surprised… that nobody… has noted the parallels between the movie and Nietzsche's famous work, *Also Sprach Zarathustra*.' Even I struggled with that one.

Matt Walton (that class geek I referred to – oh, that there had been more like him) wrote, as requested, a review for the '3B Times':

'It's a collection of very long, very boring scenes DRAWN OUT SEEMINGLY FOREVER. It was… a complete waste of… what seemed like 20 hours of my life… This movie really does suck this bad. To complete this huge hunk of celluloid garbage, the filmmakers end it with scenes that… can only be compared to patients in a lunatic asylum babbling incoherently.'

Ah, yes, well. Not covered during teacher training and definitely learning on the job.

LOSING HIS TEMPER

I felt right from day one that those long, gloomy, low-ceilinged corridors that I referred to earlier in the 'new' building (1960s brutalism) were oppressive. They were also echoey when students were safely tucked away in lessons, but come the bell for break they turned into a barging scrum as classroom doors opened along both sides, and there was a rush for the canteen or one of the asphalted playground football pitches.

I was on my way to see a colleague in the physics department – walking down the longest of these corridors. It was lesson time, and it was deserted. Deserted that is until a student appeared round the corner at one end. He passed me, and as he disappeared round the corner at the other end, the tannoy crackled into life. It was a system long since rendered inoperative in most classrooms thanks to the judicious use of disabling pencils and biros. However, disabling hadn't stretched to corridors and halls.

'(Deep breath)… Everyone stop working now… (deep breath)… a disgraceful incident (deep breath)… took place this morning during (deep breath)… break. Some (deep breath)…

boys pulled pipes off (deep breath)… the wall in the new block toilets causing serious flooding. I will not tolerate this kind of behaviour (deep breath). Those responsible will be severely punished. You can get on with your work now.'

The effect was extraordinary. Kafkaesque in its scariness. What a visitor might have thought was an asthma attack was actually the head – clearly on edge. His deep breaths had every bit as much impact as his words.

The whole corridor echoed with the sound. No doubt the intention was to cow the entire student population into submission at the same time as flushing out the culprits. Already, in the minds of older students at least, fear was quickly replaced by derision. This very public outburst (by no means the first) was likely to further reduce any lingering respect. I wondered how long he would last.

His first week hadn't gone too well as, amongst other things, he hadn't really taken on board the issue of university gowns – those I'd rejected even as a university student. Instead, he'd continued the absurd tradition set by senior staff of wearing them. It was an ill-judged, not to say risible, attempt to invest what was effectively a secondary modern with academic status. Barely disguised cries of 'Batman' showed what the students thought of the charade. It was in no way present as an agent of change.

Given how challenging he was finding his role, the head's outburst was not a particular surprise. I tried to imagine what had triggered this one. I needn't have bothered. Mr Stephens – the senior master, whose party piece, as we have heard, was an account of how he threw a boy through a door – was only too keen to talk about his involvement. Early on, it had been clear that he had little time for the head. His attempts to give rule-breaking students a second chance, for example, (even to provide counselling for the naughtiest) were anathema to him.

'Make sure they know who's boss.'

'Always be one step ahead.'

This was a sample of the kind of advice we regularly got at lunchtime when Mr Stephens gatecrashed our table of new staff. I was waiting for him to come out with 'Don't smile until April', but he rarely smiled except when narrating one of his tales of terror. And he certainly didn't brook dissent from staff or students. By the time we'd heard his version of what led up to the tannoy outburst, it wasn't hard to piece the scene together...

Philip was at his desk. His office door open as always – a wavering but fast-eroding determination to appear approachable. He was desperately trying to catch up with paperwork – much of it emanating from the highly bureaucratic local authority. This was not what he'd come into headship for, and, increasingly, he'd been wondering about his latest move. The idea of working in London had seemed attractive. He'd heard talk of gentrification in the King's Cross area, but, as I described earlier, that image bore little relation to reality. Any meaningful developments were still on architects' drawing boards. Ideally, he'd been after a mixed school but had convinced himself that single-sex education had many advantages. These had rapidly evaporated as he witnessed levels of violence he'd never encountered in Swindon. Only the previous week, a boy had been taken to hospital following a playground fight. On Monday, he'd been faced with the sudden resignation of a teacher whose class control had disappeared completely.

A knock on the open door.

'Headmaster. I need a word.' Mr Stephens walked up to the head's desk and stood in front of him. There was no denying Mr Stephens. Philip was totally reliant on his ability to bring the hardest nuts to heel. At the same time, he shared none of Philip's concern for student welfare, for encouragement rather than oppression, for discussion rather than direction. Philip hated himself for being in thrall to such a man.

'Come in, Mark. I'm just dealing with yet more forms to fill in.' There were, indeed, numerous piles of paper covering much of a very large desk.

'Headmaster.' Lurking behind the apparent deference was a complete lack of respect which Philip had sensed right from day one – but could do nothing about. 'There's been an incident in the new block toilets. It seems that pipes have been pulled off the wall, and it's caused serious flooding. We're trying to find the culprits; meanwhile, I think you need to take action.'

Philip could feel the colour drain from his face, his heart thumping, and his breaths coming faster. Frustration and anger boiled up inside him. He felt, yet again, unable to get on top of the school's culture of defiance and violence. And he knew he was being put through yet another test. He was desperate to show he wasn't out of his depth. However, wanting to take charge of a serious situation and actually doing it were two completely different things.

'What do you suggest?' The initiative was lost.

'You need to make it clear that we won't tolerate this kind of behaviour – and that severe punishment awaits those responsible.' Mr Stephens continued standing in front of Philip's desk – lining up the bullets for Philip to fire. A decisive response was needed.

'Absolutely. Thank you, Mark. I'm going to put out a message now. We can't be having this.'

His determination to put his words into action meant logic was put on hold. As the red mist descended, he reached for the tannoy button before any thoughts about what he was going to say crossed his mind. He tried to compose himself, but his anger and frustration only increased under the critical eye of Mr Stephens – still standing in front of his desk.

'I'll show them all – including Mr Stephens,' he thought as his finger came down on the button.

His words, punctuated by deep breaths, came tumbling out. When he'd finished…

'How was that, Mark?' Had he at last shown his mettle?

'Excellent. Well done, Headmaster. We need to show the little bastards that they won't get away with that kind of behaviour.'

Mr Stephens, behind a crocodile smile, managed to hide the horror he had felt witnessing the head's uncontrolled outburst.

For me, the Somers Town school was an ordeal by fire, but I emerged relatively unscathed. I learnt the art of bluff – looking as though you were in control when you weren't. I learnt that the surface of the toughest kids is often a veneer and that it was worth trying to peel it off to get to the vulnerabilities and needs beneath. That teenagers are funny even if their humour is often scatological. Most important of all, I learnt that they wanted to learn and responded positively when you got it right, viz. Tony, the head of physics, who ran after-school classes in his lab every afternoon with always more takers than he could accommodate. There were other like-minded staff and we naturally gravitated towards each other but few friendships developed – unlike my next school in Peckham.

THREE

PECKHAM

INTRODUCTION

Southwark is long and thin – stretching from the river as far as the boundary with Croydon. Peckham is roughly in the middle – divided in two by the A202. It's just north of leafy Dulwich. As with so many London areas, poverty and affluence were, and still are, cheek by jowl. In the 1970s, Peckham was an area of mass immigration. Between 1948 and 1970, nearly half a million people left their homes in the West Indies to live in Britain. They were part of the Windrush generation – invited by successive governments to relocate to Britain from their homes in the Caribbean to address labour shortages. The Peckham school was roughly fifty per cent white British and fifty per cent black British. Many of the latter were born in Britain, others came over with their parents, and a third category was left behind with aunts, uncles and grandparents to come at a later date when their parents were settled. These parents came from homes where discipline was strict and often included beatings. They found it hard to adjust to the fairly liberal culture at the school, and with corporal punishment still legal in London, they expected their offspring to be caned if they misbehaved. The Peckham school had long since abandoned caning, and we had to find a way of convincing parents that our sanctions were effective.

Although comprehensives had been introduced in the 1960s, the school was effectively a secondary modern in all but name, with the top end of the ability range 'creamed off' by more 'upmarket' schools. If, as a parent, you could find one of those, you would. Every morning we had a reminder of this as we watched two boys from adjoining houses, right on the school's doorstep, set off up the road for that more prestigious school.

The school itself was a split site, consisting, as it did, of two, decaying, Victorian 'three deckers' – three floors with a large hall and classrooms around each one. Above that, there was often a warren of small offices and stockrooms. The two buildings were about half a mile apart and, depending on age and fitness, a sweaty ten-minute walk between them. Pace was certainly an issue if you were unlucky enough to have classes in separate buildings on either side of the twenty-minute break.

Playground space was minimal. The lower school playground had a large mature oak tree taking up a chunk of it. 'Games' took place on a pitch in Eltham – so far away that, having arrived, it was almost time to return. In my second year at the school, ROSLA (Raising of the School Leaving Age) was introduced – going from fifteen to sixteen. As a token of the change and courtesy of the generous local authority, we were the recipients of a 'ROSLA hut' – mainly plywood and plasterboard. It had a drinking fountain just inside the door with a tap and a small sink which was about the height of a fifteen-year-old's seated bottom. It lasted two days. ROSLA was long overdue but certainly a challenge for many students itching to get away from school and from the staff who were trying to hang on to them. The students wanted the 'real' world.

The Peckham school was the most formative of the three I taught in prior to headship. I found many kindred spirits – all left-leaning politically. Somewhat arrogantly, the large English department considered itself a school within a school. They were passionate, gifted, and creative – and certainly more effective in the classroom than myself. We were determined to provide a more relevant curriculum than had been the case and to include in it proper recognition of all cultures – not just white British. 'Woke' fifty years before the word entered the lexicon. We were not about to repeat the mistakes of colonialists in West Africa with their daffodils and dogfish!

I saw my role as helping to bring together the team as a coherent unit – setting direction but encouraging everyone's input and not being afraid of dissent. It was my first real taste of management and one I thoroughly enjoyed. Mr Godstone (see below) was my first role model. He taught me the value of organisation and of trusting people. I was very lucky.

Until I became head, this was the most exciting time in my career, and many of us in the department made friends for life.

APPLICATION AND APPOINTMENT

I'd heard that in the Peckham school I was interested in, there were frequent culture clashes with staff – well-meaning, well-educated white teachers bent on missionary work, talking through student misdemeanours (of which there were many) on the lines of:

'Devon, can you explain why you smashed that door?'

Such gentle probing made no sense to Devon's parents. 'Why you no just give him de licks, man?'

Our West Indian parents in the 1970s certainly stood no nonsense. Threats to send children back to Jamaica, or any of the islands, were not uncommon.

Anyway, I decided to visit. To this day, I'm not quite sure why, although I guess the fact that it was mixed and multicultural were important factors. I was told to present myself at the end of the school day when I'd meet the head of English. I arrived at the wrong site (good start!) and was redirected by a friendly secretary to the lower school – tucked away behind Peckham market. I found the school office and was told the head of English, Mr Godstone, was waiting for me in the classroom on the ground floor. Fortunately, and unusually in my case, I'd left plenty of time and didn't arrive hot and sweaty.

I made my way down the stairs I had just come up and found myself at one end of a large hall – high ceilinged, polished woodblock floor, classrooms all down one side with wired glass windows. At the far end, there were two more classrooms. The one on the right had its door open, and I could see a middle-aged man wearing a suit and tie sticking pieces of paper onto a large pinboard. I knocked quietly on the open door. As he looked up, I announced myself.

'I'm Andrew Macalpine – come about the deputy head of English post.'

Trevor, as by invitation I was soon calling him, said nothing but bowled me an imaginary cricket ball. 'Do you play cricket, lad?' This is a gruff no-nonsense Yorkshire accent unsoftened by years in Peckham.

I mumbled something in reply about being my school's only off-spinner but really wanting to bat. With that, we were away. Trevor was delightfully blunt. He was also incredibly organised – thus the pinboard. A lovely man who became my mentor during my time at the school. I came away from that opening encounter happy to apply. Soon I received a letter inviting me for an interview.

Unlike Somers Town, this time I had some competition. Already seated outside the interview room was a rather effete-looking young man in his twenties with long hair and a longer coat. He was reading a book of poetry, and I could imagine him inspiring a class of bright A-level students with his love of literature.

I was soon called and found myself facing a panel of three men – none of whom, to my dismay, were the lovely Trevor Godstone.

However, my interview seemed to be going OK, until…

'Tell us, Mr Macalpine. How would you teach Macbeth?'

This is from the chair of governors – a senior figure in the academic world. Sweater, no tie and half glasses, which were perched on the end of his nose. I wasn't quite sure what he was doing there, but mine wasn't to reason why. It was to answer the question. It flashed through my mind that the opposition would have had a much better grasp of The Bard than myself. I stumbled through the various themes which I had loosely absorbed – ambition, guilt, tyranny, blood etc.

However, my heart was starting to beat faster, and my words were becoming increasingly disjointed. I sensed I was beginning to sweat. Finally, relief, the chair took a breath. Next question coming. Surely I'll do better.

'I meant the poet. George MacBeth…'

This is on top of my Shakespeare stumbles. I could feel my face reddening, and my brain freezing.

A blustered 'Oh, sorry. Yes – well… George MacBeth.' I'd never read a word of his poetry. The floor opened up. Silence.

'Alright. Don't worry. We'll move on.'

The rest of the interview was a blur. I got the job – probably by default – the least unlikely of the two candidates!

GETTING GOING

My post-appointment introduction to the school and its students was no less scary than the interview itself. The tour was courtesy of a long-standing, formidable and not-to-be-trifled-with head of Year 8. Her bearing was almost military. She never smiled, and neither students nor staff crossed her path. Miss Wright (for, indeed, she was a 'Miss') was conducting this part of my initiation because one of my responsibilities was the supervision of all Year 8 reading classes. Each week, a lesson was given over to 'silent reading' using a book box scheme that relied on cards (rather than actual books!) geared to different levels of ability. All that was required of the teacher was to check off cards as they were read – and maintain quiet. A doddle, really – even if a fairly meaningless one.

I met Miss Wright downstairs by the school office.

'Hello, Mr Macalpine.' No congratulations on my appointment. 'I gather you'll be responsible for the Year 8 reading classes. It's their reading period now, and I'll take you upstairs and introduce you to one of them.'

We climbed the stone stairs and found ourselves in a long corridor. The classrooms had those wired glass windows I mentioned earlier that enabled you to look in. However, Miss Wright didn't bother with that. She'd clearly already decided which class we were going into.

'Right 8C, you can put your cards down. Miss Wright wants to talk to you.' This is from the class teacher – the polar opposite of the 'intruder'. She was young, dark-haired with a ponytail, wearing a bright yellow sweater and a grey pencil skirt. Her face, whatever she was thinking inside, betrayed no surprise or shock at the appearance of the visitor. The cards were down by the time she got to 'you'. Miss Wright placed herself at the front of the class and delivered a short spiel.

'Quiet please.' It was already 'pin-drop' silence. 'I want to introduce Mr Macalpine, our new second in English. He will be responsible for your silent reading classes each week. Mr Macalpine comes to us from a boys' school in north London and is very strict. He will stand no nonsense, so make sure you concentrate on your work in his classes. You can get on with your reading now.'

With that, she marched out with the class teacher ignored.

'Mr Macalpine' had been, throughout the above, hovering in the background, trying to look as though he and Miss Wright were from the same stable – tough, serious, and not to be trifled with. Of course, this wasn't me, and I half wondered whether she was setting me up – a hint of sadism? My introduction of self might have been rather different:

'Reading is crucial to all your futures. I want to help you make the best possible use of these sessions. If you have any questions or queries, please don't hesitate to ask.'

Miss Wright's introduction of the new 'strict' teacher was quickly seen for the fiction it was.

At the time, in the Peckham school, all classes were streamed so that, on the basis, say, of tests in maths and English, children were grouped together for all their subjects, i.e., if you're good at maths and English, you must also be good at art and P.E. The 'most able' were put in Class 1 and the 'dunces' in Class 8. It was a system that gradually fell into disrepute for obvious reasons – not least of which was that it didn't work and was immoral. Many people confuse streaming with 'setting' whereby you might be in one group for science and another for French. Arguments about setting and mixed ability still abound, but I can't imagine that in 2025, there is any school that still streams.

At Peckham, the eighth stream (the 'dunces' – those with no hope) had long since given up on learning.

'Why do we have to do this? It's baby stuff.'

'Sir, what's the point?'

'My dad works in a garage. He can't read, but he can mend cars.'

And so on.

Meanwhile, the 'top' stream was told on a daily (if not hourly) basis that they were the 'crème de la crème'.

'We expect great things of you.'

'You can go to university if you want.'

'You're in the top stream, you know.'

And they exhibited an arrogance as befitted their exalted status.

'Sir, did you go to university?'

'What degree did you get, Sir?'

'My dad thinks teachers are underpaid. How much do you get paid, Sir?'

I never stood a chance with any of them. With that unnerving ability to home in on weakness, there were students in every class who took no more than a nanosecond to expose Miss Wright's introduction of their new teacher. Reading cards were flicked, dropped, and damaged. Off-task chat was the norm. Students wandered around the room, making huge and unnecessary detours en route to and from the card boxes. I was unable to project any personal belief in the system – because I had none. Damage limitation became my sole aim. If there had been CCTV in the classrooms, it might have picked up something on the following lines:

Me: 'George, pick that up please, and get back to your seat.'

George moves very slowly towards his seat, ruffling Mittal's hair as he does so.

Mittal: 'Get off.'

Me: 'George. Come back here and pick that card up. And Seb, please sit down. I'll be with you in a minute.'

Seb: 'You said that ten minutes ago.' 'Sir', noticeable by its absence.

Me. 'Jenny, please put that away. This isn't a beauty parlour.'

Joke about Jenny's lipstick met with sarcastic laughter. 'Very good, Sir. You should be a comic.'

With ten minutes to go, I try the only weapon left at my disposal. 'Right. If you can't settle down, you'll all stay behind at the end of the lesson.'

This brings forward a chorus of:

'I've finished all my cards.'

'It's them at the back. Keep them in.'

35

'I've got to see Mr Watson.'

'This isn't fair.'

And if CCTV were being fed back to the head's office, there would, in all probability, have been a severe reprimand – maybe a sacking.

But there were no witnesses to what went on and I somehow managed a kind of accommodation – not quite on a par with one of the school's supply teachers who would just stand at the classroom door for an hour, blocking the exit while mayhem ensued. For me, a mix of turning a blind eye, threats, and even help with reading (!) just about worked. Nevertheless, I dreaded the lessons.

WE TAKE ON THE EXAM BOARD

In my introduction to Peckham, I talked about my role as head of English. We were determined to move away from what we saw as the exam board's Gradgrindish approach to English teaching. Mode 3 gave us the opportunity to do just that. Within the rubric, there was a provision for us to write our own syllabus. Once drafted, we had to present it to the exam board. The usual form was for the head of department to present alone, confronted by an array of exam board luminaries whilst nervous colleagues waited back at school to see if the syllabus had passed muster. We had a large department, and I decided, instead of being the traditional sacrificial lamb, we should go mob-handed with each of us responsible for explaining different aspects of our approach. The tables were turned. We outnumbered them! When any one of us seemed to be faltering, someone else would step in. Our numerical superiority worked, and the syllabus was accepted.

We introduced three main elements – Oral, Creative and Practical. There had been some concession to 'Practical' in the board's official syllabus, e.g., how to write a letter of application or how to follow the instruction on a piece of IKEA's self-assembly kit. No mention of the other two.

The Oral element consisted of presentations by students to their fellow class members – followed by questions from them. It all went well until one of the candidates, having made her presentation, refused to answer any of the, admittedly rather unhelpful, questions put to her by her classmates. No amount of persuasion seemed to work, and she was at risk of failing. The trek back from where the exam room was via a narrow, echoey stone staircase – glazed tiles on the one-hundred-year-old walls. Our previously mute candidate suddenly, in her best fishwife voice, started to berate her classmates – some ahead of her and some behind. The gist of it was that they hadn't supported her and hadn't asked the right questions. Her rant was laden with expletives. My colleague in charge of the group had been wondering how to rescue her from failing and now had something to work on. Our candidate was being direct and explicit, and amongst the four-letter tirade was a not unfair analysis of her classmates' lack of support. All this was enough, in my colleague's eyes at least, to justify the award of just enough marks to see her through! No visiting inspector present!

The Creative element was the most exciting. As part of the syllabus, children had to write 'long stories'. We 'published' many of these as booklets with coloured covers and so created a library of students' writing. Exciting for the students – and for us.

THE DEATH OF PIGGY

For teachers of English literature, there are times when even the most screen-addicted youngsters sit up and take notice, e.g., moments of shocking racism in *Gone with the Wind*, Tom

Robinson getting shot in *To Kill a Mockingbird*, Harry learning that Dumbledore has planned to kill him in *Harry Potter and the Deathly Hallows*.

The death of Piggy in William Golding's bestseller *Lord of the Flies* is one such passage. A group of boys have been stranded on an uninhabited island, and it hasn't taken long for all remnants of civilised behaviour to disappear. Simon has just been speared to death by children turned monsters. The evil Jack's second-in-command, Roger, is standing atop a cliff, at the bottom of which Piggy is attempting to bring the warring tribes of boys together – using the conch which, up until now, has symbolised reason and maturity. Roger deliberately prises free an enormous boulder that rumbles down the cliff face, gathering speed as it does so. It lands squarely on Piggy – killing him instantly. The conch is shattered into a thousand pieces.

A shocking moment that represents the climax of Golding's dark tale.

It's the lesson before the break and, as head of English, I am on a walkabout – peering into my colleagues' classrooms. I've had to reschedule the weekly department meeting, and the walkabout is a good excuse not only to check on the team's availability but also to get a flavour of what's going on in each class (hopefully not being seen as mirroring Mr Wathen from Somers Town – waiting to pounce). I reach Joan's. She's standing at the front with the class facing her. Young, slim and blonde with a distinctive ponytail, Joan is a newcomer to the department – and a very conscientious one. This is her first teaching post, and she has been remarkably successful in engaging some of the most challenging classes and students. Through the door's wired glass window, I see, mainly, the backs of students. They are unusually still. She's clearly reading to them, and the faces I can see are focussed on her. I didn't know it, but each one is seeing themselves on the island, waiting for disaster. I should have waited before entering… but… I didn't.

Readers tend to identify strongly with Piggy despite him being overweight, short-sighted and asthmatic. He is the only boy who is managing to bring about any sense of order. All the class know is that Roger has prised free this enormous boulder. The suspense is palpable. Well, palpable to anyone with any sensitivity. At that moment, that excluded me. Courtesy of Golding, what happens next always generates a gasp of shock from any class.

I stand at the back of the room. Heads turn. The lump of rock hangs in the air.

'So sorry to trouble you, Miss Broadhurst. I can see everyone is really involved. Just checking you can make the department meeting on Tuesday.'

There's a pause. She looks up at me. 'Yes, I can.' Uncharacteristically terse. Her face reddens slightly, which I take to be an embarrassment, but it could just as easily be anger. Actually, 'seething' as I discovered subsequently. I make my way out of the classroom, sensing a thread has been broken. And, yes, Joan's class's rapt attention has already slumped as the drama slips away. Despite her valiant attempt to retrieve the situation by carrying on to the climax, she has lost some of the students, and there is just the whiff of fidgeting and muttering, replacing the silence and stillness that were there before.

Joan eventually forgave me. Meanwhile, my gaff entered departmental folklore. For a long time after, I felt guilty and disappointed with myself. Introducing working-class children to literature is an exciting challenge, and, as a department, we worked hard to find books (not reading cards!) that stimulated and gripped our teenage audiences. As for me, I vowed never again to interrupt a class unless it was clear what they were doing and that my presence would not undermine learning.

Years later, as Inspector for Secondary Education in Havering, I was being taken round one of 'my' schools by the head. I had been in his shoes many times – hoping I had chosen the right classes and right teachers to impress my visitor. When such tours work well, the visitor has a chance to engage with students.

'So tell me what you're doing here.'

'How long have you been working on this project?'

'That looks like a lovely piece of work. How are you getting along generally?'

Ice-breakers that enable the visitor to explore the learning that's taking place.

However, in this school and with this head, the custom was that whenever he walked into a class, all the students stood up – no matter what they were doing. His behaviour somehow turned the attention on him – rather than on what learning was taking place. It seemed to me that he'd got his priorities wrong. I was keen to see the school's next set of results. It was no surprise to me that they were still struggling along the bottom.

If, on my tour of that school, learning had been taking place, it would certainly have been disrupted – as it was with Joan's class and *Lord of the Flies*.

The term 'Teaching and Learning' used to trip off teachers' tongues but, for many, it began to be replaced by 'Learning and Teaching' – shifting the emphasis from the instructor at the front of their class (viz. black and white photos of teachers doing just that –replicating university lectures) to classes where learning situations were set up by the teacher who could then work with individual children or groups of children.

FIGHT IN THE CLASSROOM

School disputes – and full-blown fights – can erupt anytime and anywhere. Schools are a heady cocktail: large numbers of testosterone-fuelled teenagers crammed into a small space. Experienced teachers can pick up the vibes when trouble is brewing – the pushing and shoving on the way into the classroom, muttered threats, the scramble for seats – behaviours that need to be nipped in the bud.

Although I had developed defusing tactics at my Somers Town school, there were still times when I was too slow to spot warning signs and take appropriate action. One day, at the end of a break, a simmering dispute came into my class. My eye was certainly not on the ball and I didn't manage to stop it. At least I had them all sitting down – but that wasn't enough.

An argument began.

'You're a wanker. You know that, Peter.'

This was Amanda – large with bushy, unkempt hair. A permanently angry face – and manner – that went with her reputation for trouble. She was often to be seen standing outside the classroom – or outside the head's office. On those frequent occasions when she was absent, I felt calmer and more confident. Amazing how one student can affect the atmosphere. Today she was there, making her presence felt. Going for the same seat as Peter. At the back of the class, of course. I'd already lost some ground.

'Right, Peter, you can sit there.'

I gestured towards an empty chair near the front of the class. I was taking the line of least resistance. Peter, tall, pale, and skinny, was easier prey than Amanda. Or so I thought. He had a devious streak, and my impression had always been that he managed to melt away when there was trouble. Not on this occasion though. He had clearly been sufficiently riled by Amanda to take action. As I backed my way down the room towards the whiteboard, Peter produced what was recognisably an imitation pistol. It was a cap gun and just made a bang. However, it was enough to be scary. Peter turned round and fired it in Amanda's direction, managing two 'shots' before I got to him and took it away. Sadly, that was just the start. Before the echoes of the bangs had died away, Amanda was advancing down the classroom, brandishing an umbrella that she'd produced from her bag. I was unable to stop her before she'd hit Peter in the face with it.

'You fucking tosser!' Amanda never minced her words.

I rushed in to separate the two of them, knocking over a chair as I did, and managed to get between them. At that point, I should have taken both students out of the lesson and sent another to fetch a senior member of staff. Instead, I chose what might be termed the 'optimistic' route (it'll all simmer down and be fine). So, between audible breaths and a raised pulse, I tried to reassert some authority.

'Right, both of you. Back to your seats.'

Peter was immediately compliant, but it seemed an eternity before Amanda sat down.

'That was completely unacceptable. I shall need to see both of you at the end of the lesson.'

The situation seemed to have calmed. And just when I thought we might be getting on with *Roll of Thunder, Hear My Cry* – Mildred Taylor's very aptly named book – and just as it seemed the class was going from transfixed spectators to readers, Amanda's friend, Alex, sitting three seats away from Peter, joined in. She was an unlikely aggressor. Open, smiley, freckly face. Always in full school uniform. Always ready to help. I could never quite understand her friendship with Amanda. On this occasion, she had decided to join in, repeatedly provoking Peter.

'Who you going to hit next then. Come on. Who's it going to be?'

'That's not helpful, Alex. Can we get back to the book, please.' Weasel words that didn't convince me – or the class.

Peter appeared not to rise to Alex's bait but had obviously said something to her and, abruptly, it all began again. Amanda marched back down the class and, before I could get to her, swung at Peter once more with her umbrella. Of course, I should have taken it off her earlier but, in hindsight... There was a tussle

– another chair going over and students swaying out of the way as Peter prised the umbrella from Amanda's fingers and then hit her in the face with it.

'Sir, you need to stop this. Someone's going to get hurt.' This was Jenny, sitting at the front, as usual, and wise beyond her years.

Meanwhile, 'You little shit.' Amanda's face was now crimson as she confronted Peter yet again.

'Right, that's enough. You both need to come outside – NOW.' I had managed to place myself between the two of them, grab Peter's arm and march him out into the corridor with Amanda, at last looking relatively subdued, trailing behind.

As I made my way towards the door past Jenny, I took her advice.

'Yes, Jenny, can you go to the office and ask the senior member of staff on duty to come as soon as possible.' Jenny, of course, complied straight away.

'Right, Peter. Don't you move.' He was now standing in the corridor. I returned to the class.

'Come on, Amanda. Hurry up. You need to come out too.' She made her way slowly towards the door, and the three of us stood outside – me hoping that the rest of the class was by now a bit more subdued, although the excited chatter coming through the open door suggested otherwise. Certainly, the steam seemed to have gone out of the two miscreants while we waited for the duty staff member, who then took the two of them off.

For me, there was a lesson to be learnt about being more alert and more organised. Orderly lining up and seating plans, for example. I don't think Amanda or Peter learnt much despite being excluded from school for three days – with dire warnings about their future behaviour. More than likely, they kept out of each other's way rather than continue the aggro.

THE STAFFROOM BRIDGE CLUB

The school's upper and lower split resulted in a kind of pecking order, with the lower school not only having the younger children but also, predominately, younger staff. There was a third category – the 'homeless' – those who frequently had to commute the fifteen-minute fast walk between the two sites. Another feature of this ageist set-up was the apparent bias, in terms of timetabling, towards the senior (i.e., older) staff. Somehow they seemed to have lighter timetables. At least that was the impression commuters got as they arrived at the upper school puffing and panting at the end of break (often minus some vital lesson plan) only to find two utterly relaxed tables of deputy heads and heads of department finishing off their bridge hands.

'How do they manage it?' was a common thought going through the minds of these commuters as they downed a quick coffee before getting themselves together for their next lesson. That commute meant, of course, that they missed the start of a break when the two bridge tables were being set up, and some staff were already seated and waiting to play. At each table, cards being shuffled.

I'm chatting to Anne, my deputy head of the department, by the coffee machine. She has her back to the bridge tables. Looking over her shoulder, I experience a familiar sense of unease. These card sessions are probably the high point of the participants' days – as opposed to anything to do with children.

Rob, the head of Maths, rushes in. He's tall, with an unkempt beard and a suit that looks like he's worn it since the day he started – too long ago for anyone to remember.

'Sorry, chaps. 4H again. My God! What a collection! Talk about no-hopers... Alright, where do you want me?'

'Over there, partnering Mick.'

Mick, head of art – paint-spattered apron, corduroy trousers, sandals, and socks – is rarely to be seen in the art room. His students are usually left to 'get on with it' while Mick wanders the school looking for someone to chat to.

'You're lucky. We were about to recruit young Dave.' This is from Geoff, a senior master and bridge organiser. He looks the part with his neat haircut, smart suit, and tie. He seems relaxed at the bridge table – far removed from his role as school disciplinarian.

Most staff have an image of him standing on a bench in the playground during fire drills, waiting for what seems like forever to instruct or harangue – long after the assembled pupils have become silent. No one else on the staff would have been able to sustain that.

Geoff's table is mirrored by the group of four next to them. They conform closely to the ageist character of the upper school staff. Bridge is second only to discussions about pensions.

Back to 'young Dave' who lets out a sotto voce sigh of relief at his narrow escape. I take all this in a while, standing by the coffee machine. I remember that, a few weeks ago, Dave had been asked whether he played and, in his innocence, had admitted to having played a few times. Subsequently, he had found it difficult to refuse whenever they were one short. Despite having become increasingly irritated by the way the staffroom was commandeered by the bridge players, I couldn't completely absolve myself, having once been roped in in an unguarded moment. Following that isolated but shameful lapse, I managed a sufficient range of excuses for Geoff, and Bill, the other main organiser, to give up on me.

The game starts. In each round, there is always someone who observes but doesn't play – known as 'dummy'. In this case, it's Andy who has time to survey the staffroom. He notices Jenny, who has just arrived from the younger, more innocent world of the lower school. She is perched on one of the few remaining chairs with a precariously balanced pile of books in her lap.

'Get them to mark their own. Saves a lot of hassle.' Andy looks quite lively in his tracksuit and sports shirt. He teaches P.E. and is actually one of the younger members of the staff. However, it hasn't taken long for him to be sucked into the bridge players' culture. He certainly never marks books and rarely prepares his lessons.

A knock on the staffroom door. Nobody moves for what seems an eternity. None of the bridge players even appears to have heard. I'm just about to go myself when Jenny somehow deposits her books on the floor without toppling them and goes to the door.

'Yes, what do you want?' She's already on her way to adopting the 'Why are you troubling us?' tone.

'Is Mr McKay there?' I recognise Jamie from my fourth-year English group. He's a quiet, friendly boy who has probably been put up to this errand.

Mr McKay (aka Danny) from the bridge table only a few feet from the door: 'Ask him what he wants.'

'What do you want, Jamie?' Jenny has now become the intermediary.

'It's break time. We need the ball, please, to play football.'

'He needs the ball to play football.' Jenny defers to Danny for a decision.

'Tell him after school. I'm busy.' He wonders why his partner has led hearts rather than spades.

'You'll have to come back after school, Jamie.' Jenny adopts a more conciliatory tone as she begins to realise there's something unsavoury about this whole scene. Which, of course, there is. I am, however, slightly more relaxed than usual, knowing that a few of us have arranged to meet after school to discuss what we can do about it.

*

So the plotters assemble – bridge players long since departed. Gordon, chair of the Staff Association and head of R.E, always respectably dressed – jacket and tie – but underneath a determined reformer; Steve, NUT rep – a bit of a caricature with his beard and denim jacket; Lucy, head of Year 9 – tough, fierce and forceful as befits a head of year; and myself. Having waited for the cleaner to leave, we seat ourselves round one of the bridge tables, still positioned where they always are.

Gordon kicks off. 'This is ridiculous. They're monopolising the staffroom.'

I chip in. 'They certainly are. I was there this morning. I felt really sorry for Dave – and Jenny – and for that lot squeezed around the coffee machine.'

Lucy. 'So... what do we do about it?'

'Ask them to stop playing. Explain that the staffroom isn't designed for bridge.' Gordon's idea is met with silence.

'Well... rather you than me. And it won't get us anywhere. You'll just be another young Trotskyist. What about rearranging the tables first thing before they get here so they can't play? It'll have to be crack of dawn. Ann Marie (head of history) gets here about six thirty. In fact, I reckon she sleeps here.'

Lucy's suggestion is met with murmurs of assent, and it's agreed that we'd be early birds.

Bleary-eyed but determined, we assemble twelve hours later at six a.m.

'That should do it.' Gordon seems satisfied with the rearranged room – tables together and chairs dotted around. We stand admiring our handiwork and head off to our respective departmental areas.

Morning break arrives, and I head for the staffroom. Lucy falls into step alongside me.

'I can't wait to see their faces.' She echoes my thoughts.

As we enter, we realise our plan has failed. The tables are back in bridge formation, and games are already underway. Other staff, as usual, are forced to the edges of the staffroom or bunched round the coffee machine. Our team exchange looks. I'm sure that, like me, they're seething.

Lunchtime comes. Quick debrief in the canteen.

'Bastards! What now?' Steve bristles, face reddening.

'We should put it to the Staff Association.' Gordon is determined to play it by the book.

'I agree with Gordon,' I said. Gordon, as well as being a close friend, is also someone whose judgement I trust.

'That'll go down well. They already see it as a left-wing cell.' Lucy's having none of it.

However, we eventually all agree that the Staff Association is the only recourse.

'OK. How do we word it then?' Gordon asks.

'Let me have a go.' Steve starts scribbling while we look on. 'Shall I read it?'

'Yeah, go on.' I'm not confident that Steve's really the best person for the task, but he's obviously keen.

Steve reads: 'We the undersigned propose banning the following staff from the staffroom until further notice. The ban to extend to their alternative staffroom at The Five Bells[1]. [Here follows a list of the main culprits – all senior staff – including one of the deputy heads]. Furthermore, their playing cards should be confiscated and a process of re-education to take place to include:

Point one: Introductory course in human relations.

Point two: Attendance at a local teacher training centre.'

'Yes, thanks Steve – really helpful. Can we be serious for a minute?' Gordon is not about to be deflected.

'We need to make this short, to the point and reasonable; otherwise no one will support it.'

After further discussion, the following is agreed:

'We, the undersigned members of the Staff Association, propose that the playing of bridge in the upper school staffroom be banned on the following grounds:

It is exclusive – confined to a small number of bridge-playing staff.

---

1   Local pub

It dictates the layout of the staffroom – pushing those who don't play to corners.

It places the onus of answering the staffroom door on non-players.'

Staff Association meetings are scheduled once a month and, as luck would have it, there is one due the following week. The agenda is always printed in advance, together with any resolutions. It's not difficult to predict the heated exchanges that will precede the meeting.

However, come the day, the resolution is passed overwhelmingly. A refreshing move into the twentieth century as then was! It brought together the left and the far left, who constituted the bulk of the Peckham staff. The staffroom bridge ceased. For a short while, there was a petulant boycott of the staffroom by some of the erstwhile regular bridge players. Contact between the old and the new round the coffee machine was awkward, and an icy atmosphere prevailed – as opposed to the earlier heat. Eventually, the balance of power shifted from old lags to young bloods, and a visitor might even have detected some harmony.

Postscript: Later in my career, I applied for a deputy headship in another London school. My visit suggested a moribund establishment stuck in a bygone age, all summed up by the presence of a half-size snooker table in the middle of the staffroom. What a wonderful distraction from the rigours of the classroom, but not quite the next step I was looking for.

FOUR

ISLE OF DOGS

INTRODUCTION

Five years on and having made friends for life and having had
my own life transformed, I was looking for the next stage. This
was as Director of Studies at a brand-new comprehensive on
the southern tip of the Isle of Dogs. The school had replaced
a grammar school in Poplar, and James, a close friend of mine,
had been appointed as its first head. It would be his first senior
appointment with comprehensive school experience.

The Isle of Dogs is not quite an island. If you look at a map
of London, you'll see it as a distinctive loop in the Thames.
It's bounded on three sides by the river. However, the top
end (north) is effectively the fourth side and consists of what
was, up until the 1970s, dockland. However, the advent of
containerisation and the increasing size of cargo ships, which
the docks could not handle, meant that they gradually became
redundant. They closed progressively during the 1970s, and the
last two – the West India and Millwall docks – closed down in
1980. This left the area in a severely dilapidated state, derelict
and effectively abandoned – as were the white working-class
dockers whose jobs had disappeared. Naturally, unemployment

became widespread. And no funding was allocated to improve housing, with many families living in rundown council tower blocks.

The school was located in the London Borough of Tower Hamlets – right opposite leafy Greenwich, just the other side of the river. As if to emphasise the disparity between the boroughs, the foot tunnel under the Thames, which joins the two, had a steel handrail on the north side and a brass one on the south side. That's still the case in 2025.

The school's bare breeze blocks, both inside and out, gave it a crude and rather forbidding look. Inside there were split levels going from the dark, dingy, difficult-to-supervise locker area on the ground floor, up to level seven where there were 'social areas' designed for the kind of well-behaved child who could only live in an architect's imagination. These were even harder to supervise (see 'Chair Bombs') and frequently wrecked.

The school had won an architects' award but not a users' one, and, in my experience, school architects have a lot to answer for. Of course, they can't work in a school that's still on the drawing board, but they *can* get advice from those who actually use them, i.e., teachers. And, of course, they can visit other schools. Quite often, they have little conception of what enables a school to function. Just as students home in on teachers' weaknesses, so they do with buildings. For example, 'behind the bike sheds' is a phrase everyone knows. For bike sheds, read nooks and crannies where all sorts can take place, from smoking and fighting to kissing and plotting – or just becoming invisible for a while.

Another issue was that the school was north/south, with the back facing south over the Thames towards Greenwich. The large windows, with their non-existent or inadequate blinds, meant that on hot summer days, classrooms reached over thirty degrees and children had to be sent home at lunchtime. In winter, the north side never heated up. It wasn't just the unions that objected!

51

The transition from grammar to 'comprehensive' was not smooth as the small number of middle-class families on the island tended to send their children elsewhere. Grammar school staff had not encountered many pupils who bucked authority and whose families rated jobs over academic qualifications. Many of them found it hard to adapt. This was also the time when corporal punishment was about to be abolished in ILEA (Inner London Education Authority) schools, and James, appointed as head to lead the school into comprehensivisation, was making sure the cane was no longer an acceptable sanction – no matter how unruly and difficult the children were. Many of the senior staff felt naked without the cane to fall back on.

However, I had plenty of support from staff who'd seen the writing on the wall and welcomed the new era. It was my job to work with them and try to bring them on board. Or subtly hasten their departure!

APPLICATION AND APPOINTMENT

Our little group of shortlisted (and freshly interviewed) candidates sat around in the staffroom, waiting to see who would be called. Meanwhile, over in a corner, the room's only other occupant – young, tall, and rake thin – appeared to be about to have a breakdown. He was talking to himself or to anyone who'd listen as he marked a huge pile of books.

'These kids are impossible… What's the point… I might just as well leave them to it.'

This did nothing to quell our nervous anticipation. Did we really want to join this school? Morning break came with still no white smoke but an influx of current staff. They included the head of geography – an infamous figure who, I quickly learnt, was one of the school's longest-standing members. He had a pronounced stoop and a red face that looked permanently angry. He had written a book about his experiences teaching in the school's predecessor in Poplar. Putting it mildly, he was not a fan of the change. He was also renowned for his short fuse and abrupt manner.

He addressed no one in particular.

'So…Director of Studies. Who's going to direct me then?'

He barked this at the staffroom in general. Definitely rhetorical and not to be answered. No one seemed to take much notice. Obviously, no one from our little group stationed around a table on one side of the room was going to rise to the challenge. We all stayed put – and silent, once again wondering what we might be letting ourselves in for. I think I felt that having gotten that far I wasn't going to bow out. Anyway, some thirty minutes later, the white smoke rose in my direction. I like to think it was my experience that swayed it, but nepotism must have played a large part.

GETTING GOING

My reward, as an appointee, was to find my office sandwiched between two reluctant residuals from the grammar school – Howard on my left and sweet Jill on my right. Howard was white-haired, burly, and bullish. Jill – petite, kind, and rather frail. They were both heading for retirement as fast as they could. Both, for different reasons, were hopelessly out of their depth with a range of children they never knew existed and had certainly never encountered. Until my arrival, they had constituted James's senior team. Howard's job was to deal with discipline – or rather indiscipline. His subtle approach consisted of shouting at the numerous children sent to his office. Questions were mostly rhetorical.

'You don't know what work is, do you? At your age, I had to go out and get a job.'

'When are you going to grow up and behave yourself?'

'You wouldn't have lasted five minutes at the old school.'

'Don't your parents teach you manners?'

'You don't deserve to be in a school at all.'

His tirades were often peppered with worse abuse: 'Guttersnipe' (shades of Somers Town), 'You're just rubbish', etc. – all the while, I'm sure, harking back nostalgically to the aspiring, upwardly mobile parents in Poplar, as opposed to the workshy dockers on the island.

Even though I had been in two challenging schools for almost ten years, I wasn't prepared for my toughest assignment to date. The island had some 150 stolen cars being driven, bowdlerised, and customised at any one time (see below 'Inspecting Technology'), and this rather summed up the challenge the school faced.

'CALL ME NICK'

Having set the school up, my friend James had resigned and was moving on.

We made every effort to suspend judgement on our new leader, Nick Washbourn. If accomplishments were anything to go by, the interviewing team had picked a winner. Physically, however, the signs were less promising. Fiftyish, well-built but rather overweight, Nick had a heavy-jowled and pock-marked face. There was a sense of over-indulgence.

'We've heard about your CV, Nick.' Tony, one of the deputy heads, dived in. 'Seven A levels. Fluent in French and Italian. Plays the clarinet. And still, time to run a school (this was his second headship). Amazing.'

'Oh, and I've written a novel. Not a very good one.' This seemed like an airily unimportant afterthought. He might just as easily have been shuffling through some papers on his desk. After what had gone before, was this false modesty?

I was finding the list hard to stomach. I should have kept quiet.

Instead… 'What about sport?' In my time, I had been a good amateur golfer. I had, immodestly, managed to communicate this to most of my colleagues.

Nick hesitated. 'Oh, sport. I'm afraid those days are behind me. In my time, I was a scratch golfer…' I didn't hear the rest. *My* consuming passion had just been a side-line for *him* – and a more impressive one. Throughout the session, eyebrows had been raised, and glances exchanged, but, hey, these were early days. Despite a CV verging on the incredible, we felt obliged to give him the benefit of the doubt.

On to the first staff meeting. The opportunity for Nick to lay out his stall – elements of the CV subtly inserted.

'Good morning, everyone. My name is Nick Washbourn, but you can call me Nick.'

Sadly the rest of 'Nick's address' – 'heard great things', 'huge potential', 'doing a great job' – was lost on the majority of the audience as, almost immediately, whispered 'Call me Nicks' were making their way around the staffroom.

It was not long before 'Call me Nick' – as he came to be known – was quite often to be found in his office studying holiday brochures. No doubt looking for ways to escape. Our team was looking for ways to run the school without him. The five of us started with clandestine team meetings, which, initially, were held in one of our offices. Increasingly, we were able to use his own office as a result of his frequent, unexplained absences – or his lateness. On important issues, the tactic the five of us adopted was to come into discussions apparently independently but with one or two rehearsed disagreements. We'd then reach a conclusion that he would be forced to go along with. His only responsibility was to promulgate the decision to the staff. Machiavelli had nothing on us. He was still there when I moved on to my first headship – having experienced another example of how not to do it.

CHAIR BOMBS

My introduction to the Isle of Dogs school referred to 'social areas' on level seven, which were largely unsupervised and subject to vandalism. Staff duty patrols were mostly along corridors and in the playground. Another brilliant piece of design was that you could make your way along the whole of the top of the school via the interconnecting doors that linked the five areas. Wreck an area and move on.

Regular use of the landing outside the level seven area was made by caretakers stacking chairs there – metal frames and solid wooden seats. They could pile up at least a dozen without them falling over.

Meanwhile, walkie-talkies for recreational use were starting to become popular in the late 1970s and early 1980s, and students had begun to bring them into school. They found they could talk through walls and floors (even the school's thick breeze blocks) with little fear of discovery. Whether the plotting took place behind the bike sheds or elsewhere, the idea took root amongst a small group of boys (for they were, we suspected, all boys) that one person could stand behind the stacked chairs at the top of the level seven staircase while waiting for a walkie-talkie signal from the lookout stationed down the corridor on level six. Once a member of staff appeared, the boy at the top would push over the chairs, which would crash down the stairs with a thunderous cacophony of metal and hardwood as they did so. The unsuspecting member of staff would be terrified and leap back out of the way.

I was in my office when Amish Patel appeared. Amish was a recent addition to the maths department and had just started to get to grips with the school's challenges. He was in his early twenties, small and slight. So much so that, on occasions, he was mistaken for a pupil. He was shaking violently.

'Amish, what's wrong? You look as though you've seen a ghost.' He started to stutter a reply but couldn't continue.

'Amish, sit down. What on earth has happened?'

He told me he'd been at the bottom of the staircase when the chairs came cascading down. Once I'd got the story out of him and made him a cup of tea, I left him where he was and went to investigate. By the time I got up to level six, two caretakers – Winston and Chris – had already arrived and were disentangling what could just as well have been the result of an earthquake. In Chris's case, this was carried out with much puffing and wheezing, given his weight and his aversion to anything strenuous.

'What's happened here, Winston?' He straightened up.

'I've no idea, Andrew. They must just have been stacked too high.'

This didn't seem very convincing, and Winston sensed that he'd need to do better.

'Maybe a gust of wind – a door slamming. I don't know.'

'Well, I suggest you don't stack them so high next time.' With that, I walked off.

It took another deadly episode, with a reduced stack, before they were persuaded to store their chairs *inside* the social area.

Meanwhile, as senior staff, we started to investigate. We had found the caretakers' explanations unconvincing and started to pursue the theory that students were behind the 'attack'. A certain Bradley Miller had been spotted by a member of staff loitering around the corridor just before the first incident. I hauled him in.

Bradley was a small thin boy with mean, weasel eyes that looked at you unwaveringly. He was always in trouble, both in and out of school. Although there was nothing remotely innocent about him, Dickens' line in reference to poor Oliver Twist popped into my mind: 'That boy will be hung.'

'Right, Bradley, I'm sure you know that, twice, a stack of chairs has fallen down the stairs from level seven.'

'No idea. What chairs?' Bradley's face betrayed nothing. He was used to interrogations.

'You were seen hanging around level six Tuesday break time.'

'So? What's the law against that? There's always loads of us in the corridor.'

I ignored the challenge. 'There's no law against it, Bradley. So you're saying you know nothing about it?'

'No. Can I go now?'

We quizzed one or two more likely culprits but got nowhere. None of the plotters were ever caught, and no staff were injured, although those nearby, like poor Mr Patel, were traumatised by the experience.

I'm sure the boys didn't seek to kill – or maim – just to frighten and shock – or just to have a laugh. However, in my thirty years working in schools, it was certainly the scariest moment I came across.

CRAZINESS

Galleon House is a ten-storey block of flats facing the school on the Isle of Dogs. It's on the 'Schooner' estate – completed in 1963. These are names designed to conjure images of unfurled sails and open seas. Names are considerably more relevant, however, on the south side of the river where the Royal Naval College is located with all its accompanying history. Gentrification in Greenwich has been taking place since the first of its royal palaces was built there in the fifteenth century. 'Gentrification' was not a word that had ever been applied to the Isle of Dogs by the time I got there in 1976. Indeed, as the Schooner estate was being opened, so were the docks closing. I described the impact in my introduction to the Isle of Dogs. Massive unemployment resulted in many families experiencing real hardship. At the time, there were protests at the lack of social provision in the area – the area we drew the majority of our students from. Households were struggling to make ends meet, and one-parent families were the norm.

By the mid-1970s, a number of our students lived in Galleon

House. The school had no policy on school uniforms, and this only served to emphasise the distinction between children of parents still employed and the rest. Fashionable clothes v. 'hand-me-downs'. And you were lucky if they appeared with anything to write with – let alone books.

There were many kids whose attendance was rare. They hung about street corners, shopped for their mums, and learnt how to nick sweets from the corner shop. The older ones learnt how to hotwire cars.

All those living on the Schooner estate had to do to get to school – assuming they turned up at all – was cross Manchester Road, a couple of minutes from flats on the ground floor and longer if you lived on the tenth floor with graffitied, vandalised lifts that didn't work. Still, the proximity meant less expense for the unemployed breadwinner (assuming he was still resident) than having to fork out the bus fare from the top of the island.

This episode concerns one of the Schooner residents – an ex-student.

I was in the school office one day – about to do some photocopying. The windows of the office overlooked the block.

Suddenly a startled cry from Dawn – one of the school secretaries. She'd been typing away one minute, and the next she was standing by the window, her glasses in her hand, beckoning to us.

'Everyone! Look up there!'

The noise of the other rattling keyboards ceased as we all made our way over to the window and homed in on the target of Dawn's pointing finger.

When we did, my blood ran cold. Horrified looks on colleagues' faces suggested similar reactions. We could clearly see what seemed to be a young man sitting astride a corner of Galleon's flat roof, a leg dangling over each side of the corner. He was some one hundred feet up in the air but could have been sitting on the corner of a table, rather than on a rooftop.

'That's Rory Johns' brother, Darren. I'd recognise him anywhere.' Jeff, a long-standing head of the department who seemed to know every child – especially the naughty ones – was standing next to me. He was one of the old guard, tough but no flogger, and hugely respected by students and staff alike. I didn't recognise Darren, but I certainly recognised the name – a name that cropped up from time to time and was remembered with little affection by longer-standing staff. I certainly knew Rory. He was in one of my classes – difficult but not in his brother's league.

Darren, meanwhile, remained sitting on the roof.

'He was always completely crazy. We need to call the police before he falls – or jumps,' Jeff said.

I wanted to add 'or even moves'. Vertigo transference had kicked in, and while not being able to take my eyes off the boy, I had an overwhelming sense of nausea – as though it were me up there.

Jeff, however, was not standing transfixed as many of us in the office were. 'Dawn, can you ring 999, please.'

Dawn got on the phone straight away, and the police, amazingly, given how much crime there was on the island, were quick to arrive. Not quick enough, however. In the meantime, Darren had disappeared – leaving some rather red-faced witnesses convincing the police that we weren't all delusional.

They said they'd investigate, although, as we explained, we were pretty sure Darren would be gone by the time they got up to the roof. It was now after four – too late to get hold of brother Rory, assuming he'd been in school at all that day. However, the following day I tracked down his class – not really expecting to find him there, given his attendance record. Anyway, there he was at the back of the room, as far away from the teacher as possible – in Roger McGough's words… 'where those who skive hang out.' Rory was sharing a joke with the boy next to him.

I went in and asked Gill, the recently appointed deputy head of history, if we could take Rory out.

'You're welcome to him.' Gill had long since stopped pretending all was perfect. I beckoned to Rory, who immediately put on his 'Who me?' face. He had an innocence about him that belied his reputation for trouble. He sloped towards me. I gestured towards the door and followed him out.

'Come with me, Rory.'

He trailed behind. 'What's it for now?'

'Don't worry. Just a couple of questions.'

We got down to my office. I closed the door and stood in front of my desk. We both stayed standing.

'Rory, where do you live?'

'Galleon. You know where I live.' This was true.

'Did you know your brother was sitting on the roof yesterday afternoon and that we called the police to get him down?'

'If you mean Darren, I ain't seen him for months. He stays with my dad in Wapping.'

And that was as far as we got with Rory or, for that matter, Darren. We next heard, via the island's grapevine, that Darren was serving time for a violent robbery. Even old lags like myself found the incident involving Darren shocking. For a good part of the younger staff, it opened their eyes to the family backgrounds of a significant minority of students – where education took second place to survival, whether it be threats from other teenagers or from the deprivations of everyday life.

Postscript: Some thirty years later, a man actually jumped from the top floor of Galleon House and killed himself. Darren's escapade, however, was clearly more bravado than a death wish.

A TRIBUTE TO DANIEL

Aged 15, he stole a London Transport double-decker bus
When no one was looking
Slightly overweight

Rather geeky
Breaktime footie's
Not for you
Nor hanging around with knots of girls
Who stroke their hair
And talk about boys
The ones not there
Your mind's on
The 277
The Island's lifeline
To the wider world
Its timetable
And many others
Chunter through your brain
A London Transport professor
Bugger exams
Sadly – double-decker buses are unwieldy beasts
With no training, Daniel's bronco bucked
And bashed and crashed
Bus and pride dented
Reputation enhanced

FIVE

ISLE OF DOGS – SECOND POST

APPOINTMENT AND MORE TALES

Interviews – like meetings – can make participants heavy-lidded. I had a taste of this when going for a promotion at the Isle of Dogs school some four years later. This was the vacant deputy headship – Howard having finally retired. The chair of governors at the time was one John Braithwaite, a feared GLC councillor – perhaps the most famous London Labour politician of his day. Dark-suited, steel grey hair slicked back and fox-like eyes. Years of Labour Party politics had left him with all the flexibility and warmth of a Stalin. He was not to be trifled with. While being questioned by another member of the panel, I would catch a glimpse of his closed lids. If you'd been able to get up from the hot seat and walk over, you would have seen just the tiniest gap between the top and bottom lid. I was wary of him – not taken in by his apparent insomnia. The interview was over and I got up to leave. As I reached the door and was halfway out, I heard him say:

'Did you hear that? He said, "Goodbye, Braithwaite."' Implying I'd behaved like some cheeky kid. Of course, I didn't say 'Goodbye Braithwaite.' I wasn't that stupid. I got the job but probably only by the tiniest margin.

INSPECTING TECHNOLOGY

Ofsted's rubric on school inspections starts as follows: 'The inspection of a school provides an independent external evaluation of its effectiveness and a diagnosis of what it should do to improve.' That sounds so reasonable – unless you're actually *working* in a school. There, all you'll be thinking about is which category you're going to fall into. The categories have changed over the years, but at the time of writing, they are:

Outstanding

Good

Requires Improvement

Inadequate

School staff will interpret anything less than 'Good' as a failure. The inspections are high-stress for all – but particularly for those struggling at the bottom end of league tables.

Technology – not the school's strongest suit – was the target for the inspection in this case. As ever, there had been the usual attempts to display strengths and hide weaknesses. The tension was palpable – dropped tools and snappy conversations:

'Are you sure you marked 3H's books?'

'That broken cupboard door still swings open. We need to fix it.'

'Who's got the Year 11 scheme of work?'

In a smooth-running high-achieving department, there would have been no need for such panic, but, despite the arrival of a new head of the department, technology was still a 'work in progress'.

The inspector was Mr Khan. He was quite small, but there were signs of middle-age spread, and he had a rather dishevelled air. At least he was punctual – arriving at the agreed time of ten a.m. Annie, the newly appointed head of the department, and I (the newly appointed deputy head) were waiting to greet him. Annie was tall, blonde, and always had a friendly smile. She had been an external candidate, and her appointment meant she had leapfrogged two internal 'would be's'. There was a lot on her shoulders.

'Mr Khan?' I knew who it was but just checking.

'Yes, that's right.'

'I'm Andrew Macalpine – one of the deputies. Can I introduce Annie Barnett, our head of department? She'll be looking after you.'

Mr Khan stretched out his hand. 'Pleased to meet you, Miss Barnett. Shall we get going?'

'Would you like a coffee before you start?' I suggested.

'No, I'm fine, thank you.' We were still standing at the entrance.

Mr Khan seemed friendly enough, although with inspectors, it's always good to bear in mind that 'crocodiles appear to be smiling'.

'Well, I suggest Annie takes you off, and I'll see you later. I hope you have a profitable morning.' In this case, 'hope' was more accurate than 'expectation'.

With that, Annie led him off down the corridor to the technology area.

Just before one, she reappeared at my office door. Mr Khan was hovering behind.

'We've finished. Do you want to have a word with Mr Khan before he goes?' I detected a slight nervousness. Annie did not seem like her usual confident and upbeat self.

I got up from my desk and came around so that the three of us were standing facing each other.

'So, how did it go?' What I really meant was, 'What grade have you given the department?'

'It went fine. I'll be sending you my report within the next few days.' Mr Khan's expression gave nothing away. He would have been a good poker player.

'Good,' I said. 'We'll look forward to it. It's one o'clock now. You're welcome to stay for lunch if you want.'

'That's very kind, but I've got another inspection over in Hackney this afternoon, so I'd better be going.'

We took Mr Khan back down to the front entrance and bade him farewell.

As he disappeared out of sight, Annie said, 'I thought we got told straight away?' There was an agitation about her. Her question was directed at anyone who might be able to answer it.

'I'm sure it was fine.' My reassurance was tinged with a certain amount of concern, given that Annie was right. We *were* usually told immediately.

'How was 2H? They're tricky at the best of times.' 2H had at least three members who could wreck an inspection.

'They were good as gold. Put on a great performance. Probably helped that Helen Coles was away.' Helen could wreck a lesson single-handed.

'Well, that's great. Go and have some lunch and try to relax.'

'I'll do my best.' Annie disappeared back to her workshops. I hoped I'd helped her relax a little.

Any relaxation *I* might have had didn't last long. I was at my desk halfway through a tuna sandwich when I got a call from Deidre in reception.

'Andrew. Mr Khan's back. He says he can't find his car.'

'Can't find his car?' Could it be that Mr Khan's dishevelled appearance went alongside a dishevelled brain?

'I'll be right down.' It sounded ridiculous. He would have parked in a nearby side road – not a multi-storey car park.

I made my way downstairs, and there was Mr Khan standing, holding his rather worn leather document case. He was talking to Maggie Rundell, one of the other deputies, breathing heavily and looking around him – a significant contrast with his arrival at the school some three hours previously. There were now chattering students everywhere on their way to the first lesson of the afternoon. Any boisterousness might counter the image of quiet and orderliness that I hoped he'd witnessed earlier.

'What's the problem?' I asked.

'Mr Khan can't find his car.' Maggie was as bright as her curly blonde hair and colourful dresses. She had a mischievous streak, and I could tell what might be going through her mind. However, she was managing to keep a straight face.

'Are you sure, Mr Khan?' I asked. 'Would you like us to come and help you look for it? The streets around here can be a bit confusing.'

'Yes, please.'

On the way out, I told Deidre we wouldn't be long, and, with Mr Khan leading the way, we set off towards the first turning on the right off the main road in front of the school. Maggie shrugged her shoulders and raised her eyebrows, seriously questioning what was happening. We turned the corner.

About four cars up the road, there was a gap. Mr Khan pointed to it.

'Are you sure this was the spot?' Maggie asked.

'Absolutely, I remember being right opposite that playground.' Mr Khan indicated a forlorn-looking area of swings and slides the other side of the road with wrappers being blown hither and thither by the wind.

There was silence for a minute. Surely Mr Khan's car wasn't one of those 150 or so stolen ones being driven around the island. That wouldn't look good.

'What sort of car were you driving?' I asked.

'A red Nissan.'

Maggie and I both looked around, half-expecting to see a red Nissan parked a few yards away.

'Registration number?'

A lengthy pause. By now, a rather flustered Mr Khan was having difficulty thinking straight.

'CX6 9BH.'

'Theft' was obviously starting to cross his mind. It was

already lodged in ours. I'd certainly progressed from 'wouldn't look good' to 'doesn't look good'.

'Alright, let's go back inside and see what we can do,' I suggested.

'Shouldn't we phone the police? It looks like it's been stolen.' Mr Khan was still looking around hopefully.

'Of course,' Maggie and I echoed as one, although we had no desire to call the police at that stage. We needed more time to solve the situation ourselves.

We retraced our steps, took Mr Khan back inside, and made him comfortable in the secretary's office. He seemed in a daze – not quite taking in what was happening.

'I'm going to need to phone my Hackney school.'

'That's fine,' I said. 'We'll go and phone the police.'

On the way back to my office Maggie took my arm and stopped me.

'Didn't Billy Lambert's brother just get put inside for car theft?'

'Yes,' I replied, 'but I don't see where that gets us. He can't do much from a prison cell.'

Maggie pursued her train of thought. 'That whole family's bent – including Billy. He might be able to help. *If* he's in school – a big if, I agree.' This was shades of Rory and Darren and the rooftop horror. Criminality on the island often ran in families.

I thought Maggie's suggestion was worth a shot. 'Let's see if he signed in this morning.'

I was conscious that Mr Khan's view of the school was probably falling by the minute. Would he be able to put that out of his head while writing his report? We went back to the secretary's office where he was still sitting – a cup of coffee, untouched, on the table beside him.

'Well? Are the police coming?'

'My PA's on to it. I'm afraid it's a common occurrence on the island. The police tend to put car crime low down the priority list.'

Mr Khan sat up in his chair, and I was sure he was about to express his concern, so I added, 'But we have got another avenue to explore.' He relaxed back down.

Maggie and I both knew which form Billy was in. It was common knowledge for most of the senior staff ever since he arrived from primary school – already the proud owner of a reputation for causing trouble. Irene, an assistant in the office, handed over the relevant register. A quick scan showed a tick next to Billy's name. Didn't mean he hadn't bunked off at lunchtime – but a promising start.

'Looks like he's got maths with Mrs McCready...' Maggie was already on to 2H's timetable.

Fortunately, the class was only twenty yards away down the corridor. I knocked on the door and walked in while Maggie waited outside. It smelt stuffy – south facing and no windows open. The class was obviously doing some sort of exercise or test, and Mrs McCready was going around checking their work. She turned round as I walked in.

'Sorry to disturb your class, Mrs McCready, but is Billy Lambert with you?' A number of heads turned towards the back of the class.

'Alright, 2H. No need to stop working.' She gestured towards a slumped figure at the back of the room. Mrs McCready was a long-standing member of staff. Her slim frame, short silvery grey hair, and restrained dress gave her the look of a librarian. She had a quiet and gentle manner but 'Do take him out if you need to' was less sotto voce than I might have expected.

She called out. 'Billy.'

Billy looked up. 'What?' Usual aggressive tone.

'Mr Macalpine needs a word.'

People often 'needed a word' with Billy.

He traipsed his way to the front of the class – managing to knock a couple of classmates' books on the floor as he did. We got outside.

'What I done now?' He looked from Maggie to me.

'Nothing, Billy. We just need a bit of help.' I could see his shoulders drop and his face relax. Being asked for help was almost certainly a first for Billy.

We took him down to Maggie's office.

'You can have a seat, Billy.' I pointed to one of the low chairs.

Maggie and I sat on the other two facing him.

'Billy. We've got an inspector in school, and we think his car's been stolen.'

Billy went red and bristled. 'How can I nick a fucking motor when I'm sat in school? And my brother's inside, so you can't blame him.' Not a good start.

Maggie took over the interrogation. 'Calm down, Billy. No one's blaming you or your brother. You've done nothing wrong.' These words were new to Billy. 'We just wondered which was the most likely estate for a stolen car to end up in.'

'I'm not going to grass anyone up.' Honour amongst thieves but misguided at the best of times and certainly not helpful here.

'Billy, there's no one to grass up. There's no way you could have known about this.' I tried to calm him.

Billy was now thinking – his furrowed brow revealing the fact that this was a painful process. Meanwhile, a knock on the door. It was Deidre.

'Mr Khan's wondering what's going on.' As in, he's getting a little impatient.

'Alright, tell him we'll be with him in a minute.' We were playing for time, but I sensed Billy just might help us.

'So, Billy. Let's just say one of the visitors to the school had their car stolen. Where might it end up?'

'Well... not on our estate. Since Joe got put away, we've kept clear of that stuff.'

Maggie persisted. 'OK, fair enough. So where then?'

A long pause. 'You could try Altringham. Right load of cunts they are.' The island was known for its inter-estate wars.

'Alright, Billy. Anywhere else?'

'Maybe Carlton, although people are always being nicked there, and they've backed off.' Billy was getting into his stride and starting to go through the island's estates.

I stopped him. 'That's very helpful, Billy. Miss Butt (Maggie) will take you back to your class now.' I felt we had enough information to start a drive round. We all got up, and Maggie took Billy back to his class while I made my way back to where Mr Khan was still sitting. A couple of minutes later Maggie joined us. Mr Khan had gotten out of his seat and was clearly expecting some news.

'Mr Khan, we think we have an idea where your car might be.'

Was that a bead of sweat on his brow? Whatever was going on in his head couldn't have been pleasant.

I turned to Maggie. 'Maggie, can we use your car? I know mine'll be boxed in.' That was a daily occurrence, with staff arriving much later than me.

'Where are we going?' Understandably, Mr Khan was following none of this.

'We're just going to visit a couple of estates. If we draw a blank, we'll certainly give the police another call,' I explained.

'How come?' Mr Khan asked.

'We have one or two unpaid informers on our roll and we're going to follow up on a lead.' I was in danger of making us sound like a school for scoundrels.

He looked doubtful. 'Do you need me to come with you?'

'Yes, please. If that's OK.'

We made our way down to the car park and Maggie's car. Mr Khan was a couple of yards behind.

I gestured to him to sit in the front. 'You'll be in a better position to see.'

I got in the back, and Maggie, ignoring Mr Khan, turned to me. 'Where shall we try first, Andrew?'

'Why not Altringham? That was the one Billy mentioned first.'

'OK.' Maggie started the engine, and we drove out onto the main road – high-rise blocks and rundown estates on our left, a shabby-looking pub on our right.

'Do you know the way?' I asked her.

'Just past "The Sailors Return" (another pub with paint peeling from its sign) on the right?'

'That's the one.'

'Tough place to work.' Mr Khan was sitting clutching his briefcase and taking in the sense of neglect that characterised the island.

'Not easy,' I replied. 'But on the whole, the kids are great. Mostly ex-dockers' children now plus increasing numbers of immigrants.'

'I think this is it.' Maggie interrupted our conversation as she turned off into an open area surrounded on three sides by typical four-storey estates with walkways outside the front doors of the upper storeys. There were cars everywhere – mostly old bangers. Some were obviously abandoned – wheels missing, windscreens smashed. The occasional newer number plate. Huge wheelie bins overflowing with rubbish dotted the area. There were a number of kids on bikes and a few in that central grassy area playing football. Under the inquisitive gaze of some of the cyclists who had stopped to look at these strangers, we took a bowl round. No sign of a red Nissan. We were just about to drive off when I spotted what looked like a red nose peeping out of a garage with its door up. My heart missed a beat.

I turned to Mr Khan, who seemed to have retreated into himself. 'Could that be yours?'

Mr Khan sat up and followed my pointing finger. 'Maybe. We'd need to get closer. Yes. That's it. CX6 9BH.' He suddenly came to life. 'That's it. That's my car. What do we do now? We can't just take it away.'

'Mr Khan,' I said. 'It's your car. Of course you can. But we need to check it first.' Remembering Billy's description of the Altringham estate, I started to wonder who we might encounter when we started sniffing around the car.

Apart from the kids who seemed to have lost interest in us, there was no one around. We all got out to inspect the Nissan for any signs of damage. Happily, there seemed to be none. Mr Khan was peering into the car.

Maggie turned to me and whispered, 'What happens if our thief turns up?'

'Cross that bridge when we get to it,' I replied, although I had no strategy in mind. We were nervously scanning the area.

Mr Khan had turned back to us, and I ventured a crucial question. 'Have you got your keys?'

Momentary panic crossed his face as he started to feel in his various pockets. To our relief, and no doubt his, they were suddenly in his hand.

A short, scruffy-looking boy with a curly mop of black hair walked past. He looked as though he should have been in school – although too young for ours. 'Nice car, mate. Is it yours?'

'It's his,' Maggie replied, nodding her head towards Mr Khan. 'Stolen about thirty minutes ago.'

'That's not the only one around here. Any decent motor and someone's nicked it.' This was a throwaway line over his shoulder as he walked away. I resisted the temptation to ask him what school, if any, he went to. Almost certainly, that's where he should have been rather than wandering around the estate.

By this time, Mr Khan was very gingerly testing his keys in the Nissan's door.

'I don't think it's going to be locked,' Maggie volunteered.

'No, stupid me. Of course not.' He got into the driver's seat and turned the ignition. The Nissan started immediately. He wound the window and I went over.

'Any signs of damage?' I asked.

Mr Khan was looking around the inside. 'None that I can see,' came the reply.

'Well then. Off you go, and do please accept our apologies for all the hassle.'

'You've done brilliantly to find it. I think next time I'll come by public transport. Oh, and tell Miss Barnett she did very well. There'll be official confirmation in the next few days.' For the first time in the day, Mr Khan relaxed – and was that just a hint of a smile?

And with that, somewhat later than anticipated, the technology inspection was over. Thanks to Billy, we'd certainly discovered more about the island – and we made a point of thanking him for his help.

Oh – and the result of the inspection. It was 'Good' not 'Outstanding', but it was a feather in Annie's cap. She was very pleased – as were we.

UNDER YOUR SKIN

Any thoughts that, having reached the dizzy heights of Senior Master – capital S, capital M – I could hide away shuffling papers and making important telephone calls in my office (yes, my own office) were quickly banished. The timetable had gaps, and I was needed to help fill them. At least it was my own subject, English, and not science or technology, where I might have been as much a liability as the naughtiest student. The class was Year 9 – fourteen-year-olds. By this time, I had been teaching for ten years and teaching English throughout that time. You should never take anything for granted working with children. Thus WC Fields' famous dictum – 'You should never work with children or animals.' That's pretty challenging when you're a teacher, although, more recently, I have encountered 'teachers' who get close – burying their heads in marking or playing computer games on their phones instead of actually engaging with the students in front of them. I certainly wasn't going to let complacency creep in when facing my new class.

As with the school, the class was mixed, but the boys might not have existed, overshadowed as they were by a trio of girls ranged along the back – all bright and friends with each other. One particular girl stood out – curly red hair, piercing blue eyes, smiley when engaging with her two friends – one on each side – but defiantly stern-faced when looking at me. Looking back, I don't really understand why I didn't separate the trio – but then hindsight's a wonderful thing. Emasculation at their hands kicked in early, and I came to dread lessons with them. Some say that animals can smell fear. Children are certainly adept at sussing out their teachers' weak points. I'm sure the trio sensed they had me on the run – if not the rack. However, rather than trying to describe their behaviour and what might have been going through their teenage heads, I quote what I found on a loose piece of paper that one of them must have dropped on the floor:

How we drove our teacher mad

In our school, we have a teacher whom I hate, so my friends Beverley, Carol, and myself decided to drive him mad, and these are just some of the things we did.
  1. *Stamp on his toes.*
  2. *Bump into him on purpose.*
  3. *Give him dirty looks.*
  4. *Ignore him when he's talking.*
  5. *Call him names outside the classroom.*
  6. *Knock on his door and run away.*
  7. *Every time he goes by, you say, 'I feel sick.'*
  8. *When he asks us a question, say an entirely different thing.*

9. Talk when he's talking.

10. When he walks into the class, you BOO!

11. Don't join in any drama or game.

I expect when he walks in the door, he feels hate just as we do; he probably thinks, 'Oh, not them three again.' But if he knew some of his pupils wouldn't behave, why did he take up teaching? We didn't ask him to.

The trio learnt little at my hands, but I learnt something at theirs – that is, not to be so thin-skinned. I'm not sure they realised my next stop was headship. Probably better for me that they didn't. I dread to think what sort of leaving present they would have come up with!

SIX

HEADSHIP APPLICATIONS

Eventually, I started to apply for headships. There was plenty going on in what was then ILEA, but the Chief Inspector, who was central to all ILEA headship appointments, popped up every time I got shortlisted and had clearly decided headship wasn't for me.

'You can't have done everything you claim to have done,' was one explanation he gave me. I like to think that in listing my varied experience, I was being honest. However, I was still a poor interviewee. I could feel myself tighten up under interrogation. Not an attractive quality in a potential employee.

My quest for promotion was taking me further and further , to outer London boroughs going east – Barking and Dagenham, Ilford, Havering. However, I was lucky; it seemed the chief inspector's assessment word hadn't extended that far. Like buses, three shortlistings came in quick succession. I decided to spend a day driving out into Essex to get a sense of the communities the three schools on my list served – and of what the schools looked like from the outside. First stop Barking and Dagenham. From the Isle of Dogs to Barking had a nice ring about it. I had a vague idea of where to find Erkenwald School, but the warren of streets was confusing, and I was struggling. No satnav to guide me in the 1980s. Eventually, I came across what I recognised as a typical three-storey Victorian school building. It took up a whole block with streets on all four sides, but there seemed to be no signs to indicate what its function was and what it was called. I made two trips around the block, searching for any indication that this might be what I was looking for. Eventually, and I nearly missed it, I spotted a narrow pedestrian entrance with a small tarnished brass plaque – about two feet by one.

Engraved on it were two words: 'Erkenwald School'.

Underneath, someone had scrawled, in thick black felt tip, 'is shit'. It seemed to sum up the desolation of the building and the area.

Desperate as I was for a headship, I decided not to apply!

I did, however, apply for a school in Ilford – the next stop out east. It was a school with well-known discipline problems. There were three of us shortlisted, and there were the usual openers.

'Tell me, Mr Macalpine. What makes you think you're the person for this post?'

'Mr Macalpine. What's your vision for the school moving forward?'

The questions got around to a fascist-looking governor – steely eyes and an expressionless face. All that was missing was the SS uniform. He could certainly have been Braithwaite's brother (that Labour councillor who interviewed me).

'Mr Macalpine. Would you reintroduce caning?' Retaining caning, if it was already in use in the school, would have been bad enough, but 'reintroduce'…

I hesitated a fraction before replying. I really wanted to run him through my caning history (See 'Corporal Punishment'), finishing on a self-righteous and rather pompous note – 'So you can see why I think corporal punishment is barbaric and why the Inner London Education Authority banished it three years ago.'

Instead, all that came out of my mouth was, 'No, I wouldn't.'

There were three of us shortlisted. Two said they wouldn't, and one said he would. Guess who got the job.

Two schools down – one to go.

I had also been shortlisted, along with six others, for a school in Hornchurch in the London Borough of Havering. Prior to the interview, we were given a conducted tour of the school by the outgoing head and a borough inspector. It was not a promising start. Every time I opened my mouth to ask what I knew would be an intelligent and interesting question, I found one of my fellow shortlisted had got there first, and I was left open-mouthed. I could only hope to do better at the interview.

SEVEN

HORNCHURCH

INTRODUCTION

Hornchurch is located within the London Borough of Havering.
Along with Bromley, it's one of London's least diverse boroughs.
A 2015 census showed it to be eighty-eight per cent white. That
was certainly how it felt in the 1980s when I was there.

The extension of the District Line in the 1930s mainly
benefitted areas in the north of the borough, e.g., Upminster,
Emerson Park, and Gidea Park. Havering extends right down
to the river and becomes less prosperous as you move south,
with Hornchurch somewhere in the middle. The area developed
partly as a result of urban sprawl, with a significant proportion
of the population, when I worked there in the 1980s, employed
by Ford at their Dagenham factory. There were forty thousand
workers there in 1953, dwindling to around two thousand in
2020.

The majority of parents were homeowners living in post-war
housing. No high-rise blocks. All very different from the Isle
of Dogs, Peckham, and Somers Town. I hadn't wanted to leave
Inner London schools, and looking back, I may have felt a slight
sense of betrayal. All three of my schools, up to that time, had

been challenging. However, I needn't worry about settling for a cushy number. The intake was predominantly skilled working class, and the lower middle class and aspirations were low. My predecessor's task, when he arrived, was to throw off the poor reputation. In his ten years in charge, he chipped away bit by bit, and things improved. Eventually, the number of prospective parents saying, 'I wouldn't send my child to that X (name of old school)' had reduced to a trickle. However, the school was still underachieving on a significant scale, and there was a sense of complacency among staff which meant sufficient demands weren't being made on students. The focus was on the pastoral (make sure they're happy) and not on the academic (ensure tangible achievement). You need the courage to make demands on students and to reject unsatisfactory work and behaviour, and this was what was missing in Hornchurch – and what I hoped to be able to inject.

The school itself was the 1930s – neo-Georgian. It was square and solid and definitely designed to last – unlike so many post-war efforts.

Once inside the imposing entrance, you found yourself in the middle of a long corridor – one side of a square that enclosed the school. The design provided a reasonable working environment despite lengthy treks if you wanted to see anyone on the 'other' side. As has been common with many schools that survived because of their robust build, there eventually came a need for expansion. Often that meant a new building alongside the existing one. Frequently, the term 'new building' stuck long after the buildings themselves came into being (often decades).

The school's history is littered with name changes. In the early days, these reflected the educational climate at the time. For example, in 1952, as a 'secondary mixed', it had rigid streaming.

Imagine the gap between those in the bottom stream and the brightest Etonians! The British class system was functioning at its 'best', i.e., worst. Classes of forty were still common.

In the early 1960s, another school opened in the same catchment area. The result was seepage of girls – still, in 2025 – a characteristic of a failing school. In effect, it became a secondary modern taking 'eleven-plus failures' – children thought more suitable for practical education. Although the playground became mixed, attempts to do the same with the staffroom were successfully resisted by male staff who felt the presence of 'ladies' might inhibit them!

In 1965, Harold Wilson and the Labour government stepped in with the introduction of comprehensives and the ending of the tripartite system. The school started to shed its image as an 'also ran' and was soon on its way to becoming a proper comprehensive.

It was renamed for the umpteenth time in 1973 after an American pilot whose plane crashed on the grassy area just in front of the main building. Sadly, he was killed, but his name, and variations on it, have outlasted all others and remain to this day. Parents usually see school name changes for the charades they are. They're interested in results and behaviour and are not fooled by fancy blazers and tacking on 'The' at the beginning of a school's name, nor 'College' at the end. As evidence of this, from 2012 to 2020, the Hornchurch school had three name changes (all variations on the American pilot's first name and surname). The nomenclature didn't work. Ofsted's assessment of each one was RI (Requires Improvement) – not the bottom category but next to it.

So… I became head in January 1984. My first headship! I was thrilled, despite rejections en route, that I'd made it at last. I had worked under four heads in my three previous schools, and I like to think I learnt from all of them. However, I was arrogant enough to believe there were some things I could do better. The time had come for me to put my money where my mouth was. I approached the challenge with that nervous excitement that people who play sports experience before a big match.

APPLICATION AND APPOINTMENT

In 'Headship Applications', I described the rather depressing tour of the Hornchurch school arranged for those shortlisted candidates when I was upstaged by a fellow candidate. I knew I needed to be more forceful in the interview.

In common with most boroughs at the time, headship interviews were scheduled to take place in council offices. In this case, Romford – of market trader fame.

The day came. A smart suit, a nice tie. No last-minute rush (a particular challenge for me). I got to the council offices in good time, up to Floor 8.

There was a young man in an open-necked shirt and no tie, sitting at his desk near the lift. There was no one else in the open-plan office. He was busy typing and didn't see me at first. He got up and came across to where I was standing. He seemed surprised to see me.

'Can I help you?'

'Yes. I'm here for the headship interview for (I gave him the name of the school).'

Blank look.

I checked my letter. Right date. Right time...

'Can I have a look at that?'

I passed the letter over.

'I'm afraid you're in the wrong building. You should be at the Town Hall.' His voice was sympathetic but firm, and I started to feel prickles of sweat. What had been 'in good time' no longer seemed to be the case.

'Here, let me show you. This is probably the easiest way.' He took me over to one of the large plate glass windows that characterised the building. The view was over the entirety of what I later discovered was north Romford. He pointed to another tall office block which seemed terrifyingly far away.

'That's where you should be. Take you about ten minutes.'

I thanked him for his help and hurried back towards the lift. The light above showed it on the second floor – not moving! I was just about to take the stairs when it started to come up.

Reaching pavement level, things looked very different from how they were on Floor 8, and it took me a moment or two to orientate myself – with a little help from a passer-by who, to my relief, was a local.

Hot, sweaty, and a little late, I finally made it to the Town Hall. Fortunately, there were still five minutes to go before my appointed time – just enough to straighten my tie and get my breath back. I must have been able to get across some of my recent experience on the Isle of Dogs as, not long after, I was celebrating my first headship. There was certainly a sense of achievement, given the various setbacks along the way. Many failed applications would have deterred all but the most bloody-minded. But much more than that was the sense of excitement at being given the opportunity to make a difference for both students and staff. Put my money where my mouth was, as it were.

GETTING GOING

The school was all I could have hoped for. Apart from the building providing a positive working environment, I soon discovered that there was just enough bright-eyed and bushy-tailed staff to provide a platform for change.

At the same time as feeling my way and getting a sense of the school's strengths and weaknesses, I needed to make an impact. In football, there's the 'new manager bounce'. A short honeymoon. I interpret that as meaning that you can make an impact just by walking through the door. You haven't done anything, but there is the perception that change has taken place. I've no idea if that was the staff's perception. Probably not! After all, the outgoing head had certainly moved the school forward, and I sensed he was popular. Popularity helped by having a famous brother who fronted a well-known TV game show! My job was to continue his work – but at a faster pace. My sights, of course, were set on the long term, but I sensed a 'quick fix' wouldn't do any harm.

MCDONALD'S

I had already suggested a drinks dispenser as a means of bolstering school funds. That, quite rightly, was roundly vetoed. Sugary drinks, the large cabinet an eyesore, exploitative. I retired chastened, but not deterred, to think again. I homed in on rewards for good schoolwork. Already in place were 'credits', but neither staff nor students really valued them. How about if credits were attached, in students' eyes at least, to something more tangible? I pondered this and tried to think of external treats which might spur them on, e.g., trips to the cinema (God forbid after my *2001* experience!), ice skating, or a theme park, but they would require so many 'credits' that only a tiny minority would benefit. Something much simpler was needed. A typical Friday night treat, for example. So what's the most prized reward parents come up with when they want to acknowledge their children's efforts? McDonald's, of course! At that time in the mid-1980s, McDonald's hadn't been set upon by health experts and environmentalists quite rightly demanding improvements to the product.

I put the idea to our senior team.

'What if we linked up with McDonald's whereby credits could be exchanged for McDonald's vouchers?'

'Seems to me that's no better than a drinks dispenser.' Carl, our newly appointed senior teacher, had quickly gotten his feet under the table.

'At least it's encouraging learning.' I could rely on Gill, my deputy, to support anything entrepreneurial.

'I'm wondering what our parents would think.' Mike, the other deputy, was always thoughtful – on occasions, a little too much so. I always liked to think my brilliant ideas would go through on the nod.

'Well… if you think about it… where do our parents take their children for treats and celebrations? It's McDonald's, isn't it.' This was Liz, who had attended a local school and worked her way up from probationer to a member of the senior team. Her voice carried weight.

The discussion went back and forth for a while – but increasingly forth. Finally, it was agreed I should contact McDonald's and put the idea to them.

That was in the summer. Over the course of the summer break, I was able to arrange a meeting at the local McDonald's office. They liked the idea, and by the beginning of the autumn term we had vouchers printed and introduced them to students. They didn't just like them – they loved them. Obviously, no figures exist for the impact on learning, but the scheme survived for a few years until, around the time I was moving on, environmental issues started to surface.

In 1989, the Sustainability Institute showed that McDonald's produced 8,500 polystyrene-packaged hamburgers every minute of every day. They also pointed out how the flow of materials from the forest, paper mill, mine, oil well, and chemical plant generated pollution every step of the way. Including all the greenhouse gas McDonald's' 350,000 farting cattle produced.

Times have changed, and, quite rightly, I'd never get such a scheme through now. My sixteen-year-old 'climate warrior' granddaughter, Orla, might find family loyalty severely strained!

I, foolishly and irresponsibly, made a half-hearted attempt to repeat the 'wheeze' when I became head of Barnet's 'Fresh Start' school in the early 1990s but was howled down publicly. The loud voices I have referred to elsewhere prevailed. I imagined private conversations:

86

'You heard what Andrew's suggesting? Bringing in McDonald's – and drinks machines. Trying to poison the kids for the sake of a bit of extra cash and bribe them with food that should be banned. I thought this was supposed to be a "Fresh Start" school.'

Anyway, getting ahead of myself. Back to Hornchurch. What opposition there was had been overcome, and so it came about that the local McDonald's was prepared to sponsor our rewards system and provide vouchers in return for a specified number of credits. Overnight, credits became prized ('Miss/Sir, isn't that worth a credit?'), and student work improved. We should have termed it 'Hamburgers for Homework'.

Our gradual climb up the Borough league table wasn't solely attributable to unhealthy eating, but it helped!

UNIFORM

The other area which seemed to indicate the need for a quick fix was uniform. I'd moved a long way from my public school days (see 'Broken Arm and Hypocrisy'), where I had revelled in shedding my blazer. Be that as it may, the Year 11 students' attire was as scruffy as their exam results. This merely confirmed the impression of many parents that the school was not to be taken seriously as a place of learning. What uniform there was stopped at the end of Year 10, and it wasn't easy to spot the difference between Year 11s and sixth formers who, in theory at least, dressed as though ready for the world outside. I floated the idea of blazers and ties for all in Years 7 to 11. Although it was clear change was needed, in the eyes of many it should start with Year 7. But then total implementation would take four years. I suggested we start with all years simultaneously.

'That'll never work,' was the cry, and loud staffroom voices were raised. I wasn't convinced by the clamour and decided to put the issue to a vote. I had already conceded a point re. Year 11s for whom costly blazers would be redundant in four or five months' time when they started their exams and got ready to move on.

The vote showed overwhelming support for the change, and that was a salutary lesson for me: 'Don't listen to the loudest voices.' And the best thing was the implementation. The change worked and gave staff the confidence that moving forward was possible. And parents, too, once they had gotten over the cost, were very supportive.

Once I'd got my feet under the table, I tested my perception that the school was underperforming. There were no league tables at the time and certainly no value added. With the help of local authority data, I put together my own table – getting every school's raw scores. There were twenty schools in Havering, ranging from the highly selective, masquerading as comprehensives, to those at the south end of the borough, which reflected high levels of deprivation. We came out sixteenth. I knew the staff had little understanding of where the school was in the borough pecking order and called a staff meeting to explain what I'd done. The reaction was great. There was enough staff who suspected we were well below par. They just needed the confidence to challenge students. In other words, make demands on them. Not to accept second best. To reject unacceptable work. To set high standards of behaviour.

My role was to encourage the belief that all this could be done. I like to think that that staff meeting was a galvanising moment that resulted in the school going from sixteenth to sixth in the space of six years.

There were other challenges along the way, e.g., the Great Storm of 1987 when we had to close the school because so few staff were able to get in.

January 1988 saw a particularly cold winter, and pipes froze. The thaw brought flooding and the collapse of the drama studio roof. And if that wasn't enough, part of the 'new' building was torn away by more high winds – with more water damage. The school emerged from these disasters with redecorated rooms and a push-button phone system – all courtesy of the local authority's insurance policy. At least I didn't have to vandalise the school myself to get things done (see below 'Headteachers of All Sorts').

BROKEN TOE

Why would a headteacher trying to impress parents at a PTA (Parent Teacher Association) committee meeting sit for an hour with his right foot in a bowl of cold water?

This wasn't a question at six p.m. on a 'well dark' (as the locals might say), chilly, wintry evening in Essex. On most days, it would be tidy-up time and the grim drive back to south London. Instead, I was nipping off to the local pub for a sandwich and a shandy. The monthly committee meeting had come round – always faster than anticipated – or desired. I had to attend – if only to show my face. Returning to school with some ten minutes to spare, I noticed three or four cars parked where before there had been none. The early birds. The committee consisted entirely of parents, and for most of them, this was the only time they came to school. They were always keen. As I walked through the front door, I was pleased to see that Frank, the caretaker, had put out a blackboard and easel to which he'd Blu-Tacked a large notice directing parents to the meeting room down the long corridor to the right. With an eye for detail – or just plain obsessiveness – I saw that the notice was ever so slightly crooked. My fingers were well used to prising Blu Tack off surfaces, and I went to straighten it. What I didn't realise was that Frank had been unable to find any of the wooden pegs that would normally slot into the easel's legs to support the blackboard. Instead, he had cleverly improvised with a felt tip pen in each hole. Not quite clever enough. As I leaned forward to prise off the first piece of Blu Tack, the large, thick wooden blackboard slid gracefully and silently off the shiny felt tips and landed with full force on the big toe of my right foot! There were no witnesses, but I still managed to muffle the scream and the expletives. The burning pain was excruciating. The meeting room now seemed light years off as I limped my way down the corridor.

I reached the open door of the classroom come meeting room. My face and gait couldn't disguise the fact that all was not well. There were startled looks all round. A couple of members got to their feet.

'So sorry I'm late. I had a slight accident with the blackboard at the entrance. It slipped off its pegs and landed on my big toe.'

'Right. Let's have you seated, and we'll have a look then.' This was Phyllis, one of those who'd got up as soon as I entered the room. She was large, red-faced, curly-haired, and sported outsize horn-rimmed glasses. A decade before, she might have been wearing tweeds. Now it was a big woolly jumper and a long skirt. She had three children at the school and took no prisoners at our monthly meetings, i.e., she took charge. She was taking charge now. Sister Harsh.

'Tell me exactly what happened.' She started to feel my big toe. I flinched as though an electric shock had passed through me – my eyes beginning to water with the pain.

Between convulsed breaths, I repeated my earlier account. 'There's not much more to say. The blackboard just fell off its easel.' Most of the small group had remained seated – their eyes on the examination I was getting. Pam got up and came over. I knew she had actually been a nurse. She had none of Phyliss's rather scary briskness – more a well-practised bedside manner.

'You should get his sock off,' Pam said. Uncharacteristically, Phyllis deferred and moved aside while Pam knelt down and gently started to peel the sock off my right foot. On many a day,

I wouldn't have wanted my socks inspected, but at least this pair was clean on that morning. The toe was red, inflamed, and starting to swell.

'That doesn't look good.' I loved Pam, but she was stating the bleeding obvious. 'You should go straight home.'

Murmurs of assent all round.

Most of the group had now got up and surrounded the patient. Only one parent remained seated. It was Roger, the only male on the PTA (often, there were none). His capacity for empathy had never been apparent.

Stoicism – probably unconvincing – surfaced. 'I'll be fine.' Tuts all round.

'Andrew, that's ridiculous. You'll only make it worse.' Mavis had joined the nursing team.

I dug my heels in. 'Let's get on with the meeting. I'm sorry it's been hijacked.'

'Well, if you're going to be stubborn, you should at least keep it as cold as possible.' Phyliss had not gone away.

'Good idea, Phyllis. I'll see what I can find.' Pam disappeared and came back a few minutes later with a bowl of cold water.

I spent the rest of the meeting sitting with my foot in the bowl, failing miserably to look dignified – the burning sensation becoming just about tolerable. With Phyllis briskly chairing, the business was over quickly. Grimacing, I squeezed my foot into the sockless shoe and was escorted to my car with generous offers of lifts. I might have accepted, but for most parents, it would have meant a two-hour round trip.

'I'll be fine, really.' I manoeuvred myself into the driver's seat, and having discovered I could just about depress the accelerator – and, more importantly, the brake – I wound down the window, thanked the nursing team profusely, and drove off.

It was a very long sixty minutes, but I made it.

I liked to think that I had shown sufficient bravery to impress the committee. 'He's crazy' was much more likely.

The following day, A&E confirmed a clean break – no longer a link between the front and back of my big toe.

There is no moral to this story. Coming to work in steel toe-capped boots might have been seen as sensible in Somers Town but not in Hornchurch.

INTERVIEWING CANDIDATES

The First

I'd had plenty of experience interviewing candidates on the Isle of Dogs – and even some at my second school in Peckham. I was also familiar with being on the other side of the table – being assessed! Two interviews stick in my mind from my Hornchurch headship. The first was for a Scale 1 history teacher; probably going to be a probationer starting out in their career. The interviewing panel consisted of the chair of governors, the vice chair of the PTA, who was also a governor, the head of history, and myself. A large panel would not be needed now in 2025. The chair of governors, Raymond, was elderly, thin and rather frail. At governing body meetings, his eyes would glaze over from time to time, and he would have to be gently reminded of the next item on the agenda. He had been chair even prior to my predecessor's appointment – some ten years before. The vice chair of the PTA, Joan, had been around even longer than Raymond. She was grey-haired, unsmiley, and 'old school'. As a teenager, she had attended a nearby grammar school and never seemed to quite understand how different comprehensives were. Richard, the head of history, was fortyish, always in a brown suit and never without a brightly coloured tie – a tie which belied his essential conservatism. He was a loyal member of the school community and had even written a history of the school.

There were three candidates for the post. Richard and I had already decided, on the basis of their supporting statements and experience, who we saw as the front runner. However, as I well knew, first impressions (in this case, on paper) are not to be trusted, and candidates have to survive the interview grilling. The first two candidates came and went. Neither impressed any of us. The first was tall and confident – overconfident in that he was quite unable to convince us he knew how to teach. The second was a very small, thin woman with oversize glasses who presented more as a timid sixth former than a recent teacher-training graduate. I brought in our third. Bright eyes, firm handshake. She had a positive air about her. This could be the fresh blood the school desperately needed. After the introductions were over, we moved to our agreed questions. The chair of governors was to go last. I got the ball rolling, followed by the vice chair of the PTA. Halfway through her first question, we became aware of what seemed like heavy breathing. Almost as one, we realised Raymond had fallen asleep. I had a sinking feeling in the pit of my stomach. I glanced at the candidate who was sitting directly opposite him. She would have been perfectly entitled to walk out. To her credit, she kept her composure, although she must have wondered, 'What now?' It was some consolation that Raymond was still upright – rather than slumped to one side or the other. I had actually seen him nod off in governing body meetings (reasonable enough given the tedium some of them generated), but this was different. What to do now? Joan was sitting opposite me, and, as discretely as I could, I indicated with a rolling hand motion, as though filming, that we should carry on. The slumber continued throughout Joan's questions and right to the end of Richard's. As the interview finished, and I was thanking the candidate, the chair woke up and, behaving as though nothing untoward had happened, added his own thanks. Our front runner had fulfilled our expectations with her answers – and, just as important, her composure, given the strange situation she had found herself in. I took her back to the staffroom and then returned to my office. We went round the table summarising our impressions – which were all positive. We got to Raymond.

'Raymond – what's your view?'

We held our collective breath. What if he raised objections, tried to put up a case, and questioned our judgements?

Instead – 'You all seem agreed, and I'm happy with that.'

Phew! Inward sighs of relief. Even better, our candidate accepted.

The Second

We were looking for a biology teacher. Although not quite on par with physics or chemistry, it was still hard to find suitable candidates. This time it was just me and the head of the department, John. Short with a ruddy complexion and a waist that had disappeared, John was not far off retirement, and his department would benefit from the injection of fresh blood. We shortlisted three applicants. All looked promising on paper which was a miracle in itself. All were female (bearing out many studies over decades which show that far more men than women teach physics and chemistry and far more women than men teach biology, e.g., 'Gender study on the relationships between science interest and future career perspectives' – J. Kang, 2019).

At the interview, all lived up to our expectations. The decision wasn't easy. Eventually, we agreed on the front runner, and I went up to the staffroom to offer her the post.

The three were in armchairs positioned in a row and facing slightly towards each other – sitting as though they were watching TV and chatting about what they were watching. I stood in front of them, and they looked up expectantly.

'First – thank you for coming. You all did excellently, and we were very impressed.' This was to stand me in good stead.

'However, we have made a choice and would like to offer the post to Miss Baxter. Congratulations, Miss Baxter. Commiserations to you both.'

They all got up, and I went to shake Miss Baxter's hand. I expected her face to light up. She did shake my hand while the other two looked on, and I waited for the thanks which I knew were coming my way. There was a seriousness in her demeanour that I hadn't noticed before.

'I'm very sorry, Mr Macalpine, but I've decided to withdraw my application. Nothing to do with the school but just not right for me at this moment.' Miss Baxter's face hadn't lit up – nor did mine on getting this news.

I tried to disguise my combination of anger and disappointment. Disappointment that our chosen one was turning us down. Anger that she had wasted everyone's time – and that included the other two candidates.

Through gritted teeth. 'Well, I'm sure you've got your reasons.' I turned to the other two. 'Would you both mind waiting a moment while I go back downstairs?'

The taller of the two, Miss Anand, clad in a sari, said, 'That's fine with me.' The third candidate, Miss Wright, echoed this.

'I'll see Miss Baxter out and come back as soon as I can. Miss Baxter, do you want to come with me?'

We made our way downstairs to the entrance. 'Any particular reason?' I asked.

'I think the whole process convinced me that I'm not ready to settle down yet. I don't know if you picked up from my application that I've already had a gap year and been travelling. I loved that, and I just feel that if I get on the work ladder now, there won't be any more travel opportunities.'

'Well, I can sympathise with that. I had a gap year in France. I loved France, learnt French, and have never regretted it.'

By this time, my annoyance had dissipated, and I was feeling much more understanding. School, college, school is a very narrow path, and while some brilliant teachers have emerged from it, if it was a choice between two seeming equals, I'd tend towards the candidate who'd 'knocked around a bit'.

We had reached the entrance, and I bade Miss Baxter farewell and made my way back to John, who was still sitting in my office. I sat down.

'Do you want the good news or the bad news?'

'OK, tell me.' John was not going to play games.

'Well, the bad news is that Miss Baxter has turned the job down.' I proceeded to relay the events of the previous few minutes. There was a pause while John absorbed this.

'The good news is that the other two are still there – and still candidates.'

'So, what next?' John asked.

'Well,' I replied, 'who do you think came second?'

'Well, we did agree they were all appointable. If anything, I've a preference for Miss Anand, but I'd be happy with either.'

It was a toss-up between the two, but the school, and the borough, were predominately white, and the appointment of Miss Anand, all other things being equal, would be a step towards a more diverse school community.

Holding my breath, I went back to the staffroom. Miss Anand and Miss Wright were still sitting chatting. I stood in front of them once more.

'Thank you both so much for waiting. You've obviously seen what's happened, and we really hope you're still candidates.' At this point, I should have paused and waited for nods. I ploughed on. 'We've had a further discussion and decided we'd like to offer the post to you, Miss Anand. We do hope you'll accept.'

Seconds passed.

'Well, obviously I've had time to think and, bearing in mind the journey – it took me over an hour to get here, and that wasn't even the rush hour, I'm afraid I'm also going to have to withdraw. I do hope I haven't wasted your time.' If teeth could have been gritted any tighter… However, I was determined, once again, to be gracious.

'I do understand, Miss Anand. It is a trek from Peckham, as I know only too well.'

She got up to leave, and I turned my attention to Miss Wright. She was not the most prepossessing of people. She was short and on the dumpy side and was well beyond any gap year, being a late entrant to teaching. There was almost something mumsy about her. 'Well, Miss Wright. You've seen everything that's gone on. I hardly dare to ask if you're still a candidate. If you are, I'd love you to stay.' I held what breath I had left. Miss Anand had stayed – hovering by the door.

'Alright. Yes,' Miss Wright replied.

'I'll just show Miss Anand out and be back shortly. Can I get you a cup of coffee?'

'No thanks. I'm fine,' Miss Wright replied.

This time the descent to the entrance took place in silence. When we got there, I shook Miss Anand's hand and told her I hoped her journey home wouldn't be too difficult, and we said our goodbyes.

Back to the office with the news.

'Are we going to go for number three?' There was a note of resignation in John's voice.

'Not ideal' was our consensus, but we reminded each other that all three had been appointable – and we certainly didn't want to re-advertise.

I made my way slowly back to the staffroom. I could feel beads of sweat beginning to form.

It wouldn't have surprised me if Miss Wright had disappeared, but, no, there she was.

'Miss Wright. Thank you so much for staying. You may feel you came third, but I can assure you it was a very close run thing between the three of you. What do you think? Would you be prepared to join us.'

I tried to keep my breath even. I hardly heard, 'Yes, I'd love to.'

'That's brilliant. Let's go downstairs and complete the formalities.' We passed the front door without Miss Wright making a bolt for it. We sat her down in my office and made our formal offer which was accepted.

It wasn't long before she succeeded John as head of the department, and over her years at the school, she proved to be a great appointment.

Sometimes you have an agonising choice between candidates. Quite often, you just want to roll them into one – take the best bits of each! And, as with Miss Wright, just because someone has come second, third, or even fourth in your deliberations, it doesn't mean they won't grow into the job and prove themselves.

QUIZ NIGHTS

School quiz nights are a staple. Usually organised by the PTA and designed to generate funds for the school. Although competitive, they are mainly light-hearted affairs with winners congratulated and no one too worried about losing.

This particular year, halfway through the quiz, and at the end of a round, two members of staff, the Naylors – a husband and wife team – queried one of the answers. It was a full hall with tables of six. The other four on the Naylors' table consisted of two friends they'd invited and two other members of staff. Ken Naylor (the head of technology) and his wife, Sue (the head of science), had been at the school for ever and represented the 'trundling along nicely' group of staff who had lost sight of the school's potential. Whenever I saw Sue, I tried to banish 'lumpen' from my brain. They were both, however, puzzle addicts – often to be seen in the staffroom at break poring over a crossword. They took quizzes and quiz nights very seriously. Fair enough, and not completely out of order to have a quiet word with the quizmaster at the end of a round. But this was not a quiet word. It was voiced, by Sue, from their table in the middle of the hall and was loud enough for everyone to hear. For a minute, there was a stunned silence.

I felt a mixture of irritation, embarrassment, and, of course, sympathy for the quizmaster, Dave, who was a supportive and generous parent. From his position at the front of the hall, he handled the complaint with aplomb.

'I'm sorry, Sue. Quizmaster's word final.'

Sue sat up, and I sensed she was about to pursue her complaint when I saw Ken put his hand on her arm. His restraining gesture had the desired effect, and she sat back in her chair. Despite some muttering from the Naylors' table, the quiz continued. In the end, when the results were announced, their table had come second. I saw them approach Dave and was horrified to hear them querying the final scores. They were not happy with the result, and I was certainly not happy with their behaviour. The scores remained, and tempted as I was to waylay them as they came out of the hall, I didn't want parents to witness what might well have been an unseemly confrontation.

The following day, as staff were leaving the morning briefing, I managed to catch Ken by the door.

'Hi, Ken. I wonder if you and Sue could pop in and see me at the break.'

'Sure, Andrew. What's it about?'

'It won't take long, but I don't really want to discuss it now,' I said as staff filed past the two of us.

Eleven o'clock came, and I was in the office checking some typing with my secretary when Sue and Ken appeared. We stood in the office.

'Hi. You said you wanted to see us,' Ken said.

'Yes, of course. Do you want to come through?' I led the way across the short corridor to my office, sat down behind my desk, and gestured to the two chairs in front.

'It's just about last night – at the quiz evening. I'm afraid your objections didn't go down too well.'

'What do you mean?' Sue could be quite sharp. She was certainly more forthright than her husband.

'PTA quizzes are meant to be friendly affairs – not be taken too seriously, and certainly not by members of staff.'

'But they clearly got the scoring wrong,' Sue protested. I could see her face redden.

'That's as maybe, Sue, but if you were going to say anything – which I wished you hadn't – you should have had a discrete word with Dave, and not done it so publicly. I know that if we had parents behaving in the same way, Dave would have had a word with them. As it was, he was just acutely embarrassed and instead spoke to me.'

All this time, Ken was just looking at Sue, who was staring, unblinkingly, at me. She was clearly the spokesperson and leaned forward in her chair. 'Well, I'm sorry you feel like this. No one complained to us.'

'They weren't likely to, were they? But I'm surprised you didn't pick up on the silence in the hall when you objected.'

'But Dave did get it wrong on a couple of occasions,' Sue persisted.

'That's really not the point. The idea is for everyone to have a bit of fun and make money for the school.'

There was silence – but no comeback.

'Can we please make sure there's no repeat next time?'

'Is that it, then?' Ken spoke up at last. There were no concessions and no apologies, but I was pretty confident the message had gotten through.

'Yes, that's it.'

They both got up and left my office. The next quiz night, the Naylors were noticeable by their absence.

RISKING ARREST

Issues of fire safety followed me around from school to school. This was Hornchurch, and it's now the afternoon prior to the annual open evening in October. As I had done for the previous three years, I was furtively sneaking into the small, low-ceilinged cupboard under the stairs by the school's front entrance. I had to bow low to stop my head from banging against the cupboard's roof. If any passing member of staff had seen me, they would certainly have raised an eyebrow. Any senior colleague would probably have asked an awkward question.

To understand why I was crouched in that cupboard, we have to go back those three years before I started as a head. Geoff, my predecessor, had kindly agreed to meet with me. Perhaps the thought of retirement after forty years in education had made him slightly demob happy but, whatever the reason, he had been extremely generous. He was a large, genial man with a friendly face, and I knew staff were going to miss him – making my job even more challenging. He'd already taken me through the staff list and, breaching every confidentiality, given me a thumbnail sketch of each member. But the greatest gift came just before the last time I saw him.

I was starting as head in January, and our meeting took place on a late afternoon in December. Most staff had gone home, and there seemed to be no one about.

'Come with me. I want to show you something.' I sensed we had suddenly become conspirators.

We crossed the entrance hall from Geoff's office, heading towards the stairs. At the last minute, he veered off towards that door under the stairs. I wondered where he was leading me, and I followed as best I could into the narrow space. Over his shoulder, I could see the various levers, switches, fuse boxes, and meters. This was the school's electricity hub.

Geoff indicated a couple of what looked like black plastic pegs – small and seemingly insignificant.

'These two fuses are the ones that govern the fire alarm.'

He started to unscrew the larger of the two and handed me what was clearly a fuse. He turned his attention to the smaller one and unscrewed that too. Just then, footsteps sounded, and he froze. So did I. The sounds died away. Once again, we were on our own. Geoff's shoulders relaxed, and we carried on talking – albeit sotto voce.

'These two fuses incapacitate the fire alarm. I suggest you take them out when you have the open evening in October. The last thing you want is the alarm going off.'

We emerged from the cupboard and returned to his office. No further mention of the conspiracy. We chatted about life post-retirement.

'I just wanted to say, Geoff, how much I've appreciated your help over the past few weeks. I really hope you have a happy retirement and get to do all those things you've planned.'

'And you, Andrew. I'm sure you'll enjoy working here.' We wandered out to the car park and said our farewells.

I reflected on Geoff's advice. The annual open evening was a unique opportunity to showcase the school and boost what had been flagging numbers. Any head would be desperate to present their school as calm and well-ordered. A screeching alarm (as happened when the first inspection took place at the Barnet school) generating chaos and confusion could well destroy that impression. I had to weigh the odds which, of course, is what these safety issues are about. Had there ever been an actual fire at the school? If there were, would it be during school time? Most school fires aren't. On top of all that, would it be likely to be on that one day out of 365? I'd never been a betting man, but it seemed the odds were definitely on my side. Prison or the sack figured low down in my thoughts. And so, from year one of my headship, any scruples I might have had were put to one side. All the school's open evenings went off without a hitch. I was able to walk around extolling its virtues to prospective parents – the fuses safe in my jacket pocket.

*

Following my third Open Evening – some three years after my first foray into the under-stair cupboard – I happened to be around when one of the borough's electricians came in to carry out his annual test. Greying hair, blue overalls, and armed with his usual heavy toolbox, I met him as he crossed the hall towards the under-stairs. I couldn't remember his name, but we'd certainly met before and were on 'chatting' terms.

'How's it going then? What are you here for this time?'

'It's just the annual test, Headmaster. Won't take long.' He lugged his toolbox and various instruments into the cupboard.

I squeezed in behind him and feigned interest in the testing procedures he was carrying out.

'I expect you see some strange things on your travels?'

'Bloody hell – excuse my French – but you wouldn't believe it. I've seen plenty of dummy alarms. The worst was what looked like a proper alarm, but when I unscrewed it, I found all the wires had been disconnected. These are heads doing this. They ought to be locked up.' Rising indignation in his voice. I was relieved he was talking to the bank of dials and switches rather than me. If he'd turned round, he might have detected guilt etched on my face.

Innocently I pointed to the larger of the two fuses, which I had been religiously removing once a year.

'What does that do?'

'Nothing. It's redundant.' My heart missed a beat.

'What about that smaller one?'

'That. That's just a backup.'

The electrician carried on with his testing. I started to wonder how close those Open Evenings had been to disaster.

He finished, and we backed out of the cupboard. I thanked him for sharing his work with me and bade him farewell.

All that cloak-and-dagger behaviour. If I *had* been caught, it would have been for nothing. My last three Open Evenings did go off without incident, but I could never completely relax.

TEACHING SPANISH

In the twenty-first century, heads are leaders and managers – not teachers. However, in the 1980s, most heads did some teaching. Some did a lot more than that. A bit of a cop-out, I thought – even then.

Very occasionally, *I* found myself back in the classroom. Most likely a cover lesson that there was absolutely no one else available for. Although anyone else free could have been hiding in that cupboard in the staffroom.

We were now well into the summer term and planning for the coming year. The timetable was almost complete, and I wasn't aware of any issues.

Three weeks before the end of the term, there was a knock on my open office door. Sandrine's head appeared. She was the acting head of languages – small and bubbly with her dark plait always bouncing around. She was actually a French assistante (trainee teacher) but, with two members of staff away, was having to step in and run the department – and doing a great job.

'Do you have a minute?'

'Yes,' I said. 'Come in. What is it, Sandrine?'

She came and stood in front of my desk. She had on a serious face, so I guessed it was important. Up until then, she had needed little help taking over. Had she come up against a problem?

'Well... I was just wondering...' To my relief, that didn't

sound like a crisis. 'I seem to remember you talking about your time in Salamanca – learning Spanish?' Sandrine, for all her youth and inexperience, had a knack for approaching matters from the side.

'Yeees.' My hesitance betrayed just a tad of apprehension about what was to come.

'We've got a Year 7 Spanish class – 7C – and no one to cover it. Would you be willing?'

'Sandrine, I'm really not sure my Spanish is up to it.'

'I'm sure you'll be fine. They'll all be complete beginners. You'll always be well ahead of them.'

'Is there really no one else?' I asked forlornly, knowing the answer that was coming.

'No one with any knowledge of Spanish, Andrew.' That did seem a bit of a clincher. Sandrine stood, waiting. There was no triumphalism, but Sandrine was smiling as though she knew she'd won.

'OK, Sandrine, but you'll have to show me what the Year 7s are doing.' I was already feeling apprehensive. My time in Salamanca had been less productive than I'd hoped, and I still hadn't mastered the verbs – let alone the vocabulary. I knew I would need a prop – if not regular help.

'Is there a textbook?' I asked.

'Don't worry. I'll take you through the syllabus and… I'm really grateful. Oh… and it is only for one term. Felipe will be back after Christmas.'

That was some consolation, although Sandrine's innocent reassurance was quickly overtaken by the calculation I was making. Thirteen weeks times two lessons a week. Twenty-six lessons! Gulp!!

Fast forward to September. Sandrine and I had managed a couple of sessions, so I didn't feel completely unprepared, although I wasn't sure which was more demanding – teaching Spanish or getting the school ready for another year.

First lesson. I stood by the door as all twenty-five girls and boys trooped in. This was in the days before seating plans, and students could sit where they wanted. Quite often, there was an unseemly rush – more often than not, boys jostling for the seats at the back of the classroom. However, as you might expect, this pristine group, under the eye of their head, came in quiet as mice, and as they did, I said, 'Right. As quick as you can. One girl and one boy standing at each table.'

Once they'd sorted themselves out – with a bit of help from me – I sat them down.

For the first few lessons, all went well. They were a delight to teach – as shiny and new as their textbooks. Innocent, excited – and *very* keen. Hands would go up before I'd even ask a question.

'Sir, Sir.'

'Me, me.'

I even had them sitting in groups for oral work and games – a sure sign that, for me, things were under control. We played number games, learnt the days of the week, translated their first names into Spanish, and learnt something about Spanish culture and geography.

However, as early as week four, their capacity for learning, and my Spanish, were coming together at an alarming rate. The first sign was when I found Jemma, as bright and conscientious as any of them, waiting by my desk after the class had been dismissed.

'What is it, Jemma?' I asked.

She dipped into her school bag and produced a Spanish CD. 'My parents said you might like to listen to this.'

To my relief, I saw it was music, and I took it with thanks – promising to do as requested. I did manage to listen to some of it and handed it back the next lesson. However, this innocent exchange seemed to open the floodgates.

The next lesson, it was Illic – a recent arrival from what was then Yugoslavia. He was already a conscientious student and turned up with a book of short stories – in Spanish, of course. He wanted to lend it to me, and, as graciously as possible, I took it. Illic's book was followed by a CD from Pratish – 'Conversational Spanish'. It was possible my enthusiasm had rubbed off on them. They could never have guessed that the time was fast approaching when the charlatan would be exposed!

I borrowed Pratish's CD as well – wondering about the extent to which I could play for time before both Illic and Pratish quizzed me on their loans. However, I knew I couldn't keep on 'confiscating' these symbols of enthusiasm.

It even got to the point whereby I longed for window blinds so that students couldn't persistently ask questions like:

'Sir, what's the Spanish for thunder/cloud/storm/downpour/ rainbow…?'

Fortunately for me, window cleaners, for obvious reasons, were only permitted in school holidays. There was no way I would have known the Spanish for 'window cleaner'.

I realised I had to up my game – but it was a game of bluff which had me sweating until the end of the term. I became increasingly reliant on Sandrine, who must have wondered what on earth I did in Salamanca. I probably did more homework than the Illics, the Pratishes and the Jemmas of 7C. I certainly spent less time running the school on the basis that staff would notice my absence less than 7C would!

EIGHT

HAVERING

INSPECTOR FOR SECONDARY EDUCATION

Next stop after my Hornchurch headship? I wasn't quite sure. I almost applied for the vacant post of inspector for secondary education in the same borough (Havering) but, on reflection, decided not to. A second headship seemed the obvious choice, but I was about to turn fifty, and although I really didn't consider myself on the scrap heap, I did feel the time was running out. Too early to retire and too late for a new, significant post. We live now, and did then, in an ageist world, viz. the 2020 study published by the National Bureau of Economic Research, which found that workers over the age of forty were only about half as likely to get a job offer as younger ones. No room for experience. However, I wasn't panicking – wasn't yet at the point where I could feel 'Time's wingèd chariot hurrying near'. That would be overdramatic.

I was still considering my options when, having decided the inspector job wasn't for me, I got a message from the man who was still my boss – Havering's director of education. It was flattering – 'We're disappointed you haven't applied.'

At that point, I should have taken US Senator Adlai Stevenson's wise words on board: 'Flattery is fine as long as you don't inhale.'

I inhaled and fairly quickly realised that inspection was not for me – especially with Havering's tough, no-nonsense, not-to-be-trifled-with collection of heads – my ex-colleagues. These were heads who terrified the Director of Education on those rare occasions that he braved their meetings. With his moon face and round rimless glasses, he could have been taken for the borough's accounting officer – not one of its senior executives. Amongst Havering's heads, he was more likely to inspire derision than respect. Many had been in post for years. A number were about to retire. They'd seen it all. Although nearing fifty, I had often felt like a new boy in their company despite their friendliness. With my new appointment, responsible for inspecting their schools – many of which were underperforming – I guessed that relationship might be about to change.

I didn't choose the schedule of inspections. If I had, it certainly wouldn't have been my ex-school's nearest neighbour. The two schools had been rivals for years, with the neighbour always having the upper hand. The head, Gerald Loxton, was a smooth-talking classicist with a rather supercilious air. He usually wore a pinstripe suit with a colourful bow tie to match the silk handkerchief in his breast pocket. He was an autocrat and a difficult man to deal with. His school grew out of one of the old technical high schools – some of which became grammar schools. I think they would have suited him better than the comprehensive he found himself in.

I was determined to introduce 'management' into the inspection criteria. Strangely, it had never been figured before. The focus had always been on subject teaching – central, of course, but only part of the whole picture. It was just unfortunate, both for him and for me, that he and his team were the 'guinea pigs'.

The inspection completed, I wrote a first draft that referred to Gerald as 'autocratic' – no beating about the bush there but hardly the most sensitive of approaches! However, I had support from a colleague adviser who quoted his management style as being 'one of benevolent dictatorship...'

The Director of Education would carry the can for any challenge to my report, and he *certainly* wouldn't want to ruffle Gerald's feathers. I was asked to rewrite, tone down and perjure myself. It was a distasteful process, and I was torn between my determination to see the inspection through – and pulling out altogether. I decided to persist at the same time, knowing the final version would only reflect partial 'reality'. Some *four drafts* later, a significantly emasculated and watered-down version was sanctioned by the chief inspector and the director of education. Extracts as follows with my comments in parenthesis:

Management at ...School
'...there is a role in the decision-making processes for the other seven members of (his) team.' (Not true.)

The Senior Management Team
'There is a tendency for short-term and day-to-day matters to dominate (meetings), and additional space could be left for major issues.' (But space never was.)

My recommendations that followed could only be described as 'pussyfooting' using words such as... 'might be' rather than 'should be' and... 'should be considered' rather than 'should be implemented'.

Even this fourth draft was treading on eggshells. Actually, was it the fourth? It had become increasingly hard to keep track of the iterations. There was another difficult conversation over which report the head had seen and, of course, over his management style.

Finally, the chief inspector, Tim, and I met with the head to discuss the report.

We were ushered into Gerald's office by his secretary.

'Mr Loxton, your visitors are here.' No use of his first name by underlings – formal as I would have expected.

Gerald got up and motioned to the two chairs in front of his intimidatingly large desk. This had what I took to be the traditional family photos with their back to us, except for one. As we sat down, Tim nodded towards the photo, which had been turned round and was now facing us. It meant little to me at the time, but, as I subsequently discovered, it meant plenty to Tim. It was of the *Pietà* by Michelangelo. It depicts the Virgin Mary sorrowfully contemplating the dead body of her son. Gerald knew that Tim, as a fellow classicist, would understand its significance. He clearly intended it to evoke sympathy for his plight as the victim of my vicious and erroneous report. At that point, I felt a little bit of an outsider with Gerald and Tim sharing their understanding of Renaissance art.

We moved to the report itself. Amongst other complaints, there was the accusation that I had had a private conversation with the Deputy Head (no fan of the Head) prior to writing it. His accusation was unfounded, but it was a clever ploy as, in the interim, the Deputy had died – and couldn't be confronted.

Before we left, with nothing having been resolved, Gerald summed up his distorted view of my report with the following:

'Andrew, you should know that the involvement of staff at all levels is called anarchy.' This was Gerald's defence of dictatorship.

There was a subplot to this dispute about leadership, and that was the introduction, in 1988 and just two years before the dispute itself, of the Conservative government's 'Education Reform Act'. Amongst other things, it enabled schools to opt out of local authority control. Schools up and down the country had had enough of their inefficiency and bureaucracy. Even Labour was forced to recognise this. Gerald Loxton and his governing body were not alone in their opposition to the way Havering was running its schools and were eagerly heading for the exit.

As if to signal his intent, Gerald took steps to bring a libel action against me. I was forced to instruct solicitors. In their desperate attempts to lower the temperature, the local authority offered Gerald early retirement (in itself worth a considerable amount) if he apologised to me. Up until then, I had only *read* about people being 'paid off' – rather than seeing corruption first hand.

He was being made too good an offer to refuse, and almost immediately an apology was received. There was one consolation that came out of such an unsavoury episode – the school would get a new head.

My life as a local authority inspector went a little more smoothly after that. It couldn't really fail! However, I had no control over the way schools were run. At the same time, a large part of my job was pushing paper round my desk.

I stuck it out for two years, and then decided I really wanted to get back on the other side of the fence – as it were. I had had 'responsibility' for the borough's twenty secondary schools but never felt I was changing anything. As a head, as I had discovered, you're in the unique position of influencing the lives of staff and students. It's a position of great power and, of course, open to abuse. My first experience of headship had been very rewarding, and my two years as an inspector made me realise I wanted to get back to it.

NINE

BARNET

INTRODUCTION

The London Borough of Barnet is in north London, sandwiched between Harrow and Enfield. It is often referred to as 'leafy Barnet'. The truth is that it ranks almost exactly halfway between the wealthiest and poorest boroughs in London. It has the largest Jewish population of any area in the UK, with no less than four Jewish secondary schools. It also has the largest Chinese population in London.

The school, like the Hornchurch one, went through umpteen incarnations before opening as a 'Fresh Start' in September 1992 with me as head. 'Fresh Start' was a scheme the government had introduced to turn around failing schools. To enable the school to begin again, its predecessor was closed in July 1991. That gave me a year to set up the new one. I say 'me' as I inherited no staff and no pupils. An amazingly exciting prospect. I did, however, inherit the 1960s buildings, which had been neglected for years – as had the grounds. Dangerous metal windows with catches able to remove the fingers of the unwary. Antiquated heating with one side of the school too hot and the other too cold. What were most striking were the classrooms. Whatever displays had existed – and we guessed they had been minimal – had been yanked away from their Blu-Tacked fastenings, leaving, in many cases, paint ripped off and holes in plaster. The tables were the prize exhibits, with four legs of every one in every classroom graffitied. When we turned them over and looked at the undersides, we found them covered with chewing gum. And looking up – always important – we saw ceilings plastered with paper pellets, i.e., paper softened in the mouth and spat upwards. A skill, admittedly, but not really what schooling was designed for. There was no sign that any learning or teaching had taken place while the last cohort of the old school was going through. There were no books and no useable equipment.

Buildings aside, the excitement and the challenge were in establishing a school from scratch. The last of the students and staff departed in the summer of 1991, leaving behind a very poor reputation. The 'new' Barnet school was five form entries – thirty in each class – although we were subsequently able to set up six groups of twenty-five. For that crucial first intake, we had to somehow 'garner' 150 students. If necessary, ambush them and drag them off the streets. I knew that if word got around that we were oversubscribed – or at least full – parents would be falling over themselves to get their children in. Don't you always want what you can't get? Places in popular schools are fiercely sought after. People want what they can't have. Over the decades, parents have resorted to all sorts of ploys to get their children into 'good' schools. False addresses, fake relatives, nearby accommodation rented and never used. Church schools have often been particular targets, with atheists claiming they were regular churchgoers armed with bogus baptism certificates. Schools, and the law, have, to an extent, caught up with these tactics but parents still 'try it on'.

The first task was to get the new school on the rota of open evenings. Traditionally these take place in the autumn term each year and are for children in their final year at primary school. Families trek round those they want to see. Some – the more 'clued up' – try to see beneath the surface of exhibitions and displays of bright-eyed student guides and bushy-tailed staff. Others are seduced by the razzmatazz. Occasionally, tired teachers, disengaged students, and neglected display boards can be discerned. Such schools are in the minority. Most heads, at least, realise that their and their school's future is dependent on 'bums on seats'. At this point, I had a number of challenges:

- How to get the school on to the rota of open evenings. If it wasn't, nobody would know about it.
- How to present the school given we had no students and no staff.
- Linked to the above, how to distract attention from the decaying building.

I was incredibly fortunate that the local authority (yes, I know, just been rubbishing them) inspectors came to our rescue and 'masqueraded' as staff.

APPLICATION AND APPOINTMENT

Almost from the start as an inspector, I realised that that was not how I wanted to end my career – paper shuffling and inspecting ex-colleagues schools.

I decided to try and get back into a headship. I had just turned fifty-one and hoped that I might be seen as a bottle of expensive wine that had matured – rather than one that had gone off!

As luck would have it, I just happened to be the right person, in the right place at the right time when the 'new' school came up in Barnet. There were four of us shortlisted – sitting in the rather cramped office-come-waiting room in the neglected school building. I guessed the powers that be had chosen the interview location to drive home the challenge the successful candidate faced. The room had stained roof tiles, some windows that didn't quite close, and radiators that were cold despite it being a chilly autumn day. I was the last to arrive – being shown in by the local inspector.

'This is Andrew Macalpine. He makes up the four candidates who've been shortlisted.'

I took a chair – classroom type with plastic seats and no concession to comfort. There was a low table at which we were sitting round. While remaining seated, we all shook hands, although it seemed we were sitting a little too close to each other for comfort. Amongst other interviewees was the woman who had been acting head as the old school ran down. This was the final interview, and I recognised her from the preliminary ones at the town hall. We were clearly, in some way, the two oldest applicants, and I sensed (rather arrogantly) that she was my main rival. The other two were very different from us oldies. The man was tall, sharp-suited, and wearing pointy shoes. The woman was blonde with high heels. She was wearing an open-necked cream (and probably silk) blouse. She looked young enough to be one of my students. It didn't really occur to me at the time what they might make of a balding man and a very stern-faced, grey-haired woman. We were sitting indulging in rather meaningless chat – none of us revealing too much – when out of nowhere:

'I don't know what I'm going to do if I don't get this job.' It was the ex-acting head. Her confession was met with an embarrassed silence. Clearly, in her own mind, the post was hers.

We were called in one by one to what *had* been the stern-faced woman's office just a few months ago. The interviewing panel consisted of three governors and the local authority adviser. Two of the three governors were Barnet Conservative councillors. I had already been given a heads-up about one of them – the chair, Moira Bennett – who was also chair of Barnet's education committee. She was a little over five feet with an open, smiley face that deceived no one who worked with her or for her. She was a pocket battleship and not to be trifled with. I'm not sure why, but I felt we hit it off straight away. She spurred me into something approaching a decent interview, and I felt a positive response. It could have been my public school background. It certainly wasn't my politics which I sensibly kept under wraps. I think she saw me as someone who would recreate the school in the image of my alma mater, although, as chair of the local authority education committee, she was well aware that the school I was applying for was a state secondary. Anyway, I survived the grilling and was appointed.

My main rival, having offered perfunctory congratulations, never spoke to me again, even though she became a Barnet inspector and, in theory, at least, part of her role should have involved working with a newly appointed head!

GETTING GOING

I've already described the 'fake' open evening I ran in order to recruit a full intake of students. We also needed to run an induction morning in the summer term using the heads of department (by now appointed) who would join us in September.

Having divided the 150 students into six forms, they were allocated six classrooms. Halfway through the morning, there was a knock on my door. I was in the middle of a conversation with Moira, my new chair of governors, who'd popped in to say hello.

'Come in.' A small head appeared nervously round the door.

'What's your name?' I hadn't yet learnt the names of our new students.

'Chloe, Sir.'

'What do you want, Chloe?'

'Sir, Miss Black says can you come to her classroom.'

'Alright, Chloe. You can go back. I'll be there in a minute.' I tried to guess what might be behind the request. In normal circumstances, i.e., a fully functioning school, it might have spelled trouble. The thought flitted briefly across my mind. But, hey, these weren't normal circumstances. This was the induction session for our 150 bright-eyed new students.

I made my excuses to Moira and went down to Ms Black's classroom. I stopped for a moment before entering.

No signs or sounds of chaos. The class were all copying something off the whiteboard – all that is, except one. Liz Black nodded in the direction of a boy slumped head down on his desk.

'George,' she mouthed while continuing to write up various start-of-the-day and lesson times the students would need come September.

There were only five minutes of the session left, so I decided to sit on a spare chair in the corner of the classroom. The buzzer went, and Liz, very efficiently, got everyone tidying away and standing up. She dismissed them, table by table, sensibly, leaving George's table until last. As George shambled towards the door, I approached him from the side – deciding not to be too confrontational but at the same time wanting to cut off his exit.

'George, I just want a word.'

My request was greeted with a slight shove and a very clear 'Fuck off'. This wasn't the first time I'd been told to fuck off in my career, and I guessed it probably wouldn't be the last. However, bright-eyed and bushy-tailed George was not. I don't think either of us knew who we were dealing with. George appeared not to care. For my part, I resisted any temptation to wrestle him to the ground. An altercation – either physical or verbal – was going to get nowhere.

'Liz, I'll sort this out later. I've got the chair of governors in my office, and I need to get back to her.'

'Yes, a bit of a shock. He was slumped like that for most of the lesson. I don't know what, but there's definitely something wrong with him.' Liz was certainly one of the calmest people I'd come across and seemed unfazed by what had happened. *I* was definitely rattled. I left her tidying up the papers on her desk.

When I got back to my office, Moira was still there – standing, looking out of the window.

'You know there's a panel missing on that roof, don't you, Andrew?'

'Yes. The architect's due tomorrow,' I replied.

'Anyway, what was all that about?' I explained what had happened.

'We can't have him starting in September after that. Apart from anything else, the others would think he'd got away with it,' I said.

'Why don't I get on to the Director? See what we can do.' Moira had no hesitation in going straight to the top, and I knew she was only going to take yes for an answer.

She took out her diary and went over to my desk. 'Just dial nine and you'll have an outside line,' I said.

The number she dialled was clearly a hot line as, less than thirty seconds later, she was explaining the situation to the Director. I was standing watching, hoping there was a supportive response at the other end. After a couple of minutes, she put her hand over the mouthpiece and turned to me. 'He wants to know what you want to do.'

I thought for a moment.

'OK... I'll write to parents, explain what happened and say that George is suspended from day one in September. They'll have to bring him in to see me during the first week.'

Moira repeated the message to the director and moments later put the phone down. 'He says that's fine. You can go ahead.'

'Moira, that's really helpful. Thank you.'

This was far from the kind of support most heads get, and I knew I was very fortunate. For many, governors are merely a hindrance. Moira was an experienced politician and understood local authority politics and how local authorities work – or don't. I had a precious ally.

A few weeks later and it was the summer holiday. I was coming out of the borough offices as the director was going in. He was a large, avuncular man in his sixties – about to retire.

'Andrew. Good to see you. How's it all going?'

I went through the preparations we had made and were making for the opening of the school.

'You realise you've already got quite a reputation, don't you?'

I answered Martin's rhetorical question, 'Not sure what you mean?' Was this good or bad?

'Well, you've suspended a boy before they've even started at the school.'

I laughed, sensing, from the grin on Martin's face, that this wasn't all bad.

He continued, 'You remember I was on the receiving end when Moira Bishop phoned about the boy who told you to fuck off? Starting as you mean to go on. Can't do any harm.'

Like the head who left blood on the wall outside his office (see below 'Headteachers of All Sorts'), I saw no reason to disabuse anyone of my action.

By this time, George's mum, ironically, had been appointed to work in our new canteen. Initially, she was on the defensive – 'You're picking on my boy' – but her stance softened when she realised that I was more concerned with helping him settle down than kicking him out. She's still there thirty years later! And, wonder of wonders, George lasted the course too – just.

FIRST APPOINTMENTS

The Blank Sheet of Paper

Appointing staff is crucial wherever you are – schools no exception – but the process has to be rigorous. Phrases from panel members like 'I could tell straight away' and 'I knew from the off' are not good enough. Such mystics can sway others with their 'insights'. Thus the composition of your appointments panel is crucial, as is the range of tasks candidates are asked to perform. And even after all that, you still may not get it right.

I used to threaten to park outside any shortlisted candidate's house to check on comings and goings – night and day. Obviously, I had to withdraw that threat once senior colleagues started taking me seriously! A far-fetched example, maybe. However, in the US, the search for the right CEO can still include inviting the candidate and partner out to dinner! More often than not the husband and his wife! Knowing which knife to use, when to move on from small talk and when to kick your partner under the table is, arguably, as stressful as a formal interview!

I was incredibly lucky to find myself head of a 'new' school – able to appoint my own staff in my own way and recruit a cohort of pristine – well, almost pristine – students.

Barnet's plan was that I should work from the bottom up, i.e., make the junior appointments first. I knew that this was how some new schools had gotten off the ground. To me, it seemed an approach that made no sense. Cost-efficient but certainly not cost-effective. What I needed to embark on this amazing adventure was the able and experienced staff who would have knocked about enough to know what might work – and what wouldn't. Staff who would mirror my excitement and who would complement whatever talent I had. Staff who, themselves, would have a good eye for appointees. I had no qualms about appointing people who had more to offer than I did. And I certainly didn't find myself surrounded by 'yes men' and 'yes women'! Of course, this makes for a challenge – but it results in better decision-making.

So to the staff appointments we made.

Appointment 1. Initially, while still employed as an inspector in Havering, I found myself acting as the site manager for the new school. There was no one else. Forget education. I have already described some of the issues in my introduction to the Barnet school (see above). In addition to neglected classrooms, there were leaking roofs, dangerous electrics, broken floor tiles, and dented metal lockers looking as though the heads of mafia victims had been bashed against them. The grounds were a wasteland with chain link fencing that would no longer keep anyone out – or in. I needed to become an *ex*-site manager as quickly as possible. I asked around for suitable people and soon homed in on a retired local authority maintenance supremo. One who used to strike terror into the hearts of negligent heads and lazy caretakers. Was this gamekeeper prepared to turn poacher? I arranged a meeting, and five minutes were enough to convince me that not only did he know everyone in authority involved in buildings but that he was the person I needed. Obviously, this went against the arrogance of 'I could tell straight away' and 'I knew from the off' but there are exceptions to every rule! So that was appointment number one.

Appointment 2. I needed a caretaker to work with the site manager. Preferably someone with no caretaking background! Of course, excellent caretakers exist. I had two myself in Hornchurch. However, the caretaking 'mafia' abounded in schools, and I was wary of appointing someone who had been tainted. I elaborate on this scurrilous accusation below (see 'Caretakers and Caretaking').

In the end, three candidates presented themselves – two existing caretakers and one gravedigger (Bill)! There was definitely a whiff of jobsworth about the caretakers. We appointed the gravedigger, still in post nearly thirty years later. As part of the grand opening, we planted a tree. Bill was tasked with the manual work. He dug a perfect hole – not the rectangle he was used to, but just the one you'd expect from a professional.

Appointment 3. A secretary. A lovely Scotswoman with a broad Scots brogue, which often needed translating. There was no one else in the office, so she had to turn her hand to whatever was required. This included filling the urn with water for tea and coffee. Except she managed to convert 'urn' into 'errun'. She was wonderful with people and quickly made herself indispensable.

That covered the initial support staff. Now I needed some experienced 'managers'.

Appointments 4 and 5. Ignoring the local authority's bottom-up money-saving approach, my next stop was two deputies. We had 184 applications – many as excited as I was by the thought of starting a school from scratch. With admin help from my daughter, I got them into some sort of order. One hundred and eighty-four were whittled down to eight. Rigorous interviews followed. Down to two. It was then that I discovered that, out of 184, we had picked two, Bruce and Teresa, who had worked together previously! Each had to be asked if they minded coming together again. Fortunately, the answer was, 'That's fine.' Certainly fine for me as I ended up marrying Teresa. Still discussing education thirty years on. Both deputies played a crucial role in setting up the school, and both achieved great things following their deputy head roles. Bruce went on to two successful headships, and Teresa followed a headship with a CBE for services to education.

Appointments 6 to 11. The gradual build-up continued. Six heads of department next. For each interviewee, I pushed a blank sheet of paper across my, otherwise bare, office table.

'We can write whatever we want on this blank sheet. The future of the new school is in your hands.' Or words to that effect. Any candidate whose eyes didn't light up at the prospect didn't get any further.

Of course, it wasn't all smooth sailing. We encountered some extremely choppy waters. Nobody gets it right all of the time – least of all myself, viz. our first head of department appointee. He stole the ski money and ended up in prison (see 'Criminality').

Our second became very pally with the first at the same time as trying to set up confrontations – 'workers v. management'. He had been a union rep at his previous school, but here, with us, he was a lone voice, and it didn't work. He tried mud-slinging when he found out that I was in a relationship with one of my deputies, but as it was open knowledge, the mud didn't stick. Ironically, when he moved on to a post in a girls' school, it was where his partner was the head!

The other four made up for the first two.

Of course, there are nearly always more rejected candidates than successful ones (unless only two apply). Most of those not chosen take it on the chin and are grateful for feedback. Some refuse feedback, knowing we have got it wrong. There was even an applicant for head of maths who came into school the following day to explain, as assertively as she could, why she hadn't been appointed. I listened patiently to her harangue until it blew itself out.

CRIMINALITY

As I indicated above, our first head of the department stole the ski money. He had got to the final interview strongly recommended by the Barnet inspector linked with the school. 'The best in the borough' was his assessment. Our candidate was personable and good at his job, and his previous school wanted to keep him. What could go wrong?

What went wrong was that, obviously unbeknown to us, he had a gambling problem. He had suffered serious losses and was starting to place increasingly desperate bets. As a result of sloppy management (see below), the parental contributions for the annual school ski trip all came to him. They should have been banked immediately. Instead, they made their way to local bookmakers and gave him the opportunity to carry on with the Yankees, Doubles, Trebles, and Accumulators through which he tried to recoup his losses. Of course, the odds were heavily stacked against him, his bets became increasingly desperate, and his, or rather 'our', losses mounted.

We reached the point where the ski company required payment, and the co-organiser contacted the bank to withdraw the money – only to find there was none there! The game was up. Where parents had paid, we guaranteed the places. At the same time, we reported the theft to the police.

Next thing I knew, two policemen turned up in my office to let me know that he would be charged – unless I could provide a reason not to go ahead. I couldn't, although I found it strange that I was put in that position. If I had said he was an excellent head of department (which he was), would they have dropped the case? To my mind, a serious crime had been committed, and I didn't see how it could lead to anything other than prosecution.

Following his trial, he was sentenced to two years in prison. The case eventually reached the local press and shocked the whole school community. He lived locally and I, along with many colleagues, dreaded bumping into him. Fortunately, that hasn't happened – yet.

As to the school, all future bank payments required two signatures. *We* had learnt our lesson, and I'm sure he had.

FIGHT IN THE OFFICE

Gary Bender had a very chequered career. Like the majority of 'difficult' students we dealt with, you could trace his behaviour back to his parents – or parent. Quite often, a missing dad and a mum who was struggling to pay the bills. Stereotypical but sadly true.

He was thirteen – tall, dark-haired, and underfed. He always seemed to be on a short fuse. Unlike wealthier parents, whose children started every year with a new blazer, his mother had not been able to afford to replace the brand-new one that she'd saved up to buy before he started at the school. That and the natural growth spurt typical of that age meant that on those rare occasions he came to school with it, the blazer was clearly too short and too tight. His unwashed shirt was always hanging out of his trousers. He was the embodiment of scruffiness. If we didn't know his mother and his home (visited many times by staff following up disciplinary issues), we might have termed him 'a waif and a stray'. His attendance was spasmodic. When he did turn up, he was rarely on time. His teachers, although reluctant to admit it, breathed a sigh of relief when his seat remained vacant. His issue, at least on the surface, was his temper.

On this particular day, the head of history, Martin, was giving a lesson on the Civil War. Gary was ten minutes late, and Martin knew better than to start an interrogation so he gestured towards a vacant chair. As usual, Gary had no books or equipment and nothing to write with. 'Borrowing' a pen from his neighbour was often the trigger for a flare-up. On this occasion, and without any warning, Gary, accompanied by an expletive-laden rant, assaulted another pupil. The class was brought shuddering to a halt. Martin managed to separate the two boys at the same time as telling a girl sitting at the front to get Charlotte, my deputy. Charlotte and I were in the middle of a meeting in her office.

'Do you want me to go?' I asked Charlotte – starting to get out of my chair.

'No, it's fine. You stay there.'

Her office was right next to Martin's classroom. She went in to find him standing near the door with Gary by his side.

'Gary, you need to come with me.' Although you try never to show your frustration, dealing with challenging students is a challenge in itself. You never know if the pot is about to boil over or has been reduced to simmering. Charlotte was calmness personified in such situations, and her 'Gary, you need to come with me' had just that quality of steeliness and calmness that many of us struggled to emulate. She brought him back to the office and motioned him to sit down on the chair next to mine. Gary was looking at the floor, and he clearly didn't want to make eye contact given the many times I'd had to see him under such circumstances.

'So, what is it this time, Gary?' I asked.

Gary's head was still bowed, and he fidgeted nervously.

'Gary, look at me. What got you so angry?'

'It's Ahmed. He just winds me up.'

'How's that, Gary?' Charlotte asked. 'In what way did he wind you up?'

'He wouldn't lend me a fucking pen.'

'But Gary, you never come to school with any equipment. You're always borrowing other people's stuff. Not surprising they get fed up.'

The interrogation continued, and Gary continued to fidget – his foot tapping vigorously, nails being bitten.

'We're going to have to phone your mum, Gary,' I said.

He sat up, and his eyes widened. 'Do you have to? She's going to kill me.'

'We've no choice, Gary.' This was Charlotte's 'this is going to hurt us more than it hurts you' voice.

To me, 'I'll be back in a minute, Mr Macalpine.'

Charlotte disappeared, and I was left with Gary, who was nervously drumming his fingers on the table.

Charlotte reappeared and asked Gary to wait outside. 'What did she say, Charlotte?'

'In her own words? I'll fucking kill him; I will. Just let me get at him.'

'Not a surprise he's so difficult. Mind you, so is she. You can see where he gets it from,' I said. Charlotte nodded – a silent echo of my thoughts.

Gary's house was just round the corner, and less than ten minutes later, Mrs Bender stormed into my office with Angela from reception in hot pursuit a few steps behind. Her behaviour, and the fumes that quickly permeated the office, left the two of us in no doubt that she was drunk. I was reminded of the time we had to eject her from the sports day spectator area because she was drunk then as well. Over the years, we'd had numerous dealings with both Gary and his mum. As with so many troubled and troublesome boys (mostly boys), we'd hung on to him as long as possible. Often way beyond what any reasonable parent with a child in Gary's class would consider acceptable. That was always a balance we had to strike.

For Mrs Bender, disruption in her life was the norm. Her husband (Gary's dad) was no longer on the scene. Her eldest son was in prison.

'Please come and sit down, Mrs Bender,' I said.

Charlotte got up and managed to usher her round to sit between Gary and me. She had dark, unkempt hair, and, despite her slight frame, she had the tight, muscly look of a runner. She turned away from me and launched into an unrestrained and vitriolic attack on her son. Not unlike, I thought to myself, Gary's attack on Ahmed.

'Your fucking behaviour. I warned you what would happen. You wait until I get you home. You won't know what's fucking hit you.' Mrs Bender was well into her stride, and Gary started to cry. All the bravado he had just shown disappeared, and he shrunk into his shell. At this point, his mother drew her arm back and hit him in the face. A lot more than a slap. An assault that had to be stopped. I immediately leaned across and grabbed her arm while she continued her tirade.

I held on while she tried to twist out of my grip and then turned towards me.

'Don't you fucking touch me.'

Despite her wariness, I managed to hold on to her arm while Charlotte, sensing her moment, grabbed Gary and propelled him towards the door. She opened it, pushed Gary out, followed him, and slammed it behind her. At the same time, mum, realising what was going on (even in her drunken state), got up and went for the door. Fortunately, I was just a fraction quicker. I had to go around her, and we ended up at the door handle at the same time. We both grabbed it. There was a struggle in which her strong, sinewy arm started to pull my hand off the handle – in the process pulling my index finger back until I thought it would break. Despite her strength, with my other hand, I managed to break her hold, but as she let go, her hand slid down my forearm, and her long nails left angry scratches and drew blood. Eventually, I decided Gary had had enough time to get away, which I had no doubt Charlotte was ensuring he did. I let go of the handle and watched Gary's mum set off down the stairs opposite. In her drunken and out-of-control state, I was holding my breath in case she tripped. Slurring her words, she shouted over her shoulder as she reached the bottom:

'You lot are all the fucking same. Let them get away with what they like. He needs a good thrashing, and that's what he'll get. And if you want me, I'm in the pub.' With that, she was out of the door and gone.

There was obviously the need to pursue the incident. We wrote to Gary's mum and banned her from the site and then involved social services and governors to name but two. I won't go into detail. As a short-term measure, we kept Gary in school for the rest of the day. We let him go at four o'clock, having accepted his word that his mother would have calmed down by the time he got home.

However, there was a rather different postscript.

Some weeks later, I got a message from the cleaning company via Keith, our assistant school keeper, that my wonderful cleaner, who had kept my office spick and span for the previous four years, was retiring. We said sad goodbyes on Friday, and I anticipated seeing my new cleaner first thing Monday morning. Come Monday, Keith waylaid me to let me know that my new cleaner had started.

I made my way towards my office. The door was open and although the cleaner had her back to me dusting my keyboard, there was no mistaking who they'd sent. Mrs Bender! My pulse quickened, and I felt a hot flush come over me. I managed to beat a hasty retreat before she turned round.

I tracked down Keith, who was standing by the entrance doors.

'She's banned from the site, Keith,' I said, explaining the story. 'You need to ring the cleaning company and get her removed immediately.'

And that's what happened. Gary left at the end of that term, having reached school-leaving age, and we never saw him or his mother again. Sadly, you could be almost certain that, sooner rather than later, Gary would be in trouble with the police.

FIRST INSPECTION OF THE NEW SCHOOL

Awe and Wonder

The Barnet school had been going for some four years when we had our first inspection. It was a crunch moment, with pride, and even job security, on the line. I didn't feel I was going to be sacked, but anything less than 'Outstanding' would feel like a failure. And the final grading isn't something you can hide. It gets published by the school – and elsewhere.

We had prepared for the nth degree. However, 'the best-laid plans of mice and men often go awry'. There was certainly plenty that could go wrong. And it did. Day one, and the inspectors had barely set foot inside the building when suddenly we were assaulted by a shrill, insistent screeching that we all recognised only too well. The fire alarm had gone off. This was our worst nightmare, as it would be any school's that is undergoing an inspection. Probably a disruptive child and a sure sign of an ill-disciplined school. As teachers emerged from their classrooms, I emerged from my office – hoping a calm exterior wouldn't betray my inner panic.

I walked a few yards from my office to the top of the stairs where senior and office staff had congregated. Jeff, the assistant caretaker, came slowly up the stairs. It was the only way he ever moved, and the crisis seemed to have done nothing to change that.

I walked over to him as he reached the top of the stairs and shouted over the noise of an alarm that was right behind us.

'Do we know where it is?' I asked.

'Not yet,' Jeff replied. 'Pete's (head caretaker) looking now.' I was not reassured by this.

However, as he spoke, I could see Pete coming towards me down the corridor.

I walked to meet him. 'Well?'

'It's in the art room. No sign of any smoke, no smell of burning. I'm one hundred per cent it's either a glitch or one of the kids.'

We never found out. All we knew was that this was the inspectors' introduction to our school.

Meanwhile, I asked Sarah, one of the senior teachers, to go and reassure the inspection team in their classroom base while we carried out what we prayed was a well-rehearsed drill.

Nevertheless, I was experiencing the nightmare vision the deafening alarm conjured up of 750 students, tensions released, taking to the corridors, pushing and shoving, shouting and laughing, not knowing where to go – and not really caring. However much our fire drill had been rehearsed, we were about to fall flat on our collective faces before the inspection had even started. Rival schools and rival heads would, beneath a veneer of sympathy, revel in our misfortune.

However, even as this chaotic vision was playing out in my head, our senior team was moving towards the doors of the nearby corridor to stem the chaos.

What happened next left me speechless.

Two members of staff kept the corridor doors open as an orderly and silent procession of students made its way down the stairs towards the playground. The military training seemed to be bearing fruit!

In record time, class lines formed, roll calls were taken, and students, class by class, were returned to their rooms. Inspectors could be seen witnessing the event from the windows of their base on the first floor. Their faces showed surprise, admiration – even wonder – at the precision of the process. Miraculously, the fire alarm had done us a favour.

But there was no time to rejoice – a second event was to occur the following morning.

It was seven thirty. No slacking here. I was savouring the events of the previous day at the same time as preparing myself mentally for what was sure to be another challenging one. Just then, the lead inspector, Michael, knocked on the open door of my office. He was slim, tall, dark-haired, dark-suited – and serious. Fortyish and recently promoted. There was no chance of any informal chats with him and certainly no feedback until the last day.

'Andrew, do you have a minute?'

'Of course, Michael. Come in.' I got up and gestured politely towards a chair. At the same time, running through my mind were a range of reasons for the visit. What did he want to see? What had he seen? It turned out to be the former.

'Thanks Andrew. I won't stay. I just wanted to say we need to see an assembly at some stage.'

'That's fine, Michael. I'll let you know.'

He left, but I knew this was part of their 'awe and wonder' brief, the need to see something special – to wow them, as it were. I hoped the fire alarm response might have generated a bit of wonder. What about the 'awe'? A challenge – but if it meant that 'Very Good' became 'Outstanding'…

As luck would have it, that morning, a Year 10 assembly was being taken by a deputy who was never less than inspirational. Whether telling an illuminating story or delivering a homily, she always held her audience in the palm of her hand. I made my way to her office, and knocked on the door, which opened almost immediately. I could see she was on her way out – a couple of books in her hand.

'Sorry, Andrew. I'm just off to do my assembly.'

'Joan,' I said, trying to keep up with her as she breezed past me towards the stairs. 'Is it OK if your assembly gets observed?'

We reached the top of the stairs.

Joan stopped. 'Do I have to? I'm not really prepared.' She had left the door open a fraction.

'Joan, you're always prepared. Your assemblies are certainly better than anyone else's.'

There was a note of resignation. 'Well, I suppose so. Do you know who it'll be?'

'No idea, I'm afraid. Pot luck.'

'Alright then. I've got to go. The kids are going down already.'

We moved out of the way as a line of students emerged from the corridor behind us and, accompanied by their teacher, made its way down the stairs towards the hall.

'OK. I'll try to just to carry on as normal.' Joan followed the line of students down the stairs.

I hot-footed it to the inspectors' classroom lair. I knocked and walked in to be greeted by a warm fug and inspectors variously lounging at tables or hunched over papers. There were coffee mugs everywhere. Michael was sitting by himself at the front, and I went over to him.

'Hi, Michael. There's an assembly going on. If anyone's free, this could be a good time to experience some awe and wonder.' I'd had little time to think about all this but I was pretty confident Joan would produce the goods.

Those inspectors within earshot looked at each other. Eventually, the lay inspector, Hannah, got up. This was the same one who had tripped on a hole in the playground almost as soon as she had arrived. She had been making a tour of the outside of the school and had only just stopped herself from falling flat on her face. I could see why she'd tripped. Her diminutive stature was compensated for by frighteningly high heels – points designed to pierce. Above the shoes: full make-up and a skirt veering on the short side. I couldn't get 'Essex girl' out of my head. She might be out for revenge. Not only did she not take kindly to a pitted playground, but we'd had other concerns about her. She seemed poorly briefed and slow to establish a role for herself.

'I'll go.'

'It's just started, Hannah. I'll walk you downstairs.'

I left her at the doors to the hall, hoping Joan's assembly was still going on and that Hannah was able to bring herself to appreciate it. However, a Brian Rix farce was about to take place.

Hannah had to go in through the back of the hall with students sitting facing away from her and towards Joan at the front. There were three sets of doors to choose from and then thick curtains which came right across before you could get into the hall itself. Once through the sensibly chosen middle set of doors, Hannah then had to find the gap in the curtains. Unfortunately for her, the gaps didn't match the doors, and Hannah found herself in the dark, fumbling for an exit that she couldn't find.

Cut to Joan holding Year 10 in the palm of her hand with a 'rags to riches' story about someone who had nothing but who eventually achieved great things. However, her focus started to waver as she became aware of a strange, large, mobile bulge in the curtains at the back of the hall. The side-to-side movement was accompanied by twisting grey curtain material. The spectacle was reminiscent of some third-rate ghostly drama. Just as Joan's concentration was at breaking point and students' heads were starting to turn, a hand appeared in the gap between the curtains. Someone who, thirty minutes earlier, had been the epitome of fashion emerged into the hall totally dishevelled – her hair all over the place, her skirt twisted, and her lipstick smudged. She was just in time to catch the last few minutes.

Joan's assembly was rated 'Outstanding', and I'm sure it was. But we guessed that, in part, the result was mostly Hannah trying to avoid any discussion as to its content.

The school was also rated 'Outstanding'. The day we heard, I slept well, as, I'm sure, did all my colleagues.

SACKABLE OFFENCE?

It's eleven thirty-five a.m. Breaktime for students. And for staff. I'm sitting in my office, just about to head for the staffroom down the corridor. My second coffee of the day beckons. I get up as a rather flustered Jason Stobart knocks on the open door. He's a recently appointed physicist. He was a 'deer in the headlights' at the interview, including, poor man, managing to knock over a glass of water. He was lucky it was a field of one, and we had little choice.

He's quite small, with a jacket that's slightly too big.

'Sorry to disturb you, Headmaster...' He still struggles to call me by my first name. 'But can I have a word?'

'Please, Jason. It's Andrew. Anyway, what's the problem?'

'Sorry, yes. I've been on duty on the top floor and found three girls in the boys' toilets.'

'OK, Jason. So what did you do?'

'I wasn't really sure what to do. I think they're still there.'

'I doubt it, but we'd better go and see.'

I'm disappointed, but not totally surprised, that Jason hasn't taken the opportunity of handling this himself – but these toilets are far-flung and rarely used, and I'm grateful he's solved my recurring dilemma of not knowing which toilets are on which floor.

I set off as fast as dignity allows. (Someone, somewhere, once gave me an excellent piece of advice: 'As a head, never look as though you're in a hurry – even when you are. It conveys a sense of panic.')

We head towards the stairs, past the school office. Jason is in front of me but certainly not adhering to the maxim above. We're passing the second-floor landing and heading up the last two flights.

'OK, Jason. You can slow down. What were they doing?'

'Yes. Sorry, Headmaster.' I let that one go. Jason's no longer in a fit state for lessons on etiquette. 'Not really sure – just hanging about it seems.'

We reach the top floor and march down the empty corridor, past empty classrooms. A smell of disinfectant hits us as we near the entrance to the toilets.

There are no doors at these entrances, which makes supervision easier. There are a couple of girls hanging around – both looking rather sheepish. I recognise one of them – fourth year, I think – although, of course, I can't remember her name. The other, rather thin and pasty-faced, I don't recognise. They watch as we approach – seemingly unconcerned.

'What do you think you're doing here? You know you're supposed to be outside at break time.' And certainly nowhere near the boys' toilets, I'm thinking – but didn't say.

'What are your names?'

'Elena.'

'And you?'

'Marcia.' That's the one I recognised – although certainly not as a troublemaker.

'Who are you with?'

'Androulla,' Marcia replies.

'Where's Androulla?'

Marcia points to the end cubicle – the only one with the door closed.

'Right, both of you wait here with Mr Stobart.' Jason has been loitering behind me as all this is going on.

'You can both come and stand there.' Jason points to the wall next to the entrance. It's good to see a bit of assertiveness from him.

I move down the cubicles and stand outside the end door. What on earth is she doing in there? Drugs? I could feel myself getting angry.

'Androulla, open that door.' Stern and very clear – I hope.

No response.

'Androulla, OPEN THAT DOOR – NOW!'

I'm loud enough to hear an echo in the corridor. Again no response.

'Androulla. NOW!'

I'm on the point of exploding when I hear the lock click and the door swings open – to reveal Androulla – on the toilet – skirt and knickers down.

I look away. I think we're both equally lost for words. 'Androulla, what are you doing here? Hurry up and get out.'

Androulla is on the short side. She looks startled, and her face has turned bright red. I back away as she exits the cubicle, grabbing her blazer off the back of the door and trying to straighten her skirt at the same time. She drops her blazer.

'Right! Pick that up and come with me.'

I walk out of the toilet area with Androulla trailing behind me. I'm preparing to embark on a massive interrogation. As I reach the entrance, Jason steps forward. He seems unable to make eye contact.

'Headmaster. It seems I got this wrong.' Lengthy pause. Jason, not knowing where to look.

'These *are* the girls' toilets. As you can see, there are no urinals.'

I turned to look, and where urinals would have been in the boys', there were only basins and mirrors. I suddenly feel rather sick. I should have noticed when I went in.

I sense Androulla standing behind me. She comes out and joins Marcia and Elena. There are now the five of us standing in the corridor, with me facing the girls, and Jason, who steps to one side.

'Girls, you know you shouldn't have been here at the break.' I'm getting a feeble defence in first, but given the situation I'm now in, I realise that what they should or shouldn't be doing is no longer relevant.

'However, I can only apologise. We got this wrong. And Androulla – a particular apology to you. This shouldn't have happened.'

Pause. None of the girls say anything, although I wouldn't have been surprised if nervous giggles hadn't broken out, which would have been difficult to react to. 'Quit while the going's good.' However, the going isn't good. It's awful.

'You can go back downstairs now.'

And the three of them go down the corridor.

We're still standing by the entrance to the toilets. I turn to Jason, who has started to mumble an apology.

'Jason. Stop. We both got this wrong, and I certainly should have known. The good news is that we now know which toilets are which. Let's hope there's no bad news.'

'What do you mean?' Jason asked.

'Well, if I were their parents, particularly Androulla's, hearing this story, I wouldn't be happy. Fingers crossed, she'll be too embarrassed to mention it.'

How word got out, I don't know, but over the next few days,

both Jason and myself had to endure some good-humoured 'toilet' ribbing (from staff, I hasten to add) which, of course, we both deserved. Who the girls told – parents or friends – I never found out as, from that quarter, there were no repercussions. Nevertheless I was on tenterhooks for some time – at the very least awaiting a whispered conversation accompanied by some giggles.

I say there were no repercussions. Not true. That image of Androulla sitting on the toilet with her skirt and knickers down has haunted me ever since.

SUICIDE NOTE

My first encounter with Ritalin (used to treat ADHD) was with Mark.

Mark is one of four students photographed entering the Barnet school on day one of its formal opening. The four of them in the picture, which featured prominently in the local press, are alongside various dignitaries. As they walk up the steps towards the glass entrance doors, they look smart, eager, and ready to do themselves and the school justice.

In the picture, Mark looks at least as impressive as the other three. Unfortunately, this was only one half of a decidedly split personality. It took us longer than it should have to diagnose his behaviour as something other than sheer naughtiness. However, naughty he most decidedly was. A one-boy lesson-wrecker. Up and down. In and out.

No pen? Take someone else's.

No homework? 'Course I haven't done it. Didn't understand it.'

Textbooks and papers find their way to the floor.

'Pick it up, please, Mark.'

'Fuck off.'

'You're late, Mark.'

'So?'

To another student: 'Who are you looking at? Fuck off.'

The pattern of response was for the teacher to call for a senior member of staff. As happened with Mr Bolt.

Gill – on call to deal with emergencies – has just appeared at Mr Bolt's classroom door, not knowing what she'd be encountering. He's another recent appointment but, unlike Jason, has a confident air. He teaches with his jacket always off. He's smiley, empathetic, and funny. The kids respond to him.

'I'm afraid you need to remove Mark.' He knows that asking for him to be removed from a lesson is a regular request from many of the staff. However, there is a tinge of sadness in his voice, feeling, as he does, that he hasn't been able to engage him in his lessons.

'Why? What have I done?' Mark's antennae are twitching.

Gill takes a deep breath, wondering if he will come quietly or not. Will he come with me or won't he? Does she have another card to play with?

'Come on, Mark. You can work outside Mr Macalpine's office.'

There is a pause. Mark surveys the scene. Most students keep their heads down – not wishing to provoke a confrontation.

'Better than working with this lot of tossers.' He moves towards the door. Phew!

My office is just across the landing and down a corridor towards the staffroom. There's always a desk and chair parked outside for the school's Marks and Marias.

'Right, Mark. Just sit there, and we'll sort you out some work.' Gill then knocks on my door and enters, looking sheepish. 'Sorry to trouble you, Andrew. I've got Mark here again.' She explains what's just happened.

'Can you have a word with him while I go and get something for him to do?'

140

I've had regular dealings with Mark, and his appearance isn't a surprise.

We both go outside, where Mark is now slumped forward on the desk – head on his arms.

'Hello, Mark. I'm sorry to see you here again. Have you had your medicine this morning?'

'I told you. I'm not taking it. You know it makes me feel funny.'

'I know that, Mark, but it just helps you stay out of trouble.' I can sympathise with his aversion to the personality-altering drug, but the alternative is that we end up excluding him for his disruptive behaviour.

'I don't care. I'm not taking it.'

'Alright. I'll need to talk to your mum.'

'You can talk to her. It won't make any difference.'

Mark has got to the point where he just puts his foot down, although it's actually quite hard to hear him, slumped as he is. We've been down the same road many times.

Meanwhile, Gill brings some work back from the classroom and places it on the edge of the desk.

'He needs to finish page seventy-three and start reading the next chapter.'

'Did you hear that, Mark? Did you hear what Miss Wait said?'

'Not doing it.'

I return to my office to phone Mark's mum. There's no answer, so I leave a message for her to call me back. I leave Mark to stew while I get on with some work.

Some thirty minutes later, I decide to check on him. His exercise and textbook are there but no Mark. I wonder if perhaps he's gone to the toilet, although he would have asked first. His empty seat makes me feel uneasy. It's then that I notice a scrappy piece of paper on the edge of the desk. In Mark's scrawly handwriting, it reads:

I'm suddenly hit by a sick feeling in my stomach. Knowing Mark as I do, thirty minutes was probably too long to go without checking him. I head to the staffroom, where three or four teachers are sitting around. 'Has anyone seen Mark Carlton? He was sitting outside my office.'

'No, sorry.' Everyone shakes their heads.

'He's disappeared. If you see him, please let me know.'

Feeling sick has now been replaced by hot and cold sweats as I hurry back to his class. The students stare passively as I have a whispered conversation with Mr Bolt.

'No, sorry,' Mr Bolt says. 'Not seen him since you took him out.'

I dart from the school office to the receptionist – who then phones the school keeper. No one's seen Mark.

Back in my office, I phone the police. I also try his mum again, but there's still no reply.

'Has he done this before?' The desk sergeant is checking me out.

'No, never, although he's certainly unstable – and today seemed particularly depressed.'

'Are you sure he's not on the premises?'

'Absolutely. No one's seen him since he was put outside my office.'

'Can you just repeat what's on that piece of paper?'

'*You'll find me by the railway.*'

'And you think this is a possible suicide note?' By now, the desk sergeant is starting to sound less sceptical.

'He's capable of anything. He veers between extreme depression and hyperactivity. And he hasn't taken his medicine this morning.'

'What medicine is that?'

'Ritalin. It helps with his behaviour.'

Despite the reasonable questions, my anxiety – not to say impatience – is growing. All I want is for someone to get down to the railway tracks ASAP.

As if reading my thoughts, the next question moves us forward. 'So, the train line. Where would that be?'

I quickly consult the wall map in my office. Mark lives over by Ballards Lane – close to the Northern Line at West Finchley. I feed this back.

'Alright, we'll see if we can get a helicopter up to look for him.' The desk sergeant has suddenly come alive, moving from scepticism to serious action.

'How long will that take?'

'Should be more or less immediate.'

I sit stewing for another few minutes and then try Mark's mum again. A voice I recognise only too well answers.

'I've been trying to get hold of you. Do you know where Mark is?'

'Why, yes. He's in his room. Is there a problem?' I'm torn between relief and frustration.

'Well, yes, there is. Let me phone you back in a minute.'

My hand grips the receiver just a little more tightly. Valuable police resources have been wasted – and I need to let them know what has happened. The same desk sergeant is on duty and, again, to my relief, is remarkably understanding, although he can't see what a boy like Mark is doing still on roll at any school.

I get back to Mark's mother, who stammers out profuse apologies with a promise to talk through the incident with Mark at the same time as pursuing his ADHD issues with his local clinic.

As for me, while the suicide threat was the only one I ever received, there *was* an actual suicide while I was head in Hornchurch. It occurred during the six-week summer holidays and was a fifteen-year-old girl. Although her attendance had been sporadic, and many staff didn't know her at all, the news, when it came through, was shattering enough and, of course, terrible for her parents.

As to threats like Mark's, I realised that even if you don't believe they'll come to anything, you certainly have to take them seriously.

TEN

OTHER TALES AND REFLECTIONS

FIRE SAFETY

There is no doubt that school fires – whether accidental or arson – are serious issues.

As with all managers, heads have to have risk assessment policies and take into account:

What are the potential dangers?

Who, if anyone, would be affected?

How could they be protected?

What would that protection cost?

Could the money be better spent elsewhere?

Opportunity costs come into the picture. For example, sprinklers in all classrooms. Ideal, of course, but would the benefits justify the cost? What else might you do with that amount of money?

JOBSWORTHS

This tale is from my time in Peckham and involves my mentor, Trevor (referred to above).

A bright sunny summer's day, and I was chatting with Doreen in the school office. Devon, our assistant caretaker, slightly out of breath, appeared at the door.

'There's a fire officer who arrived in the downstairs hall. Seems concerned about the stock cupboards.'

Doreen thumbed through her diary. 'News to me. Nothing in here.'

'That's what they do now,' Devon said. 'Arrive unannounced. Catch you on the hop.'

Devon, although new, was learning fast.

'Not sure who to ask,' Doreen said. 'The head's in a meeting with the senior staff.'

Without really thinking, I dived in. 'I'll go. Those are the English department stockrooms. If necessary, I'll get Tom involved.' Tom was the head of the department, and I was his deputy.

'If you're sure?'

'Don't worry, Doreen. If I need help, I'll come back up.' I made my way down to the ground floor.

It didn't take an Einstein to spot the fire officer. Serious black uniform, booted, badged, helmeted and clipboarded. All slightly undermined by his fresh face. How quickly you get to the point in life where everyone looks so young! He was standing in the middle of our large ground-floor hall with its shiny parquet floor. Another tick for Devon. There was still a faint whiff of polish.

He turned as he heard me approach. Despite his youthful appearance, the officer had a convincingly stern look. His lips were pursed, and his brow furrowed.

'Are you the head?'

That question was probably the high point in my career up until then. 'I'm afraid all the senior staff are in a meeting. If you can tell me what the issue is?'

'I'll need to see the head, but I can tell you now. It's that store room,' he said – pointing to the middle of three similar ones, all on the same side of the hall. 'It's blocking a fire exit.'

For some reason, the hall had, within the space of thirty metres, three fire exits. One at each end and one in the middle. These had long been seen as excessive; thus, the middle one had become an English stockroom with shelves of books built around the exit door. An exit door which, unfortunately, still had 'Fire Exit' in bold red letters clearly visible on it. Two escape routes from the hall in the event of a fire had been deemed sufficient. In terms of risk assessment, no one had identified any risk as a result of the loss of the third exit.

The officer waited for a reply. He tapped his booted foot.

'If you give me a minute, I'll fetch our head of English. I'm sure he can help. He's just in that classroom there.'

I pointed to the room at the end of the hall where I knew Tom would be. Pupils were all in lessons, and he was always sorting, preparing, and marking whenever he had a spare moment. The door was ajar, and I went in. Tom looked up from his desk piled high with books. He smiled in that warm way he had – but he was not to be trifled with and could spot a jobsworth at a hundred metres.

'Hi, Andrew.'

'Tom, have you got a minute? There's a fire officer complaining about that little stockroom in the hall.'

Tom got up. 'Bloody fire officers. Haven't they got any fires to attend to?'

We left the classroom, and I introduced Tom to the fire officer, who repeated his demand.

'That store room will have to go. It's blocking a fire exit.'

Tom indicated the two uncluttered doors. He was clearly up for the encounter.

'Are you telling me that if there was a fire here (now standing in the middle of the hall opposite the store room), a child wouldn't be able to get out via either of the other fire doors?'

'I don't care how many you've got. That door is an officially designated fire exit and must be kept clear at all times.'

'I'm not here to argue. My job is to ensure that all fire exits throughout the building are kept free.' Our man had transmorphed into Jeremy Taylor's stereotype. His face reddened, and he seemed unbudging. Had Tom met his match?

'Alright. So what do you want us to do?' Was Tom climbing down?

'I want that store room removed and clear access provided to the fire door.'

Tom sighed. 'You realise that's a big job. We have no spare storage space. How long have we got?' Tom winked at me.

'I'll be back in a month. I haven't got time to see the rest of the school now, but you can tell your head I'll be sending him a copy of my report.' With that, he departed – through one of the *uncluttered* fire doors.

When he had gone, and not totally reassured by the wink, I asked, 'Tom, where's all that stuff going to go?'

'Go, lad? It's not going anywhere. We carry on as normal. He won't be back. And if he is, we'll put in a formal complaint to the fire service.'

Of course, Tom was right. Our man had ticked his box – and never returned.

It was an important lesson to me (a lesson I like to think I was temperamentally inclined towards) that *you* have to decide what's right for your circumstances – sod any consequences from bureaucrats.

MAD SAFETY OFFICER

Some years later, by which time I was in my first headship, Jim, the caretaker, and I were standing in the school office just before ten in the morning. Period 2 had just started, and it was quiet apart from the tap tap of Sarah's typewriter. We were awaiting a visit from the borough's 'Safety Officer.' Budget cuts having bundled staff together in new roles, with many experts laid off, our man was not necessarily an expert in the field – as we were to find out. It was my job to take him around the building so that he could check all was in order, and, as was customary, we also included the caretaker, Jim, on our tour. Jim, by now rather grizzled and fairly overweight, had been around forever. Despite a tendency to tetchiness, especially where 'kids' were concerned, he was my right arm as regards the site, and I had great respect for his knowledge and judgement.

I asked Ruth, our PA, if she knew who was coming.

'No idea, I'm afraid, Andrew. They just said, safety officer.'

'If it's Mr Tucker, he's been here before. He's slightly crazy.'

Jim's assessment was interrupted by the appearance of a visitor.

He arrived on the dot at ten o'clock as arranged. He was probably in his fifties, wore a suit and tie, and with his gelled-down hair, could have been mistaken for a company executive. No doubt the impression he wished to create. The clipboard under his arm was just part of the uniform.

Ruth introduced us. 'I think you're the safety officer, but we don't have a name.'

'It's Tucker.' Definitely no first name. He turned to me. 'And you are?'

'This is the head, Mr Macalpine.' Ruth was keeping it formal. 'And this is our caretaker, Jim Maitland. I believe you've met.'

'Yes, we've met many times.' Jim piped up. Just managing, I didn't doubt, to stop himself from adding, 'And you're a nutter, Mr Tucker.'

Mr Tucker took no notice of Jim.

'Right! Let's not waste any time. We should probably start with your electrics. Can you show me where the meters are?'

I turned to Jim. 'Aren't they under the stairs, Jim?' I asked innocently. Of course, I was now dissembling on two fronts. Jim, to the best of my knowledge, had never seen me crouching my way into the meter cupboard. Mr Tucker certainly hadn't. And neither of them knew about the fuses.

We moved into the hall.

'Yes, just behind you, Mr Tucker.' Jim pointed to the small cupboard door behind us.

At this point, it crossed my mind that if this safety inspection had taken place late afternoon, just before an open evening, Mr Tucker would have found two fuses missing. A slight chill went down my spine.

Mr Tucker reappeared. 'All seems in order there. Shall we carry on?'

We continued around the school, working our way through laboratories, kitchens, boiler rooms, and storage areas.

'What about fire drills? When did you last have one? Can I see the log?' Mr Tucker, as I'm sure he remembered, had caught us out on this one before. Thankfully, Jim had primed me, and like the rabbit out of the proverbial hat, I produced it. Mr Tucker wasn't the only one with a clipboard.

We stopped while Mr Tucker, ignoring us, pored over the entries for a couple of minutes. We knew it wasn't so much an eye for detail – more an attempt to find fault. I had a sense that he was conflicted. On the one hand, he could take credit for a clean bill of health. On the other, I could see fault-finding as central to his role.

'That's fine. Shall we continue?'

His chance came as we worked our way around the back of the school where, over the years, various bits had been added. We walked into an empty classroom which had a definite Portakabin feel about it – and a musty smell. Various holes in the plasterboard walls – no doubt bored students finding alternative uses for pens. A strip light that didn't work. Chairs and tables higgledy-piggledy. Paper on the floor. I knew the room hadn't been used for months.

'We don't really have much use for this room,' I commented lamely.

Mr Tucker appeared to ignore all this. His focus was on the

door at the back of the classroom with its single crash bar and a big green sign saying 'FIRE EXIT'. He put his clipboard down on a dusty table and gave the crash bar a sharp push. No movement.

He turned to us. 'Why is this fire door nailed up?' Although the question was gently put, I sensed Mr Tucker felt he'd found a chink in our armour.

'Because there's a six-foot drop on the other side?' Jim tried, unsuccessfully, to keep the sarcasm out of his voice.

Mr Tucker ignored this. At last, he was on to something. 'That's a fire door. It has to be kept clear, you have to be able to use it, and it should be tested every six months.' He fixed me with an unwavering stare. 'It needs to be put back into use immediately. Jim, you can sort this out while Mr Macalpine and I continue our tour. We'll be back in ten minutes.'

The two of us traipsed back along one of the school's long corridors. We came across an empty technology room. I stood back while Mr Tucker inspected plugs and equipment.

'Yes, that's all OK.'

We wound our way back to the Portakabin.

He stopped just before we went in. 'You realise this will have to be reported? It's completely unacceptable.'

We went in to see Jim standing by the fire door. Claw hammer in hand and a pile of nails on the table in front of him.

Mr Tucker walked over to the door and pushed the crash bar. Much to our horror, he started to topple forward towards the asphalt path six feet below. He just caught the door frame in time. He swung himself back, white-faced and breathing heavily.

'You see what we mean?' Jim was not going to back down.

Mr Tucker had managed to pull himself together. 'Not my problem. I shall be back in six months to re-inspect. Shall we move on?'

Jim and I exchanged glances and shrugged shoulders.

There was little else left to see, and we made our way down the corridor leading back to the entrance. Halfway down, Mr

Tucker stopped by a section of what looked like plastic pipe running down the wall and then disappearing.

'That electrical conduit needs to be boxed in immediately. I'll give you until tomorrow afternoon; otherwise, this corridor will be shut off.' He was off again – and in his element.

Was that a muffled snort that came from Jim? We moved on. 'I'll make sure it's been seen to'

Back at the front entrance, he handed us a copy of his summary report. Then it was a perfunctory 'Thank you' and 'Goodbye'.

Once he was safely out of the way, I turned to Jim. 'What was all that about?'

He took me back to the threatened corridor and stopped where the pipe went to the wall. Taking a screwdriver from his pocket, he started to prise it away. I watched in horror, expecting any moment to see Jim thrown back as a thousand volts sent him flying. Soon he was able to grab the pipe with both hands and pull it away from the wall.

'Nothing to worry about, Mr Macalpine. It's an old *gas* pipe – nothing to do with electrics. When Mr Tucker returns, we can tell him we've chased the whole thing into the wall. He'll like that.'

For the first time in my headship, I relished the thought of a safety officer following up on a visit.

BIG BOOTS

Barnet and my second headship. I should have had issues around jobsworths under control by this time but... The first part of the tale concerns Heather – one of my deputies and one of my original appointments. She was in her late thirties and, from the off, had shown herself to be bright, resourceful – and unflappable. This episode was to test that last quality to the full.

The first part of what happened is her account:

It was the end of school. Most staff and nearly all students had gone home. Suddenly the fire alarm went off. I rushed upstairs to look at the screen telling me the location – a technology workshop. As quickly as I could, I made my way down the main stairs and along the corridor, which ran the length of the school until I reached the workshops at the far end, all the while deafened by the screeching alarm reverberating down the low-ceilinged corridor. Jemma, deputy head of technology and a recent appointment, with dark straggly hair and still aproned, was standing near the open door on the left. The other was shut, and I could see there was no one there.

'Hi, Jemma. The fire alarm showed a fire in the workshop. Seems like you've sorted it.' I could see no signs of any damage, although there was a smell of burning. By this time, the alarm had stopped screeching. Jemma, looking slightly alarmed herself, started to explain.

'Yes – it was a spark from the grinder which just caught that pile of paper in the corner.' I could see the charred remains Jemma was referring to. Just a wisp of smoke rising up.

'Well, well done on sorting it. Seems like you took prompt action.' I was about to go back to my office, but Jemma obviously had something to add.

'I'm afraid I called 999.'

'You called 999?' I couldn't believe what I was hearing. From previous experience, I sensed what was about to happen. There'd be the sound of sirens getting louder and louder. Abruptly stopping and being followed by the tramp of booted feet up to the main office.

Sure enough, that was exactly what did happen.

As the siren stopped, I said to Jemma, 'They'll be going up to the main office, and I'd better get up there to greet them. I'm afraid you'll need to stay here. They'll definitely be wanting to see the source.'

'I'm so sorry, Heather.' Jemma looked crestfallen.

'Don't worry. We'll sort it.' I wasn't at all confident about that score, but I wanted to provide Jemma with a bit of reassurance.

I hurried back up the nearby stairs and got back to the main office just as two large uniformed men reached the top of the main staircase – our unfit and rather sweaty caretaker, Geoff, trying to keep up. They were both carrying large black helmets.

'Where's the fire then?' The taller of the two – dark-haired, moustachioed, well-built, and slightly red-faced.

'Not really a fire. Just some stuff in a bin.' I was trying to downplay it as much as I could.

'Well, whoever it was thought it was bad enough to phone 999. So we need to have a look. Please direct us.' The fireman was looking around, getting ready to march.

'Right, I'll take you down.' Geoff was still standing there, having got his breath back.

'Will you be needing me, Heather?'

'No, that's fine, Geoff. I'll see you later. I'll take… Sorry, I didn't catch your names.'

'I'm Inspector Bolt, and this is Station Officer McReady.' I felt he was getting impatient.

'Shall we go?'

Taking the lead, I took the two officers down the stairs and along the dimly lit and rather ghostly corridor, given that it was beyond the end of school and there were no students around.

Jemma was clearing up one of the workbenches and looked up as they entered.

I introduced her to the two men.

They both started looking around the workshop. The inspector came to the pile of charred paper.

'I assume this was it?' he said.

Jemma started to stammer out an explanation.

'Young lady.' I bristled at what I took to be his male

chauvinism. 'You did *exactly* the right thing. If you've any doubts, you should always call us.'

To my shame, visions of bored, card-playing, pornography-watching firemen popped into my head. I was about to pay a heavy price for such blasphemous thoughts.

'Right, we'll need to assess your safety arrangements while we're here. You can come with us if you want.'

'No – that's fine. You get on with it. The head's not here and won't be back today.' I started towards my office opposite the top of the main staircase.

'By the way, my name's Heather Stanforth.'

Neither officer seemed particularly interested in who I was and marched off down the corridor – boots clomping. I went back to my preparations for the governors' meeting that evening, having no desire to spend more time than necessary with my visitors.

Some fifty minutes later, there was a knock on my office door.

'Come in.' I knew who it was. The same two firemen came in and stood in front of my desk.

'Do sit down, please.' I gestured to the chairs they were standing by.

'That's alright, thank you.' Stern-face, looking even sterner. 'We're going back to the station now to write our report, but we'll need to return later to interview you.'

'Why do you need to do that?' This wasn't what I'd expected, and I could feel my heart starting to beat just a little faster.

'It's better you see our report first.'

'I've got a governors' meeting at seven. I hope we're going to be finished before that.'

'This has to take precedence.' Officer McReady spoke for the first time. They both turned to go.

'Alright, I think you know the way out – just down those stairs.' I pointed to the main staircase.

I went back to my office, stewing over what the report might hold.

An hour and a half later and a loud knock on my door. This time it was the inspector by himself – helmet in one hand and an A4 plastic folder in the other. He came in and, without waiting for me to get up, thrust the folder across my desk.

'It'll probably help if you go straight to the summary at the back.'

I thumbed quickly through while he stood and watched. I reached the section entitled 'Findings and Recommendations'. At a glance, I could see the list – all in black except for one starkly contrasting in red.

'Corridor fire doors propped open in clear contravention of School Fire Safety Regulation 8.'

I knew how to answer that as it had been discussed quite recently.

'If we were to close those doors, we would have total chaos at the break, at lunchtime, and at changeovers. Students shoving each other out of the way, falling over each other, trapped behind the doors.'

'That's not our problem.' Where had I heard that before?! 'Those fire doors are crucial to the prevention of fire. How you deal with that is entirely up to you.' There was now a steely tone to his voice.

'As I've said, we have a governing body meeting tonight. I'll be seeing the head beforehand, and we can bring it up at the end of the meeting under AOB. We'll obviously have to find a way around it.' I thought this might be seen as a concession.

'There is no way around this and, as things stand, we will probably have to caution you.'

'Meaning?' Caution? What was he talking about? I started to feel a little sick.

'You're breaking the law.'

Inspector Bolt got up to leave. 'You'll hear from the station commander in the next few days. Meanwhile, you need to get the issue sorted. And don't worry. I can find my own way out.'

He left, closing the door behind him. I slumped down in my seat. I needed to get in touch with Andrew but couldn't see how to do that. The governing body meeting was due to start in twenty minutes. I just hoped that he would turn up early. He usually did. I'd just have time to put him in the picture. (This ended Heather's account.)

At this point, I return from my meeting and take over the story.

Almost as soon as I got back into my office, there was a knock on the door. It was Heather. She looked flushed, and unlike her usual considered self, her words poured out. She quickly put me in the picture.

'OK, Heather. We'll bring it up under AOB,' I said.

The meeting was mercifully short, helped by the absence of one of the more garrulous members of the governing body. I went around the table asking for items for AOB. There were none. I explained what Heather had told me. There were mutterings, and various governors piped up.

'I mentioned that before you were appointed, Andrew. I thought it'd been sorted.'

'This will not look good.'

'No, certainly won't.'

'*I've* mentioned it many times.'

'We cannot play around with student safety.'

Then, thank goodness, the vice chair, Vince, sitting next to me, piped up. Vince was a barrister – fiftyish, slight in stature, always smart, and deferred to by the rest of the governing body.

'Of course, we can't dispute the finding. However, a caution? Completely over the top. Heather, I'm sorry you've been put through this. Andrew, you should get on to your police liaison office right away.'

I nodded.

'If you give me the number, *I'll* call him. What's his name? Arjan something?' Vince, as usual, was quick off the mark.

'Yes. Arjan Ladd. Thank you so much. That'd be great,' I replied.

I had his number in my diary, scribbled it down, and passed it to Vince. Meanwhile, Bessie, on the governing body since time immemorial, ever the pessimist and always ready to pour cold water on most positive suggestions, pointed out, 'You know cautions are usually accompanied by a criminal record.'

I bristled at this but stopped myself from confronting her. I caught Heather's eye and her startled look.

By this time, Vince had disappeared to make the call. He returned a few minutes later. 'I spoke to Arjan. He was horrified. He'll contact the station commander.'

'Many thanks, Vince. That's really helpful.' I felt my shoulders drop and my breathing become easier. That was the end of the meeting, and there was the usual chitchat as the room gradually emptied. Vince was the last to go.

'I'll let you know, Vince. I really appreciate your help.'

Two days later, I got a call from Arjan. I went straight to Heather's office.

'Arjan got back to me. They won't proceed with the caution, but they're giving us 48 hours to install electronic door closers, which are activated in the event of a fire. I'm sure we can manage that.'

That was another set of shoulders dropped, and the colour returned to Heather's cheeks. At the time, it felt like we were dealing with another jobsworth, but we had to concede that, potentially, safety issues were involved. In actual fact, the electronic door closers were never needed, but it was good to know they were there.

Architecture

I learnt an early lesson as head with staff wanting to personalise their space, be it offices or classrooms.

'Yes – fine, go ahead.' I felt they were showing their commitment, and I wanted to be supportive.

However, the next thing they're gone, and you're faced with introducing a successor to a pink office or a yellow classroom with dragons on the ceiling. Thus 'Any colour as long as it's magnolia' crept into my vocabulary.

When I started teaching, corridor walls, if they had anything on them at all, tended to be plastered with posters – often dog-eared and dated. By the time I left, thanks to a deputy with a keen eye for standards of presentation, it was students' work, and woe betide the teacher concerned if it wasn't triple mounted.

Important as walls were – and are – they pale into insignificance against the overall design of the school – its architecture.

The only pre-1900 school buildings still standing, are prestigious public schools and university colleges (e.g., Eton and Balliol). However, in 1870, William Forster was successful in getting a law passed which made it mandatory for all children in Britain aged between five and ten to attend school. 'Board schools' came into being and thus was initiated a massive building programme. In London alone, some four hundred schools were built over a thirty-year period. The Victorians were energetic and far-sighted.

Sir Arthur Conan Doyle's 1893 short story 'The Adventure of the Naval Treaty' contains the following exchange:

Holmes: 'Look at those big, isolated clumps of building rising up above the slates, like brick islands in a lead-coloured sea.'

Watson: 'The board-schools.'

Holmes: 'Lighthouses, my boy! Beacons of the future! Capsules with hundreds of bright little seeds in each, out of which will spring the wise, better England of the future.'

An inspiring description. Many of the schools Holmes was describing are still in existence – as schools. This is thanks to a number of factors – their solid construction, imaginative ways teachers have found to adapt them and successful campaigns to preserve them. Others have been pulled down or turned into flats.

Typically they were, and are, red-bricked three-storey buildings with a large hall on each floor and, quite frequently, a capacious fourth floor often turned into office space and store rooms. As head of English, I inherited one such fourth-floor store room – full of dusty, unread, and irrelevant sets of books that would have had no meaning for the Peckham children we were teaching. It was cathartic to position huge waste bins under the stockroom window and watch all that fiction flying down.

Classrooms round the halls were usually built with high ceilings and high windows – originally designed to stop children being distracted by the outside world.

The Somers Town school's main building was established as a board school in the 1870s. The addition – a forbidding two-storey concrete structure – opened in 1961.

For over a hundred years after Forster, there was no similar large-scale school-building programme. Different styles came and went, but no far-sighted successor appeared.

As recently as 2003, a preservation campaign was initiated by an eleven-year-old schoolgirl – Susannah Page. She wrote a letter to her head teacher requesting that her Victorian school be saved from demolition.

'It is a good strong building and will probably last longer than the new one. It is useful to learn about the Victorians; children like the building, and it seems it is only being knocked down to make a car park and part of the playground.'

Her campaign sparked an eighteen-month battle as parents, teachers, and others fought over whether the building was or was not, in the words of the county council, 'an educational nightmare'. The campaign failed, and the increasing use of technology called into question the value of the traditional classroom. At the same time, Labour's 'Building Schools for the Future' programme was being launched. The fact that it gained such momentum over a hundred years after the introduction of the board schools is largely down to a lack of comparable far-sightedness on the part of politicians in the intervening years.

Elain Harwood, in her excellent *England's Schools – History, Architecture, and Adaptation*, talks of the years from 1914 to 1940 as a 'missed opportunity.'

There was a short burst in the 1930s, characterised by a profusion of styles and including many open-air schools. The idea being that exposure to fresh air and sunlight would help combat the rise in tuberculosis. They must have been challenging to run – especially in the depths of winter!

The inter-war years also saw a number of 'neo-Georgian' schools similar to the Hornchurch one I inherited. Their solid, robust construction has meant that many, like Forster's schools, are still in existence.

Moving to the post-war period, the robustness of the Somers Town 'new building' was frequently not matched elsewhere. Sadly its aesthetics were. The New Zealand architect Paul King was asked in an online forum why the buildings from the 1960s and 1970s were so ugly. His answer was as follows:

'Because developers and building owners quickly noticed the money-saving opportunities available when 'cheap' is sold as 'modern' leaving architects with reduced budgets, and, in most cases, few attractive alternatives that would meet the client's cost brief.'

Evidence of this can still be seen up and down the country. Post-headship, I had a spell as chair of governors at a secondary school in north London. Its hotchpotch of styles, starting with the original construction in 1914 with various bits and pieces added on over the following fifty years or so, make it a nightmare to run. In the main building corridors, corners and unsupervised areas abound, putting a huge strain on staff – particularly those on duty. The final addition was opened in 1961 and perfectly demonstrates Paul King's analysis. Its prefabricated look is matched only by its leaking roofs and rotting window frames. It still stands to this day. Such schools frequently turn heads into site managers.

In my quest for a headship, I was shortlisted for Pimlico School. It was opened in 1970 and is seen as a noted example of brutalist architecture – a concrete and glass construction. A contemporary critic likened it to a battleship, describing it as a '100-odd metre long, turreted, metallic grey thing lying in its own sunken rectangle.' ('Architect's Journal 1970')

There were complaints that it was too hot in summer and too cold in winter. It had seventeen exits and entrances – impossible to secure. Like the critic above, I was also struck by the endlessly long, dark corridor with almost windowless doors, making it hard for anyone to see in, whether checking on behaviour or looking for someone. I withdrew my application before the final interview, realising as I did that dealing with the building's deficiencies would take priority over learning and teaching. As if to bear out my concerns, the school was subsequently in special measures for a number of years before being demolished in 2010. As with the Isle of Dogs school, it was given an architect's award – but certainly not an educationalist's one.

This whistle-stop tour started with William Forster and it ends with Tony Blair. In 2004, Building Schools for the Future (BSF) was announced with a planned spend of £8.2 billion by 2011. The intention was to build or refurbish two hundred schools each year – and eventually every secondary school in England. It was dubbed – with much justification – as the 'biggest school building programme since Victorian times'.

It was not just about replacing leaking roofs and crumbling brickwork. It was about initiating a 'step-change' in education – inspirational buildings that would make those who worked in them feel valued and up-to-date.

Such an ambitious programme needed huge funding, and the government thought they had got round this via what is known as the 'Private Finance Initiative' (PFI) – a way of creating 'public-private partnerships' (PPPs) where private firms are contracted to complete and manage public projects. It was, and is, highly controversial, with critics arguing that it was used simply to place a great amount of 'debt off-balance-sheet' (Commons Treasury Select Committee 2012).

A major issue for headteachers was that, while educational provision remained under their control, facilities management didn't. In practice, it meant that at four p.m., schools were handed over to private companies. A process designed to create tensions. That was 'on the ground', as it were. At government and local authority level, debt was created, which is still ongoing – in some cases for decades – even where the schools no longer exist!

Despite the above, many magnificent schools were built, which fulfilled Blair's original aim of giving teachers an exciting and up-to-date environment within which to work.

However, in 2010, following the global financial crash of 2008, the then-Conservative government embarked on 'austerity'.

For Blair's new school-building programme, the results were disastrous. It was Michael Gove, then Education Secretary, who axed the programme – leaving 715 school refurbishments being ditched and 123 academy schemes to be reviewed on a case-by-case basis.

Subsequently, in 2016, Michael Gove, when asked what mistakes he had made during his time, pointed to the cancelling of BSF.

Forster and Blair were both visionaries. Forster got there. Blair got halfway. Still leaving so many of our schools unfit for the twenty-first century and, going back to headship, so hard to run and work in.

BROKEN ARM AND HYPOCRISY

I missed National Service by one year. Nevertheless, my public school wanted to make men out of us boys, and so I found myself a reluctant attendee at the annual Army Cadet camp. There was an alternative – Scouting – but somehow Scouting had acquired a reputation for being for 'girls'. The late fifties were still the Dark Ages as far as sexual equality was concerned.

In 1958 – the year in question – the camp included an assault course with, halfway through, a scrambling net draped over the branch of an oak tree. The branch was about twenty feet up. The idea was that you climbed the net on one side, straddled the top, and climbed down the other side. Reading this description in an Army manual, I might just have thought, 'No problem there,' and moved on to the next exercise. However, the reality proved very different, and I was about to experience a life-changing moment.

The tough, no-nonsense army instructor demonstrated an alternative to the straddle whereby, once you'd reached the top, you leaned over and grabbed the net on the other side. You then flipped yourself over so that you were hanging facing outwards. You turned yourself round and climbed down.

At the time, I had a very athletic Indian friend, Krishna Devi. He was small, wiry, and a fearless scrum half for the school's first team. 'OK, Krishna – we'll have a bet. If you do it, I will.' To this day, I have no idea why I got in first with the challenge. I was certainly not fearless, and the challenge would have been far more credible coming from him.

Krishna was quick to agree and, in no time, had shinned up the net, flipped over at the top, and climbed down the other side.

There was no escape for me!

I went up fine, got to the top, reached over to grab the netting on the other side, and flipped myself over. Disaster was about to strike! I lost my grip as I flipped and plunged twenty feet to the ground – landing on my left arm. The pain was excruciating and only when the ambulance arrived and I got a shot of morphine did it subside. The drive to the hospital, with sirens blaring, seemed to take forever. Once there, breaks to both my radius and ulna were diagnosed. I suppose it could have been my neck. The arm was set, put in plaster, and my parents arrived to take me home.

That was August. The arm remained in plaster for just over three months. When I went back to the hospital in November, the surgeon put me in a sling, and I felt full recovery was in sight.

December arrived with snow and ice, and just before Christmas, I slipped on the paved area at the back of the school. I automatically put my left hand out to cushion the fall. As the hand hit the ground, I felt the bones slip apart – no physical pain, just mental anguish. I knew that, even after all that time, they hadn't knitted together properly.

Someone called an ambulance (again!) which, under the curious eyes of students and staff, manoeuvred its way round the quadrangle to where I was sitting just inside the entrance to one of the dormitory houses. Then it was back to Addenbrooke's Hospital and straight into the operating theatre. The surgeon, by coincidence, I'm sure, happened to be the very same who had allegedly set my arm in the summer and who'd then sanctioned the removal of the plaster in November. If I'd had the courage, I would have requested a substitute! Anyway, under the anaesthetic I went. When I came round, one of the nurses told me that she had never heard such ripe and robust language from an anaesthetised patient – most of it directed at the surgeon who had set my bones four months earlier in August.

Back in school, with my arm heavily plastered once more, there was an upside for me. I had never liked uniform, and as I was unable to get into my school blazer, I had to continue with my dad's sports jacket, which was comically oversized for my puny frame. That was a small price to pay for being able to jettison the blazer.

There was the added bonus that I couldn't tie my tie either – so I didn't wear one. Courtesy of the incompetence of my orthopaedic surgeon, who had failed to ensure the bones would knit properly, the powers that be had to accept what might otherwise have been seen as a serious flouting of school rules, and I was spared the school's punishment line (one that I was very familiar with!).

'Few things are more distressing to a well-regulated mind than to see a boy who ought to know better disporting himself at improper moments.'

Without wishing to sound overdramatic, the experience had a lasting effect. My left arm never recovered fully, having spent so long in plaster and being non-playing captain of the school's hockey team brought with it the realisation that there was more to life than sport. Not a lot more, obviously! However, I started to put extra effort into my A levels, to think about a possible gap year and then what I might read at university.

Hypocrisy set in about twenty-five years later when I took up my first headship. I set myself up as the Uniform Tsar (see 'Hornchurch' – 'Getting Going') and introduced a smart new uniform for Years 7 to 11.

I never owned up to the pleasure I felt at ditching my blazer and tie and wearing my dad's oversize jacket. I know that many of the students I taught, and was responsible for as head, would have felt equally delighted if they had been able to throw off their uniforms and replace them with clothes of their own choosing. And, if they ever caught wind of my past, they would have posed some tough questions, e.g., 'How come you force us into school uniform when you hated it so much?' I would have struggled with that one.

CARETAKERS AND CARETAKING

It was only when I became head that I established a close relationship with my caretaking staff. In both schools, they were loyal and hard-working. I was totally dependent on them. Many heads and senior staff in schools would echo that. They not only spot issues like broken doors and windows, holes in fences and graffiti but they also deal with them. Most of the caretakers I've known have DIY skills they're happy to use. They accost intruders. They'll even engage with students!

There are others who wouldn't, or couldn't, do any of the above. Heads find themselves bound up in red tape, thwarted by rules designed to protect employees, and unable even to get a light bulb changed. The bulb is too high up (risk of falling off the ladder), and it's broken (risk being cut or getting an electric shock). So you either do it yourself or pay an electrician.

The Institution of Engineering and Technology gave the following advice in 'Setting Standards for Electrical Installation' (May 2005):

Question: *Can a caretaker (non-technical person) replace fluorescent tubes and unscrew light fittings in a public area?*

Answer: *Yes, but… only if he or she is competent to do so and… if the person has been given information, instruction, training, and supervision as is necessary to ensure, so far as it is reasonably practical, the health and safety at work of his employees.*

An inspector would expect to see 1. A risk assessment. 2. Training records. 3. Instructions in respect of the use of access equipment and the changing of the lamps. 4. Records of an assessment of the person to do the job.

No wonder heads, or other senior staff, sigh and say: 'Alright, I'll do it myself.'

However… think, for a moment, about what caretakers have to do:

- Carry out basic repairs and set priorities for maintenance
- Manage access to the premises and maintain security
- Clean – and supervise the cleaning
- Help and plan site use
- Encourage health and safety around the school
- Supervise external contractors
- Manage site staff

And the skills they need:
- To be able to work flexibly
- To carry out basic DIY
- To be reasonably fit to cope with the lifting and carrying

And how demanding and frustrating it can be:
The journalist, Ian Wylie, wrote an article for the Guardian:

'They're the *men you love to hate, but most schools couldn't run without the janitor' (26 August 2006) and referred to:
- 'Those beautifully buffed up floors at the beginning of a new school year ruined with hundreds of teenage footmarks grinding in mud and dirt
- Inadequate staff supervision leading to damaged walls, graffitied brickwork, and chewing gum stuck anywhere and everywhere
- Corridors to be swept, toilets to be plunged
- Getting the blame when heating systems break down
- Frequently operating with little thanks from staff and little respect from students.'

*Still predominantly male even in 2023

There is no excuse, of course, for caretakers to turn to crime, as was the case in one of my schools. Large consignments come through the front door and disappear through the back – toilet paper, cleaning materials, soap, paint, light bulbs, and stationery. A lucrative black market. It was a large caretaking staff, and their rotas were so opaque that no one was ever caught. Although once we started asking questions, the thefts died down.

Given what gets dumped on their doorstep, it's no wonder that many caretakers get described as 'grumpy'. They usually bottle up their more extreme frustration – unlike Assistant Caretaker Devon, who sent this message to his boss (Jim) during my second headship:

'To Jim 9.45 pm

I've just gone to lock the music block up once again and asked them to leave the room as they found it. This time they have taken the piss.

I've left it, every piece of furniture moved. I hope it doesn't cause you any shit! But if I am expected to move the entire classroom around at the last thing, as well as other shit, then I resign!

These people make me sick.! Who the fuck do they think they are? I've tried to ask them in a polite way, but they are fucking ignorant, zen, yoga, type muppets.

Perhaps when a teacher sees what happens, they might just sort these fuckers out.

Any way

Again I hope it doesn't cause you shit, but I really have had it with these people

Devon.'

However, Devon's frustrations were as nothing compared to those of a Birmingham primary school caretaker, Terence Batters, who, according to witnesses, was patrolling the school's playgrounds with a one-hundred-thousand-volt stun gun when the alarms went off. Mr Batters said he had the weapon because he 'felt vulnerable'. Following his sentence in Birmingham City's Crown Court, he was quoted as saying,

'I'm hoping to keep my job.' (Free Online Library – November 2004)

My favourite caretaker was the deputy we had in Hornchurch. He was loyal, hard-working, resourceful, and, however late it was, would carry on until whatever he was working on was finished. He once said: 'We'd do anything for you, Mr Macalpine.' It brought tears to my eyes. No wonder he was my favourite! Sadly, he died while I was still in post, but I like to think he felt as supported by me as I did by him.

CATNAPS

My parents taught me the benefits of napping, especially on holiday – hot summer days by the sea – and, following a good lunch, happily succumbing to early afternoon torpor. I've never lost the habit – even to the point of risking a 'gross misconduct' charge.

My post-prandial dips at work (usually following a sandwich rather than a 'good lunch') were very different. They were necessary for recharging my batteries, ready for the rest of the working day.

When I was first made a head, I inherited an office and (joy!) a tiny ensuite – toilet, basin, and nothing else. Most days, around three-ish (earlier or later depending on meetings, etc.), I would retreat to my 'pod', put the toilet seat down, and head forward, trying to grab a few refreshing minutes. I was never caught, although, to this day, I don't know if my senior colleagues believed I had bowel problems or had actually fallen asleep.

Those 'pod' naps were, I always liked to think, private. However, a number of my headteacher colleagues – many long-standing and near retirement – had no such scruples when it came to the monthly meetings with a director of education who commanded nil respect. Quite soon, their eyes would glaze over, and heavy breathing, punctuated by the occasional snort, would ensue. When they awoke, suitably refreshed, they took turns to give their 'boss' the roughest possible ride.

Between headships, during my time as local authority inspector, I was based in the borough's headquarters – a large building in the centre of Romford with its own gloomy car park. It was poorly lit, and my car proved a much more comfortable, and probably less risky (fumes notwithstanding), base for my efforts at recharging.

My second headship provided nowhere for me to recharge. I just had to try and avoid, not always successfully, of course, any serious or demanding meetings around two-thirty. When there was no way out, I employed a tactic learnt from a close friend. If I felt my eyelids drooping, I would pinch my leg as hard as I could bear. That usually worked.

In the UK, napping, even at the start of the twenty-first century, could still be classed as 'gross misconduct', i.e., sleeping on the job. Attitudes have changed, and now in the 2020s, a number of well-known companies are making provision for that mid-afternoon slump. Google and Samsung have introduced pods into their offices – infinitely more civilised than toilets or car parks! Uber has 'napping rooms'. Ben & Jerry's have had a nap room for more than a decade.

And, as a 'napper', you're in 'good' company (depending on your viewpoint). Salvador Dalí, Aristotle, Winston Churchill, Eleanor Roosevelt, and Margaret Thatcher were all 'nappers'. They, of course, needed a lot more recharging than I did!

CONFLICTS AND VIOLENCE

Iona and Peter Opie's classic study *The Lore and Language of Schoolchildren* (1959 – Oxford University New York Press) looked at the behaviours, rhymes, games, and jokes of some five thousand children aged between six and fourteen across all types of school. It also paid passing reference to fights. Here's an eleven-year-old Londoner commenting on a playground brawl: 'people gather round and shout fight, fight, fight' (p.196). The Opies quote a teacher in the East End as saying, 'The boys like fighting – often with the intention of inflicting as much damage as possible.' (p.142 footnote – Opies). The TV series *Peaky Blinders*, launched in 2013, is based on the gang warfare that existed in Birmingham and other major cities in the mid to late 1800s. Researchers into the period have concluded that what we would now, in 2025, term 'postcode wars', gave men the opportunity to indulge their enjoyment of fighting.

Little has changed by the time we get to the late 1960s. Corporal punishment was rife, as was its corollary – the violence meted out to students by the students themselves. Fights were commonplace, and a circle of onlookers would gather around, lusting for blood as if they were watching a cock fight. Teenage spectators in the 1960s – and later – would often try to 'put the boot in', i.e., to kick the losing fighter while he was on the ground. And the 'boots' in those days were often 'bovver boots' – heavy and steel-toe-capped, stereotypically worn by skinheads. While the boots disappeared from schools thanks to changes in school uniform regulations (and the advent of trainers), the fights did not. In the 1980s in Hornchurch, we had to introduce a rule to the effect that anyone watching a fight was as guilty as those actually fighting. And, in that mixed school, the rules were the same for girls as for boys – the girls being quite ready to support one or other of the combatants.

Over thirty years on from *The Lore and Language of Schoolchildren*, Iona Opie did a follow-up, *The People in the Playground* (1993). She described how '...fights added to the excitement in the playground, and a fight can be the main, if not the only, event of a morning playtime.' (p.10)

While fighting has always been a predominantly male

activity, there is plenty of evidence of female involvement. The Birmingham gang warfare, referred to above, often involved women – albeit to a much lesser extent. Iona Opie again: 'Girls fight, too; not so frequently and in a feminine (sic) way with much screaming and pulling of hair.' (p.10)

The Opies talk about playgrounds. That's the normal place for fights during school time. If the school has a tight grip on discipline, then disputes can relocate outside the school gates (or even further afield) after school has finished.

As far as girls are concerned, it's often in the toilets that the build-up starts and where disputes are kept bubbling along. For decades, girls have used them as social areas. It's also the place where bullying often actually takes place – verbal and physical. It's like an underground culture – separate from the school's management policies and structures. A senior master in a London school recently explained how there's often a central figure deciding who will be picked on next. (Drugan – 2019)

Boys are more inclined to enter their toilets, relieve themselves, and exit. For them, disputes rarely start or take place in toilets.

If anyone were foolish (or brave) enough to bug student toilets, they would get an insight into the private lives of students that otherwise rarely emerges. However, being as alert as possible to what goes on there is an important role for heads and for staff in general. It's certainly not a role that would come to mind when the public at large think of teachers and their day-to-day duties!

In the classroom, we also see significant differences between girls and boys. How these manifest themselves will depend on the teacher – from those capable of establishing 'pin drop' order to those for whom every lesson with every class is a battle. In the latter, boys tend to shout out and act silly, while girls just chat as though they were in the playground during break.

Schools have always found bullying very hard to deal

with – even more so with the advent of Snapchat, Instagram, Facebook, WhatsApp, Twitter, and other social media platforms – the underground culture. Boys do look at the various sites but are less inclined than girls to take part, as an article by Kathy Doering of the Social Media and Research Association (October 2019) makes clear: '40% of girls admitted being on their social media accounts for more than three hours a day – compared to only 20% of boys.' Boys are roughly four times as likely to say they spend too much time playing video games, and their bullying will generally still be physical – rather than via social media.

It's a tough nut to crack. A friend of mine, a long-standing and experienced senior member of staff, recently attended a course on bullying at school. She was surprised to find that the 'expert' leader asked her for *her* solutions! So often, the so-called experts are either academics or ex-teachers long since out of the classroom.

As I've implied, many of the behaviours described are as common in the twenty-first century as they were fifty years ago.

A report in 'Coventry Live' (3 April 2019) – a local media outlet – describes how concerns were raised after videos emerged of fights at the Nuneaton Academy and Hartshill School:

'Education bosses have condemned videos showing fights at two schools in Nuneaton, which were uploaded onto Instagram. A group entitled 'Nuneaton Baits' encouraged teens to upload videos taken of school scraps. It promised to glorify the fights by uploading them onto the social media site.'

Or this, in 2020, from a senior teacher (Jones) in a large north London mixed comprehensive, referring to disputes. 'Boys get it over with quickly. There's a slap or a punch-up. Get it over with and move on. Girls tend to talk disputes through, although their fallings out can go on for months.' I used to take students on school journeys and noticed that, quite often, when boys arrived at the seaside, they threw stones. The girls didn't.

Perhaps we should remind ourselves that there are no girls in *Lord of the Flies*.

There have always been, and still are, occasional fights between girls, but Churchill's dictum 'jaw jaw' rather than 'war war' generally holds good for girls. The following abridged accounts, which were written (in their own words) by two girls who fell out at a secondary school early in 2000, bear this out:

Nicole: 'There's a group of fifth years (girls) that dislike Daphne going out with Lee. We've spoken and had a row about the situation of dirty looks... not a regular occurrence for Daphne and me to argue, but from that time onwards, she has received dirty looks... but we've both been in the position where we've let out our feelings to each other...'

Daphne: 'Nicole and her friends seem to dislike me. They asked me why I was giving dirty looks, and we exchanged words. Nicole seems to be understanding, and I am very willing to be her friend. Her friends seem to be very jealous... because I am going out with a fifth-year boy... I only wanted to talk to Nicole sensibly and ask what was going on... We have sorted it out and are willing to be friends, and we'll hope this doesn't occur again.'

Hard to imagine boys writing the above.

In my piece on 'Corporal Punishment', I looked at violence administered by teachers. However, often they're also the victims. In April 2019, the NAS/UWT Union reported that twenty-four per cent of the nearly five thousand teachers who sent in feedback said they were on the receiving end of physical attacks each week. Many reported that they had been 'shoved or barged', and a significant percentage said they had been hit, punched, or kicked. 'Schools Week' (2019) reported a seventy-two per cent rise in attacks on teachers in the previous four years. Many say poor behaviour is making them want to leave the profession.

Quoting Roger McGough again, they may fantasise, as did the teacher in his poem 'The Lesson':

> '...He picked on a boy who was shouting
> And throttled him then and there
> Then garrotted the girl behind him...'

So how *do* schools combat violence? As I said at the beginning of the book, this is not a blueprint for running a school. However, the following strategies worked for my schools. There are, of course, many, many others.

Number One. *Make all schools mixed.* I have never regretted my Somers Town 'all boys' experience. It was a baptism of fire, but it meant that little fazed me in the four schools that followed. What it did do was convince me that girls, for all their 'dirty looks' and toilet gossip, exercise a civilising influence over boys. They also seem to mature faster to the point where I've toyed with the idea of organising year groups so that, for example, 13-year-old boys are taught with 12-year-old girls! I guess that doesn't even make the pending tray.

Number Two. *Make the curriculum relevant* to all members of the school community – black, white, male, female, minority ethnic, etc. That probably seems obvious, but in a sizeable number of schools, it isn't the norm.

Number Three. *Ensure supervision is taken seriously,* e.g., staff turning up for break or dinner duty on time. Don't spend money on mealtime supervisors who cower in the corner of the playground, chatting to the girls and making sure they're as far away from the 'rough' boys as it's possible to get.

Number Four. *Practise tough love.* That means believing in what students can achieve and only accepting the best.

All that helps you to identify the tiny minority who present a real challenge and to create strategies for helping them and minimising the disruption they cause.

CORPORAL PUNISHMENT

'...the infliction of physical pain upon a person's body as punishment...' (Encyclopaedia Britannica)

Corporal punishment in state schools in the UK was abolished in 1986. 'Private' schools hung on for another twelve years! Long before the violence of Somers Town, my boys' school background had its rough edges, starting with my 'posh' Hampstead prep school in the early 1950s. One of my prouder memories was of taking on a much older boy in the playground. He was a bully, and I was merely flailing at him, but it was enough to ensure he never troubled me again. On that occasion, I escaped punishment. It was break time, and we were down the far end of the playground with no supervision in sight. I was rarely so lucky and frequently found myself in the head's oak-panelled study. This was long before heads were based in offices. To my young eyes, he always seemed terrifyingly fierce.

He was tall, white-haired, with a white moustache, and his name was Wharton. Mr Wharton, Sir. I thought of him as incredibly old, but he was probably no more than fifty. At that time, 'Spare the rod and spoil the child' was almost a national mantra, and he certainly didn't spare the rod. Or strap, in his case. He personally administered all punishments. The routine was that whichever teacher you had offended or had caught you up to some mischief sent you to the head's study with a note explaining your offence. The long trek down a corridor lined with photos of previous heads was nerve-racking enough, and it was hard not to scrunch up the note. Eventually, you reached his study. You knocked timidly on the forbidding door.

'Come in.' His sharp voice cut through the air. He would usually be sitting at his desk and would stretch out his hand for the note. You had to stand in front of the desk, waiting while he read it. Just occasionally, you'd be let off with a warning.

'This is unacceptable boy.' You never got a name. 'This time I'll let you off. You won't be so lucky next time. Now get back to your class.'

That was the exception. Normally he'd get up, stand behind his desk and fire the routine question:

'Small strap – trousers down? Or big strap – trousers up?' I always struggled with this choice.

'Come on, boy. Make up your mind.' In a fairly chequered prep school career, I always had ('always' indicating that this was not an infrequent event) opted for the small strap – trousers down. However, on this particular occasion, possibly wanting to ring the changes and maybe thinking that my trousers would offer some protection:

'Big strap, please, Sir.'

Over sixty years on, I can still see Mr Wharton going into his desk drawer and bringing out an enormous thick piece of leather. It was not unlike a large Scottish tawse[2] but without the split end. To my twelve-year-old popping eyes, it looked like something you might use to tame a fiery horse.

'Bend over.'

I bent over. Moments after a loud thwack, I felt a searing pain. The experience was repeated twice more. My trousers failed miserably to provide *any* protection, and I realised too late

---

2   The use of the tawse in Scottish schools goes back to the nineteenth century. An article by C. Farrell, 'The Cane and the Tawse in Scottish Schools', charts its use right up to 1980s, including a reference to a famous Fettes old boy – Tony Blair. '...he received "six of the best" there when he was a six-foot 17 year old. The caning was delivered by his exasperated housemaster who described the future PM as the most difficult boy he had ever had to deal with.' ('Rebel pupil Blair was given six of the best', *Daily Telegraph*, 28 March 2001)

my mistake. I retreated from the head's office, tears in my eyes, vowing never to repeat what was a badly judged experiment.

At that school, corporal punishment occasionally took an unofficial route. For lesser misdemeanours (e.g., pulling someone's chair out as they were about to sit on it, throwing a paper ball across the back of the class where I always tried to position myself), there were detentions. You would be sent to get the detention book from the school office, where you might get a friendly 'Not you again' from one of the secretaries. The book itself was a large, leather-bound volume that, in another guise, might have been used as a ledger by the school accountant. One teacher, Mr Rotherham, seemingly even older than the head, had a favourite trick. Instead of a copperplate entry – ('Throwing paper across the back of the class – Andrew Macalpine – September 12, 1953'), he'd take the book from you and, while still sitting down, whack you over the head with it. Stars resulted and, most likely, the many mental deficiencies which have plagued me ever since!

Prep schools were introduced in the early nineteenth century in order to prepare children for entrance to a private secondary school. Part of that preparation, it might be argued, was linked to beatings. Not quite the roasting over an open fire, as in *Tom Brown's Schooldays* nor the famous caning scene in Lindsay Anderson's 1968 film *If* where, with your head facing the wall and your bottom facing up, a prefect armed with a cane took a run at you in the school gym. But beatings nevertheless.

I moved from a 'prep' school to a middle-ranking public school where the prefect system licensed students as young as sixteen to administer corporal punishment. Indeed, discipline, as in many boys' public schools, was almost entirely in the hands of the students. It was a system hugely open to abuse.

A turning point for me came when I was about to be caned by a sub-prefect – probably only a couple of years older than myself. This was for some misdemeanour, the nature of which escapes me. I was told by the head of the house to present myself to Jason at a certain time.

I knocked on his study door (there's that 'study' again!). For a student to possess a study, albeit shared, was a sign of rank.

Again that brusque 'Come in!' He was a tall, thin-faced boy who seemed to have few friends. Was he taking this out on miscreants? I entered to find him standing there with a cane in hand – swishing it in a kind of practice movement. He had a wild look in his eyes which suggested something deeper than the objective administration of a sanction. Unfortunately, this was neither the time nor the place to offer a course in psychoanalysis. The 'psycho' element, however, was all too evident.

'Bend over!'

I couldn't see his face – bent over as I was – but I certainly felt the wild, uncontrolled swipe to the approximate region of my backside. To say I was used to being caned would be an exaggeration. However, I had experienced enough of them to know the difference between the punishment fitting the crime and sadism. I stood up and said:

'You're crazy. I'm not taking any more of this.'

Obviously, it crossed my mind that my actions might have gotten me into even more trouble, although I was perfectly prepared to defend myself. I sensed he would find it difficult to justify his behaviour, and, indeed, I heard nothing more.

That experience, and others, stayed with me to the point where, when I became house captain, I abolished corporal punishment. My first small 'p' political act.

Moving on to Somers Town, where, as I have already indicated, corporal punishment was not only the norm – but not even questioned. Somers Town was far removed from any public school – a secondary modern in all but name.

So... despite my crusading background as house captain, I found myself in a situation where both staff and students expected me to use the cane I was issued with on arrival. Of course, I could have refused and staged a protest that might, possibly, have gathered some support. I'm sure many of you reading this would have done just that. As a 'newbie', I just didn't have the courage, nor, at that point, did I have any alternative strategy to deal with the indiscipline that was rife.

It didn't take me long to discover that caning was an 'art' in itself – and one I wasn't mastering. Hitting a boy's bottom at a range of two to three feet was a challenge, and I resorted to using a plimsoll (the equivalent of slippering). This was immediately much more effective – easier to hit the target and accompanied by a thwack that would reverberate around the empty classroom. How did I feel administering such punishment? I'm confident that it wasn't incipient sadism, but rather a practical solution to a problem. At this distance, decades later, I like to feel it wasn't really me! But I know it was.

The theme of violence permeated the school. It was not uncommon to see a whole class being canned in the corridor before they went in for their lesson. One boy – certainly no troublemaker – was caned for not turning up for choir practice. And while it was only the men who seemed sanctioned to administer corporal punishment, there was at least one exception – a young female Australian supply teacher who always turned up for work in very short skirts. Naturally, boys would position themselves to take a lascivious peek – only for her to whack them on the hand with her ruler. Perversion all around.

I made an attempt to deal with misbehaviour by replacing corporal punishment with detentions. They were hated to the point where, one winter's evening, some ten minutes after I'd released a couple of miscreants, I heard the noise of stones being thrown against the metal grills which were needed to protect the school's ground-floor windows.

This hatred of detentions was reinforced one evening on a bus on my way home. As usual, I made my way up to the top deck.

'Hello, Sir.'

Three boys that I'd had numerous run-ins with were the only other people there. I couldn't just ignore what seemed a fairly friendly greeting and get as far away as possible, so I sat a couple of rows on the other side of the aisle – far enough, I thought, to deter conversation but not so far as to insult them. It didn't work. They were happy to talk across the seats.

'Sir, you know you like giving detentions.'

'It's not that I like it, Bobby; it's that I don't approve of caning.'

'Well,' this was Bobby's mate Mark, 'we'd rather be caned than kept behind.'

'I don't really understand that,' I said. 'Maybe I just don't cane you hard enough?' A feeble attempt at humour. 'What about when Mr Stephens canes you?'

'He's barmy. Should be locked up.' This was George. 'He shouldn't be teaching kids.'

'Anyway, boys. Thanks for the chat. I have to get off here.' Not true, but I couldn't think where to go next with the discussion. I also needed to get my head around the most effective way to discipline boys when they were out of order.

A cheery chorus of 'See you, Sir' followed me down the stairs. The upside was that they were happy to engage in a polite and friendly manner. I don't remember if the encounter did me any favours when next they were sitting in my class – but it didn't seem to do any harm.

Scroll forward some fifteen years, and I'm applying for the school in Ilford where, astonishingly, I was asked if I'd reintroduce caning (See 'Headship Applications'). This was at a time when it was beginning to be phased out altogether. I couldn't believe that they were trying to turn the clock back. I withdrew.

Given that corporal punishment was abolished in *all* schools by 1998, you may be thinking, 'Thank goodness – a bygone era.' But… over fifty years on, *The Times* (17 September 2018) contained an article headed 'Boarder shines a light on initiation beatings.' It referred to recordings made in a public school which appear to show older boys asking fourteen-year-olds in a boarding house how they wanted to be beaten – once on their bare buttocks or twice through their boxer shorts. While most people, including myself, would now see corporal punishment as barbaric, there are still many happy-to-quote dictums like 'Spare the rod and spoil the child' and 'Never did me any harm'. And it often starts young – witness mums dealing with fractious children in supermarkets.

Maybe not quite *plus ca change, plus c'est la meme chose* but, sadly, corporal punishment certainly hasn't disappeared completely.

COVER FOR ABSENT COLLEAGUES

'Hide in a cupboard when you're free. You're a sitting duck in the staffroom.'

In relation to staff absences, much has changed over the years – and certainly for good. In 2010, as a result of union pressure, the government introduced a policy whereby teachers would be asked to cover for absent colleagues '...rarely, and only in circumstances that are not foreseeable.' (School Teachers Pay and Conditions Document 2019)

Up until 2010, 'cover' was not a word teachers wished to hear. Office in-trays may mount while their owners are away, but they do stay in one place – unlike classes of unsupervised children. The change in policy was enthusiastically welcomed. It meant that those blank spaces on individual timetables where you could mark books, prepare lessons and contact parents were protected.

However, pre-2010, teachers who were 'free' would be in constant fear of being snared and asked to fill a gap that had arisen through a colleague's absence. More often than not, you found yourself in a strange classroom with a strange subject and students you didn't know. Thus the sage advises, 'Don't sit in the staffroom when you're free.'

First of all, if you *have* been captured, there's a dilemma. Students have to line up outside the classroom, laboratory, or workshop. If you arrive *before* the class, you can be on the front foot and are more likely to be able to exercise some modicum of control before they go in. But if you drag your feet and take that last slurp of coffee, what might have resembled some sort of orderly line-up by the classroom door has, by now, degenerated into pushing, shoving, and shouting. Let's call the class 4H. Here they are – 'lining up'.

'Oi, Pratish. You got a pen?'

'Jenny, you done your homework. Can I have a look?'

'Stop shoving, you wanker.'

'Oi, that's my bag you're kicking around.'

'Where's Butcher? She's always late. I hate her lessons. Hope she's away.'

I appear as all this is going on – realising the last slurp of coffee was a big mistake and that the imposition of what authority I might ever have had could take some time.

'Right, in you go. One at a time. Mark, stop shoving.' There's always a Mark, and you already know his name because everyone knows Mark – a truculent teenager already in trouble with the police, and always in trouble in school. He's not the only one with his shirt hanging out (a mortal sin), but he's the only one without a blazer. He's tall, spotty, and just beginning to show signs of facial hair. You know he won't have anything to write with. I don't feel like taking him on – not with an hour in his company to look forward to. As I stand by the door, the students struggle in towards the stools (this is a science lab) – a number going for the same one. I follow the last one in.

'Now, can we have everyone sitting down, please?'

'Please' can be interpreted as polite, an attempt to ingratiate yourself with the class – or an instruction. Whichever, it rarely works. There's a sluggish response from the majority, and supplementaries are needed:

'One to a stool.' You raise your voice as you see more than a couple going for the same one.

The school has seating plans for all classes. They're effective in putting students together who work well, keeping those who don't apart, and mixing up girls and boys. No one's given me one for this class, so while the more biddable head towards their usual places, the majority, revelling in the freedom they've acquired, sit with their mates.

The lab is typically rectangular, with sinks, taps, and Bunsen burners on either side of a centre console that runs the length of the room. There's a smell of chemicals.

I position myself behind the raised desk – a symbol of authority, or just a shield? From this vantage point, the lab seems impossibly long, stretching away into the distance with the stools at the back already occupied by Mark and his mates. It's hard to make out what, if anything, they're up to.

'We won't be using the Bunsen burners or the taps today, so please leave them alone.' This instruction was prompted by a hiss coming from somewhere in the lab – hard to pinpoint exactly where. If you wander towards the back from the safety of your desk at the front, you're then facing the wrong way from those behind you!

Eventually, you establish reluctance to order but realise you've no work to give them. You know you've got little time before the class gets restless.

'Have you been set any work?' Again, you anticipate a nil response. However, just occasionally, you might be saved by a self-appointed class prefect, sitting at the front of course. You mentally prostrate yourself at her feet.

'Sir, we were starting to write up the last experiment we did.'

Those nearest the front hear this. Their reaction is swift:

'I wasn't here.'

'Nor was I.'

Ignoring these voices, you latch on to the help you've been offered.

'Right, thank you. What's your name?' Name volunteered. It's Chloe, and she's the polar opposite of Mark. She has a smart pencil case, and her science book is covered with tasteful wallpaper and has no graffiti on the front. Her tie's done up, and her face is open and eager. And, of course, she's a girl. Even if she wanted to sit at the back, which she never would, there'd be no room as it's a 'boys only' area.

'Alright, listen.' No response. Chattering continues. I should say 'off task' chattering, but you haven't *set* them any tasks yet.

'I said, listen.' You raise your voice a notch. 'Chloe tells me that at the end of the last lesson, you were beginning to write up the experiment you did. You can get on with that.'

Cue more excuses:

'I was ill last week.'

'So was I.'

'I've got nothing to write with.'

'Nor have I.'

And so it goes on. You're outwardly calm and in control, going from bench to bench, helping, cajoling, reprimanding, trying to cut down that off-task chat of which there is a huge amount. Inwardly you're sweating and wondering why the hands on that clock have stopped moving.

It only takes one such experience for even the doziest of a newly qualified teacher to realise that hiding in the stockroom is infinitely preferable to being a sitting duck in the staffroom. But your harassed senior manager has been promoted for a reason. She knows the hiding places. She also knows that every minute, 4H is teacherless, and children and equipment are at risk. And,

God forbid, if the worst came to the worst, she'd have to cover the class herself.

My Peckham school had that Yorkshireman who asked me if I played cricket. He was meticulous in keeping track of how many 'free' periods each member of staff had lost. However much you hated the system, at least you knew that, in his hands, it was fair.

A particular cover lesson sticks in my mind. It was with 3.8, i.e., third year and eighth out of what were then the eight streams. The very bottom of the pile, rejected and neglected. I don't remember the subject, but I do remember that no work had been set. Par for the course. 'Containment' was the mantra. I had a couple of 'free' periods that day and, foolishly, had ventured into the staffroom at the break – rather than hiding in a cupboard. Coffee had overridden caution, and I was sitting chatting to a couple in my department when I saw Trevor making his way across the staffroom towards me. Despite his role as 'cover maister' – one of his many roles – everybody loved Trevor. Like a favourite uncle, he was gentle, reasonable, and fair. As he made his way across the staffroom, he stopped to have a friendly chat with various people. However, I had a sixth sense that I was going to be his final destination. I wasn't wrong.

'Hi, Andrew. Sorry to be the bearer of bad tidings, but I'm afraid I'm going to need you after the break. It's 3.8 with Miss Betts. Her son's not well, and she's had to go home. Sorry, it's such short notice, and I'm afraid she hasn't left any work. Hopefully, they'll have something to get on with.'

Both Trevor and I knew this was a forlorn hope.

'Good luck with them, Andrew.'

Sympathetic words from Carol, my English department deputy, as I got up to leave. Dragging my feet, I made my way from the staffroom down to the classroom off the lower hall – joining the scrum of students and staff off to their next lesson.

There was certainly no need to rush as what one colleague termed 'sheepdog trials' were still taking place, i.e., shepherding students out of the playground back into the main building and then into classrooms – a process which could comfortably (on a good day for students) cut ten minutes off the next lesson. I reached the classroom as the hall emptied to find a class of... one! He was sitting at the front in what was clearly his usual place. His neat appearance – school blazer and tie, clean shoes as opposed to trainers, neat, short, dark hair – already distinguished him from the average 3.8 student. But, then, he clearly wasn't the average 3.8 student.

I asked him his name.

'David Peatty,' came the reply.

'Where is everyone?' I asked.

'I think they knew Miss Betts was away,' David volunteered. With his help, I then went through the register.

'William Abrahart?'

'Market stall,' came the answer. Clearly, for William Abrahart, putting money in his pocket *now* was taking precedence over any future employment.

'Ross Bowman?'

'Prison.' I think David meant young offenders institution.

'Michael Christofi?'

'He's got a problem with his older brother.'

'John Fenn?'

'Oh, he left before Christmas.'

'Ronald Heyfron?'

'Sick,' David thinks.

'Leslie Issac?'

David's pretty sure he's suspended.

'Gordon Neil?'

'Was around at break, Sir.'

'Tracy O'Keefe?' The only girl on the register.

'She's never here. Can't stand the boys.'

And so it went on, although even with everyone present, it was a small class – seen as 'special needs' and needing more individual attention.

At the time, I didn't understand why David was there at all. While his classmates may have given up on formal education, and their teachers may have given up on them, there was definitely a choice of careers ahead for David – detective, stock controller, accountant – anything that required a good memory, an eye for detail, and organisational skills. Still, a class of one I could cope with. I gave David some work to do – and, of course, he did it. Or at least gave the impression of doing it. I sat at the front, catching up on marking.

I subsequently discovered David was dyslexic and that, shockingly, there was no provision for a bright boy who had trouble reading – other than to be lumped with some of the most difficult pupils in the school. It was my shame that I never checked on whether he understood the work or not.

Soon, although we still had to cover colleagues' classes, we had a list of regular supply teachers brought in specially. One of them was Mr Silverman. I never sat through one of his 'lessons', but enough of us had been in and out while he was 'teaching' to be able to build up a pretty good picture. He was beyond retirement age and just supplementing his pension. With his thinning grey hair, heavily lined face, and baggy eyes, he always looked tired. His creased suit looked equally so. He would arrive not to a neat line-up but, as I had experienced, students milling around the locked classroom door. Some even wandered around the hall.

He produces a key, and the class saunters in.

'You all need to sit down while I take the register.' He had a rather weedy, high-pitched voice which students were quick to mimic. There would be a reluctant, and noisy response, including some muffled (and not so muffled), weedy, high– pitched voices. Eventually, everyone is seated. He puts the work up on the board, and immediately there is a chorus of complaints.

'We've already done that.'

'Sir, I don't understand what we have to do.'

'Miss Andreas told us to do the next exercise in our books if she was away, but we haven't got our books.'

'Sir, can you explain what that means.' A boy points at a poster on the wall. The diversionary tactic of which there were many.

'Sir, do you get paid for this?'

'Sir, can I go to the toilet?'

'Sir, I haven't got my exercise book.'

Mr Silverman hasn't got an answer for any of this apart from: 'You'll just have to do the best you can.'

From that moment on, he would just stand by the classroom door for an hour while students did more or less as they wanted – wandering around, chatting, shouting across the room. A small group even commandeered the blackboard to play teacher. Any student trying to get work done would find his pen being 'borrowed', his chair shoved. For Mr Silverman – nice work if you can get it. Paid to be a tailor's dummy for a few hours each day.

Scrolling forward to the Isle of Dogs in the late 1970s, we had the delightful, mild-mannered, bearded and diminutive Mr Hassan on our books as a permanent cover teacher. Elsewhere he might have been mistaken for a lecturer on eastern mysticism. His teaching ability (rarely attempted) might have been called into question, but his reliability and commitment were legendary. One cold winter with snow on the ground, transport at a standstill, and some staff still snuggled up in bed, Mr Hassan walked the four miles from his home in Wapping to the school on the Isle of Dogs to present himself for duty. Dressed in a brown overcoat, thick woolly scarf, and hat, he arrived as the morning session finished. I was in the staffroom when he appeared and took his coat off.

'Mr Hassan (we all loved him, but he was never called by

his first name), how on earth did you get here? There aren't any buses, and the school is about to close for the day.' Dawn, one of the deputy heads, looked astonished.

Mr Hassan seemed bemused. I almost expected him to apologise for being late for the morning session.

'You didn't try phoning the school to check?' I asked.

'I just thought it would be normal,' Mr Hassan replied. In the meantime, the staffroom was filling up, and a few of the staff came over to find out what was happening.

'You're a hero, you know that,' said Cameron, head of maths. Mr Hassan had probably spent more time covering maths lessons than any other subject. Word had now got out about his walk to school through the snow.

Deidre, Cameron's number two, was listening to all this. 'Mr Hassan, can I give you a lift home? You can't do that trek again in this weather.'

'No, really, thank you so much, Deidre. I'll walk. It'll do me good.' With that, he put his coat back on and disappeared, leaving staff open-mouthed at his stoicism.

After the Isle of Dogs, it was off to Hornchurch (see above) where, as the newly appointed head, I inherited a fearsome deputy – rather like owning an attack dog. Her name was Jenny Bolt, and, as far as staff were concerned, she was aptly named. She was well-built but quite short. That probably explained her high heels, which click-clacked on the school's stone floor – heralding her approach. She had a sharp tongue to match those heels and was perfectly happy to do the dirty work for you. She was decisive, and, with her, there were hardly ever two sides to an argument. Part of her role was to take early morning calls from teachers unable, unwell, or unwilling to come into school. These calls took place in a colleague's office right by the school entrance and were put through by the school secretary. The office door was kept permanently open so, if, as a member of staff, you happened to be late, there was no sidling in.

When I had time, I tended to hover in the background while Jenny was dealing with calls. It was useful for me to know who was away or late and what lessons needed covering.

Calls went something like this:

Nine forty-five a.m. Well into the school day. Phone rings.

Pam (school secretary): 'I'm putting Michael Appleby through, Jenny.'

Jenny: 'Good morning, Michael. What is it?' Already a slight edge to her voice.

Michael: 'I woke up this morning feeling terrible. My temperature's over a hundred.'

Jenny – ignoring this: 'So when do you think you can get in.'

I'm flinching at this point, but, on balance, I've already decided that giving malingerers a hard time just edges it over being harsh with genuine cases. Michael's probably halfway between the two.

Michael: 'I really don't think I can make it today.'

Jenny: 'We'll see you tomorrow then.' This was definitely not, as it might have been if it were me, a question. It was as near as Jenny could get to an instruction.

Michael: 'I'll do my best.'

Jenny: 'I've no doubt you will, Michael. I see you've got a full timetable, so we don't want to have to cover it.'

Michael: 'Alright. Thank you, Jenny.'

Jenny went on to become a head and found life rather more challenging. *Her* way of dealing with pressure was to disappear off-site to buy shoes. This during the school day. As head, she could get away with, 'I've got a meeting at County Hall.' Or some equally convincing explanation. No one was going to subject *her* to the Spanish Inquisition.

Eventually, and before the legislation kicked in, good schools got to grips with the whole process of covering for absent colleagues. More and more schools started to keep a record of who had lost what 'non-teaching' periods – not 'free' periods any longer, and an assumption took hold that you might well have marking, preparation, and phone calls to parents to make when you were not teaching. You were not just lounging around the staffroom drinking coffee.

FAREWELLS ENDS OF TERMS – ENDS OF YEARS

Peckham – Staff Retirement

Irreverence characterised staff behaviour in many of the schools I worked in – in common with workplaces generally, I'm sure. In the Peckham school, there was a head of R.E., Bill Light, whose classroom happened to be next to the English stockroom. From time to time, when I had a 'free' period, I was there as the bell went for the start of the next lesson. The walls of the stockroom were plasterboard and sufficiently thin to enable me to hear students coming in next door for their R.E. class with Bill. It was all harmless teenage chatter, and I didn't really think anything of it until I remembered whose class it was. He was late – as usual. I had some sympathy. R.E. was still being taught as a separate subject, and, in most schools, that meant one lesson a week with every class in the school. Hundreds of names to remember meant resorting to 'You boy' and 'You girl' when you needed to engage with a student – and 'engage' in Bill's case meant to engage with the enemy.

You would have to be God's gift to teaching to be effective in the above circumstances. And, despite the subject being R.E., God showed no sign of intervening in the unsettled and often rowdy lessons. So Bill's frequent lateness *was* understandable. Although I could see nothing, I knew for sure when he'd arrived at the class. The decibel level shot up. There was the sound of furniture – and bodies – clattering around and Bill's voice trying desperately to instil order out of the chaos his arrival had generated. It seems cruel to highlight his deficiencies as a teacher. The fact was that he was one of a kind – drifting into teaching and then finding himself trapped with no obvious alternative. He was a sad character, and never more so than when he came to retire. He gave his farewell speech in the rather cramped school library. It was not joyous. No sense of reluctance coming to the end of a fulfilling career. His finale was a sad riff on how he would struggle with the pension he'd get. Halfway through, someone in the audience managed to land a coin at his feet. It was followed by others. To his eternal credit, Bill took it in good heart, but there were no plaudits for the staff responsible who never quite forgave themselves. A sad end to a sad career.

Isle of Dogs – Flour and Eggs

Every year in the Spanish town of Ibi, a festival takes place called Els Enfarinats. It goes back over two hundred years, with participants dressed in military garb covering each other in flour and eggs. Everyone, including bystanders, ends up coated in a sludge of batter.

Just when UK students started to emulate the Spaniards is not clear. Of course, they haven't been celebrating Els Enfarinats; they've been celebrating leaving school – and the end of the year generally. For decades now, they have challenged staff – and heads in particular.

A few years ago, a school in Woking hit the local headlines as parents (yes – parents) were blamed for dropping off flour, eggs, and ketchup as students made their way to the local park for their end-of-year celebrations (Surrey Live, 22 May 2015). You can imagine breakfast scenes in those households – 'I'll see you later, love. Shall I bring one bag of flour or two? Oh, and that's a new bottle of ketchup…'

Around the same time, a school in Rochdale had their end-of-year 'ball' cancelled as eggs, flour, and shaving foam fights spilled back into the school building.

And again, in 2015, students at the UK's largest Jewish School went beyond flour and eggs and introduced food fights in the canteen – and stink bombs. Around three hundred were escorted off the premises, and police were called when they tried to break down a security fence to get back in – and not to their next lesson.

Right at the other end of the spectrum is Winchester School's Wykeham Day – and no doubt special days at many public schools. This is the end of the autumn term rather than the end of the year.

'The autumn term at Winchester College, known as "Short Half" comes to an enchanting close with a tradition known as "Illumina". When pupils finish their lessons at quarter to five in the afternoon, they're met with the sight of scores of candles illuminating the wall enclosing the school playing fields. The festivities are a chance for parents, staff, and pupils to celebrate the end of term and enjoy some early Christmas merriment, including a bonfire, carol singing, mince pies, and punch...' (ref. Oxford Royale Academy)

The reaction of many kids I've taught to this sacred tradition would range from 'wankers' to 'nutters'. End of terms at my Isle of Dogs school were modelled much more closely on Els Enfarinats. Water 'bombs' and water fights were the norm. The air was full of flour, and students were covered in eggs. And anyone without a graffitied shirt (more often than not brought in especially for the occasion) was an outcast. We tried, but with no success at all, to bring order out of the chaos.

Grumpy caretakers, of which there were always some in the post, would retire in despair at our inability to deal with the mayhem:

'Those kids are running riot.'

'Ain't you got no control?'

Etc., etc.

Parents, far from supplying ammunition, joined the caretakers' protests – as 'fights' spilled out onto the streets. We had to come up with a strategy. We came to a decision that 'If you can't beat 'em, join 'em.' Thus we set up 'organised' (not that any of the students wanted to be organised) flour, egg, and water fights on the back terrace overlooking the Thames. It seemed to work – albeit not without some very wet, sticky corridors. Of course, caretakers were no less grumpy and felt we had just given in. It was a fair price to pay.

Isle of Dogs – The Fire Hose

Once all the students had gone home, we organised our own celebrations. Two images stick in my mind. One is of Gordon, a member of the P.E. department (tracksuit, sports shirt, and trainers), hurtling past me down the narrow senior staff corridor and past the head's office. The head who had sensibly disappeared long before – as was his custom. Gordon was being chased by Sam, a determined look on her face. She had recently arrived at the school and was a colleague of his in the P.E. department. She was similarly dressed and clutching the nozzle of a fire hose reel which trailed back some forty feet to the main entrance where it was normally housed. Emanating from the nozzle was a powerful jet of water. I pressed myself against the corridor wall to avoid being soaked. It crossed my mind that things had gotten out of hand! At the end of the corridor was the door to the staffroom. Gordon reached it and slammed it shut just in time to avoid a soaking. Not to be deterred, Sam then tried to force water through the keyhole.

'Sam, if you don't turn that hose off, you'll flood the corridor. Just twist that bit behind the nozzle.'

I was tempted to snatch it off her as she grappled with the nozzle, spraying the ceiling as she did so. Just as I was about to do just that, she got the hang of it, and the jet was reduced to a dribble. She started hauling the hose back down the corridor. Meanwhile, I slopped my way into the staffroom. Gordon seemed to have disappeared, and there was only one person there – Jonny. He had clearly witnessed much of the episode – at least from his side of the door. Jonny was very tall – well over six foot – and so thin his clothes always seemed two sizes too big for him. He was bent over a pile of exercise books and didn't look up.

'Hi, Jonny. You OK? Sorry about the chaos. The end of the year gets like this sometimes.'

'It's OK, Andrew. I just want to get these books in some sort of order before September.'

Jonny hadn't been at the school long and, to his credit, had not yet taken on board the more anarchic nature of the school. He appeared oblivious to the mayhem which had just ensued and went back to his marking.

I slopped my way back down the corridor following the sound of staff shouts and screams – indicating that the mayhem hadn't abated. Staff end of terms were a little more civilised after that.

Isle of Dogs – Staff Farewell

One year we had a colleague leaving to join the Army. This was Charlie – a popular bouncy character – small and wiry with a mischievous streak. The kids loved him – and his sense of humour. He was also an effective teacher due for promotion. We were never quite clear why he would want to subject himself to army discipline. But, whatever the reason, we wanted to give him a good send-off.

The farewells normally took place in the staffroom. There was only two other staff leaving that year, and we managed to persuade people it would make a change to do the honours in a covered courtyard at the back of the school. The centre of the courtyard was open right up to the roof. Halfway up, there was a walkway all the way around from which you could look down on the staff below. Charlie chose to give his farewell speech in full army uniform – reminding us of where he was off to next. He was standing in the middle of the open part of the courtyard. Five minutes into his speech, a loud bang was heard, and those nearest Charlie, including myself, suddenly found we were covered in a white powder that hung in the air and gave the appearance of smoke. At the same time, down each of the four walls of the courtyard, figures dressed in black and with camouflaged faces. The 'SAS' grabbed Charlie and roughly hustled him away. Newly arrived staff couldn't believe what they had just witnessed. Was this really happening? *Should* it be happening? Where had they taken him? Those, like myself, longer in the tooth, were quick to recognise one of the abseilers – even with his camouflaged face. It was a brilliant 'prank' which, no doubt, Charlie would relate (with embellishments) to his future army colleagues.

Hornchurch – More Flour and Eggs

I was still faced with the issue of student farewells when I became head of Hornchurch. However, the culture was very different, and parental expectations regarding order and control were higher. Thus we issued stern warnings that, while graffitied shirts were OK, flour and eggs, etc., were not. Anyone caught would be suspended. With exams about to start and students preparing to move on to the next stage of their education, this threat could not be taken lightly. It worked reasonably well until the last few minutes of their last day when breathless caretaker Jim came puffing through the front entrance where I was chatting to Mike and Karen, my deputies. He was red-faced and rather sweaty and angrily relayed his news.

'There's a group of Year 11s in the bottom playground chucking flour and eggs at each other. I thought you'd banned that.'

'We certainly did, Jim.' This was over my shoulder as all three of us hurried out. We *had* banned it and knew we had to move fast if we were to stop it – or catch the culprits.

By the time we arrived at the playground, there was just one student left – picking himself up off the tarmac. It was a fair cop, and he made no attempt to escape. At least we'd caught one. A result of sorts. Except… this was the son of the vice chair of the Parent Teacher Association. Sheila was a tireless supporter of the school, and her son had, until this incident, an unblemished school record. However, we had agreed to exclude whoever we caught, and, in Brian's case, that meant missing exams. Whatever the rights and wrongs, I was determined to wriggle out of this one. I arranged a meeting for the following day – still not quite sure what line to take.

It was just after morning break, and Jenny, one of the school secretaries, knocked on my door.

'Andrew, it's Sheila to see you.'

I braced myself for the encounter. There had to be some sort of sanction – otherwise, our threat would appear toothless.

Sheila was ushered in with Brian just behind her. He was taller than his mum but not now with his head down – clearly lowered in shame. It seemed like Sheila had been crying, but maybe that was just my imagination. Her normal cheery demeanour and smiley face was certainly not in evidence. However, it would have been completely out of character for her to come in with all guns blazing.

I got up from behind my desk.

'Hi, Sheila. Hello, Brian.' Neither responded, and I motioned for them to sit opposite me on the two upright chairs in front of my desk. I wanted Sheila to feel there was an air of formality about the meeting.

'I think you know why we called.'

'I do.' Sheila turned to her son. 'Brian thinks he's going to be suspended. I think you know what that would mean. He'd miss both his art exam and his French. It would be a disaster for him. There were lots of other students involved, you know.'

'I do know, but by the time we got to the middle playground, where this was all happening, he was the only one left. It was his bad luck, but he had clearly been involved. He was covered in flour,' I replied.

The evidence *had* been clear, and I was definitely holding firm on that, even though I was still looking for an escape route – halfway between punishment and reprieve.

'I find that hard to believe.'

'To be honest, Sheila, I'm extremely disappointed he was involved. We've made it absolutely clear that anyone involved with flour and eggs would be suspended. Nearly everyone heeded that warning, and in the end, it was only a tiny minority of Year 11s. We know who the others are and will be seeing their parents as well.'

'So what are you going to do?' Sheila fixed me with a stare.

'Well, it was very stupid. Wasn't it, Brian?' His head had remained bowed.

'Look at me, Brian. What on earth made you get involved?'

'I don't know. I just got carried away. It was really stupid.'

'More than stupid, Brian. You knew what the consequences would be and still went ahead – risking your future as a result.'

Brian's head had risen and then dropped again. 'Brian, look at me. What have you got to say?'

'I'm really sorry, Sir.' Brian's lips were trembling. I could see tears welling up. 'It won't happen again.'

'Of course, it won't happen again, Brian. Term's over for you, and you're about to start your exams.'

I let this sink in for a moment, and there was silence. Just the faint tapping of a typewriter in the office across the corridor.

I turned to Sheila. 'Brian's behaviour has put me in a very difficult position. He may have an unblemished school record, but some of those with him certainly haven't. If I let *him* off, I'll have to treat the others in the same way. That would make it look as though we'd issued an empty threat.'

I paused again.

'Very reluctantly, I'm prepared to compromise.'

By the time we'd got to this point in the meeting, and having witnessed what I was sure was Brian's genuine remorse, I had decided what line to take. In response, Sheila's shoulders dropped just a fraction. Brian's head remained down.

'This is what's going to happen, Brian. You're to stay at home for the rest of the term and only come in for exams. If you're seen on-site, outside of exams, that'll be it. You won't be allowed to take any more. Is that clear?' Brian nodded. 'And you are not to talk to any of the others involved. They will be dealt with in the same way.'

'Yes, Sir.'

'Thank you, Sir.'

I turned to Sheila. 'I suggest you keep him at home from now until his exams are over.'

'I am grateful, Mr Macalpine.'

She had clearly taken on board Brian's guilt and was now looking a little sheepish.

'I hope you've understood everything Mr Macalpine has said.'

Brian nodded. It was a dangerous compromise. 'Don't issue a threat you can't (or won't) carry out.' We had only carried out half our threat, and the danger was that we might have appeared weak. However, the episode seemed to have done the trick. We introduced shirt signing instead! That went down well!

Farewell Andrew

When I left the Isle of Dogs, I was departing as deputy and going on to my first headship. My farewell was in the staffroom. There was a gratifyingly large turnout, including many members of the support staff – always a good sign as they quite often felt distanced from the teachers. They included a group, about half a dozen, who worked in the school canteen. I always tried to make time for a chat when I collected my lunch and was delighted to see them in the staffroom. They stood together by the door. Halfway through my own typically moving, profound and humorous speech, they all turned and left. I managed some crack on the lines of, 'Sorry, I was boring you,' which produced a ripple of laughter. Maybe they had meals to prepare, but I had to accept that the quality of my oratory wasn't sufficient to keep them in the staffroom.

When I left Hornchurch – off to my role as an inspector in the same borough – there was a farewell in a local hotel, a good hour's drive from my home in Dulwich. It was a jolly affair, and I savoured it as I drove back along the A13. I arrived home at about midnight, parked the car, and walked towards the front door. As I did, I became aware of a newcomer in the small front garden – a fir tree! It could only be linked with my Hornchurch departure. I couldn't imagine when it was put there, but I certainly had an idea who might have been responsible. We had a head of drama who was a great practical joker. I also think he was quite sorry to see me go, and the lengthy drive and planting of the fir tree was his way of saying he'd miss me. It made my farewell especially memorable and was certainly better than any card could have been.

Farewell Mr Macalpine

Quite often, students arranged for huge farewell cards to be signed – seemingly by anyone you've ever taught. I didn't always get one of those, but I was delighted when I did. Some of the messages, however, were not on those big cards but on cards nevertheless and were rather more personal – and not always a testimony to the quality of the teaching they'd experienced. This book's title is one of those:

'All the best in the future – its been great being teached by you.'

'Cool, calm, and collected, you were alright when you excluded me.'

'...We don't get much homework *(in his new school)* like you used to give us. Plus, the standard of work has lowered...'

'...I hope you come back because it is killing me...'

'Hi, Mac. How are you keeping, fine, I hope... I know that you miss 4G being the best form in the school, and we all miss you. Mrs Hayes is a fairly good teacher, not as understanding and good-looking as you. Anyway, I must go now, the old bags nagging.'

'...It aint the same without you here as our English teacher...'

'Just a word to ask how your job is going (Traitor). I am OK. I hope you don't like your new job, then you can come back even if you make us read.'

These were not cards to go on the sideboard, but I certainly valued them, and I liked to feel they reflected the positive relationships I had with some of the less academic, naughtier kids for whom school, for the most part, was pretty unrewarding.

HEADTEACHERS OF ALL SORTS

Heads have tough jobs. They can be responsible for up to two thousand students and maybe two hundred teaching and support staff. Their roles are multi-faceted, to say the least – get results, make learning attractive and relevant, balance the books, appoint good staff, liaise with parents, ensure student safety, forward plan, look after the site – and others. An intimidating list. Many fulfil these roles brilliantly. The majority tick most but not all of the boxes.

However, for a minority, the pressures are too great, and they resort to eccentric behaviours – operating without restraint when, in theory, at least, they are under the control of local authorities, governors, and now (in 2025) in the case of academies, trustees.

What follows are a few examples of that eccentric minority.

1. This first head put out regular missives, which were lengthy and threatening. The <u>underlining</u> and CAPS were all the head's own:

'Do <u>not</u> allow boys to make their own rules. In the first instance, they are to observe the most important maxim, that pupils are here to be told what to do, to be directed, to be led.'

'<u>As a last resort</u>, corporal punishment may be used. The application of this is limited to about a dozen very experienced staff, who know what is inherent in its use.'

'Canes are kept for use in the office... and such canes are the only ones to be used.' *i.e., Don't imagine you can just pick some up in the local garden centre.*

'I realise fully that there has been an increase in STRESS and STRAIN on some members of staff (I myself am <u>constantly</u> under pressure).'

'Some members of staff need to RE-READ my documents: I have frequently urged this RE-READING. The principles and practice enunciated therein (my documents) are not VOLUNTARY; they are OBLIGATORY and fully in line with the authority's policy.'

2. Here I was applying for the role of second in charge of English:

I would describe the head as young, slick, and smooth-talking. His blond hair was parted in the middle, and he had steely blue eyes. Somehow I sensed he wasn't quite right in the head. Having met me in reception, he took me into his office, sat me down, and looking me in the eyes, said:

'I'm a direct man. I may even call you by your Christian name.'

He seemed to know very little about 'his' school, including, for example, whether classes were streamed or not.

The school's deputy had been there thirty-four years and had the ghostly appearance of someone who'd just stepped out of a cupboard into the sunlight. The head of English had a nervous tic. Politely, I withdrew my application from the asylum.

3. A few years on and I had been shortlisted for an inner London deputy headship – along with five others.

The school was in a very deprived area and not doing well and I had already heard about some of the head's eccentricities prior to my visit. Anyway, the morning arrived and the six of us were shown into her office to await her arrival. We sat there – four of us, including myself, seated round a table, the other two on a sofa. We eventually started making polite conversation. After a few minutes, we noticed a snorting noise. We looked at each other quizzically. It seemed to be coming from under the sofa.

Just then, the head walked in. Small, blonde hair (almost certainly dyed), her wrists encircled with bangles. Face heavily made up.

'There seems to be a strange noise coming from under your sofa,' one of the others commented – bravely, I thought.

At that, there was a muffled bark, and two Pekingese dogs emerged and headed for their mistress.

'Molly and Marmaduke. Come here, my lovelies.'

They scampered, yapping, over to the head, little tails wagging. Somehow she managed to sweep them both up into her arms.

'Aaaah, have you been hiding from these lovely people? There's no need to be frightened.' At this point, she nuzzled into each of them in turn, as you might comfort yourself with a furry scarf on a cold winter's day.

'I love having them. Means I get a chance to give them some exercise.'

I reflected on a head I knew whose dog provided much-valued therapy – particularly for withdrawn students. I couldn't quite see yappy Molly and Marmaduke in that role. I pictured myself as a dog walker and politely withdrew my application.

4. A head I got to know well ended his career following his fourth headship. He took no prisoners. He was big in every sense – voice, figure, assertiveness. You'd have guessed a prop forward in his youth. Typical of his approach was how he dealt with some noisy heating pipes. The local authority sent one of their surveyors around.

The conversation went something like this:-

Surveyor: 'My assistant said you had an issue with your heating pipes.'

James (head): 'Yes. You can hear it now. They're making that gurgling noise. The only time it stops is in the summer when the heating's off.'

'James, I'm sorry. You know the authority's struggling to balance the books at the moment. They're only sanctioning urgent repairs. If those pipes were hanging off the wall and threatening to burst, that'd be a different matter.'

'So you're telling me there's nothing you can do?'

'Fraid so.'

'OK, we'll just put up with it then.'

The note of resignation in James' voice as he terminated the call seemed completely out of character – an impression confirmed when James winked at me as he put the phone down.

Two days later, the local authority received a call from the school secretary.

'Can I have your emergency section, please?'

'Yes – I'll just put you through.'

There is a long wait before someone at the other end picks up the phone.

'Emergencies here. What's the problem?'

'We have a whole corridor of heating pipes just hanging off the wall. The head's terrified that we're about to get flooded.'

Somehow the secretary managed to convey the sense that she was looking around the office, expecting an onrush of water at any moment.

'OK, we'll send someone straight round.'

By then, James was already law unto himself – eventually being dismissed from his fourth headship after he'd rugby-tackled a troublesome student. I didn't find it difficult to draw the line at assaulting students. However, I could never help but admire his 'school comes first' determination.

5. The next head makes some of the more eccentric ones look positively 'normal'.

This was out in the wilds of Hertfordshire. The head is responding to a parent who's written in about school punishments suggesting alternatives such as:

'Boy! That's disgusting behaviour. Fifty lines for you.' Here are some extracts from his reply:-

'Dear Mr…

'Punishments often involve a measure of useless activity. It is often the sense of utter uselessness which is the true punishment rather than the intrinsic activity…'

(His suggestions follow):

1.   LARGE LINES. These are written in large handwriting using a double-line width, i.e., each letter has to be written twice the size one would normally use…
2.   BACKWARD LINES. Under my whole-word reversal, the sentence "I must not play around in the First Year Centre" becomes "Centre Year First the in around play not must I".
3.   A more rigorous task is the SINGLE LETTER REVERSAL – "ertnec raey tsrif eht ni dnuora yalp ton tsum I."
4.   Finally, the most tiresome but potentially the most profitable form is the "Backward Large Lines".

Yours etc.'

Of course, these punishments favoured the most literate. Twice as hard for the less able – and twice the punishment.

My own school line, which I wrote hundreds of times during my five years, was a little more sophisticated: 'Few things are more distressing to a well-regulated mind than to see a boy who ought to know better disporting himself at improper moments.' I used to be able to get it on one line, although, looking back, I can't see what good that did me.

6. Disgruntled parent avoidance.

For most of the above characters, a guardian secretary, whatever she (sadly, I never met a male one, although I've no doubt there are many around now) thought about her boss, would cover for them with a 'Sorry he's not available right now.' Chris, however, a head I got to know and like, when he got wind of an imminent and unwelcome arrival, usually an angry parent, was quick and wiry enough to climb out of his ground-floor office window and disappear.

7. Although sometimes reined in by brave governors, heads wield untrammelled power – as I indicate above. Occasionally, staff register opposition – of a sort.

One such concerned Bill, a tough and unpopular head of a very challenging London school. So tough that he was hardly ever to be seen, whether he was on the premises or not. Randomly, Bill's wife visited the school one day. Staff got wind of this and arranged with the school receptionist that, when she arrived, she would be shown up to the staffroom. The seating there had been so managed that the only chair left for her to sit on had virtually no webbing left under its cushion. Fortunately, her undignified fall to the floor did her no physical harm. A silly schoolboy prank, of course – but the staff involved derived some satisfaction from this small, vicarious token of their opposition to the head.

8. Longevity, eccentricity, and insensitivity – all in one headteacher.

These are accumulated staff memories of a home county head who was in post for twenty-seven years. Throughout that time, she wore the same two outfits – two very similar dresses. They were both polyester and knee length with a rather dull floral pattern and a frilly collar done up to the neck. Every school day (we obviously didn't know about weekends) started with a visit to the hairdresser. During any crisis, she would lock herself in her office and refuse to come out. Incredibly, this included the time when a tree was blown over in a storm, tragically killing a girl who was leaving the school. In fact, she rarely left her office at all. Staff were not allowed to email each other, and in the second decade of the 2000s, she must have been the only headteacher in the country whose office was uncluttered by any electronic device – phones, computers or printers.

9. Making your mark.

A well-known London head trying to make his mark in a challenging school had a student slip and fall right outside his office one afternoon. The student gashed his head on a noticeboard as he fell, leaving a smear of blood on the wall. The head decided to leave the dried blood there for some weeks as stories circulated amongst students, and no doubt some staff, that this was the price to pay for poor behaviour!

10. Times have changed – for the better.

The characters and their behaviours described above might just be seen as humorous eccentricities until you realise these heads have responsibility, collectively, for thousands of children – and all those who teach them. John Cleese's character in *Clockwise* was closer to the truth than might be imagined.

INSPECTIONS AND THEIR STRESSES

Inspections in the 1990s were quite different from those 'no notice' ones experienced by schools in the 2020s. Each school was inspected for a whole week every six years and given two months' notice to prepare. It was criticised as being extremely disruptive. And, in the eyes of many, it enabled schools to present a distorted picture of themselves. Such were the inspections I experienced as head.

They certainly put schools on the spot. You hoped there weren't cracks to be identified by the inspection team, but if there were, how could you paper over them without being found out? Also, you didn't want visiting inspectors encountering your naughtiest students. It was amazing how some of those managed to get a day off at crucial moments. A well-known head put together a whole coachload of her 'undesirables' and sent them far away on a field trip. She was subsequently honoured by the Queen for services to education! I have to confess I papered over a few cracks every now and then. However, I never got rid of undesirables. Another 'wheeze' was keeping permanently excluded (expelled) students off the stats. Quite rightly, that was stopped – with even those who had been sent to another school, or to a PRU (Pupil Referral Units set up to cater for the most disruptive students), being counted.

Ironically, one of the most important outcomes for schools, then and now – exam results – can be judged by your chief inspector trawling through the data with their feet up, a glass of wine by their side – at home.

In the run-up to an inspection, as with so many challenges, preparation was key. Every lesson had to be planned, every book marked, every piece of litter picked up, every graffiti scrawl removed, everyone's lines rehearsed.

The pressure was intense. I knew a head of department who would go so far as to learn her lesson plans for the week off by heart, and I once worked with a second-in-department whose anxiety about being visited increased as the week went on – to the point where she eventually collapsed with exhaustion. Inspectors, if they have ever worked in a school, often forget the stress their visits cause.

Touring your school with a member of the inspection team would be carefully planned. Constant internal reminders bounced around in your head – where to go, who to see, how to explain known defects, or those being picked up.

'At all costs, avoid Mr B's biology group – his students knowledge of anatomy owes more to the playground than to his teaching. A visit to Miss H's Year 9 Spanish class could well interrupt the umpteenth request for something no Spanish textbook would ever reveal. Don't let Mr A collar your inspector. He's on his way out and has a particularly jaundiced view of the school.'

In practice, such was the fever of expectation and excitement that most staff *wanted* that knock on the classroom door and anticipated with pleasure the discrete sidling in of whichever inspector had chosen to visit. Conversely, those not visited felt disappointed. They'd had a week of tense anticipation and no chance to show off their students – or themselves.

Students, whatever they might say publicly, really don't want to be in 'a crap school'. Thus, more often than not, there were pleasant surprises. With an inspector in tow, you couldn't keep walking past classes with a simple, 'they're doing an exam', or, 'better not disturb them', or even, 'they're rehearsing a play'. So, holding your breath, you'd walk into Mr K's Year 10 GCSE English lesson. His record isn't great, and the odds are that the class won't impress, but – lo and behold – they've magically transformed into serious students: putting their hands up to answer questions, listening attentively to each other and saying how much they enjoy the subject. You discovered their loyalty to the school, whatever they felt about it, was greater than their loyalty to this visitor. Mr K also discovered that his class had got through the forty-minute lesson plan in half an hour – leaving him desperately stranded for ten minutes!

That was then. In the intervening years, there have been regular changes to the framework – many of them designed to stop schools from putting on a well-rehearsed but misleading performance. Currently, a school will get notice between ten thirty a.m. and two p.m. on the day before the inspection starts. One day rather than two months!

Also, inspections last for two or three days rather than a week. And, where there are serious concerns, the lead inspector will normally phone the school fifteen minutes before arriving! Just time to tidy your desk.

MISTAKEN IDENTITY

I followed up my career in education with a spell as a magistrate, just squeaking in as a sixty-five-year-old after the retirement age was raised from sixty-five to seventy. It gave me an insight into the workings or otherwise of our legal system. For example, observing a range of prosecutors and managers, from impressive to incompetent. One regular CPS prosecutor we had was so hopeless we had to prompt his interrogations! There were many brilliant bench chairs, but 'wingers' (those who sit either side of the chair) often appeared not to have taken on the role of impartiality. I didn't have time to train to become a chair, but I have no doubt I wouldn't have fallen into the brilliant category. However, I did consider myself relatively impartial. The role was interesting and, I liked to think, useful.

By a bizarre coincidence, on the day of my seventieth birthday – the day I ceased to be able to sit as a magistrate – I found myself delivering my first Personal, Social and Health Education (PSHE) session at a Barnet school... invited as an active magistrate! Which, of course, I no longer was. I wasn't going to confess this masquerade to the head, Chris, nor to Neil, the deputy taking me on. His response would probably have been, 'Don't let's worry about that,' given that he was delighted to be filling a PSHE space on the timetable with a fresh face who had actual experience of what they were talking about.

Organising these sessions was challenging in the extreme. In each year group, all the sessions happened at the same time. There were eight classes to be covered. The members of staff involved were being asked to stray from the comfort of their mainstream teaching subject into such areas as puberty, mental health and personal hygiene. Plenty of scope for sniggering and inappropriate questions there.

Anyway, on day one, Neil came into the class of sixteen-year-olds with me and gave one of those fulsome introductions that always seem to set the bar just a bit too high for comfort.

After this first session, I reported back. 'How did it go?' he asked.

Talking to students about criminality is unlikely to fail, and I had put together enough slides dealing with criminality to have been pretty confident the sessions would pass muster. And so it proved. That was enough for Neil. He was always busy – finding teachers who were free (but hiding) and directing visitors like myself who didn't know where they were supposed to be. He wasn't going to waste time on a post-mortem. From then on, he would introduce my weekly session with: 'This is Mr Macalpine. He's going to talk to you about being a magistrate.' He would only just manage to complete the sentence before he left the classroom. I was quite happy with that. I just wanted to get on with the session. They were thirty minutes long and took Year 11 students through as many aspects of crime and punishment as could be crammed into the slot. Whatever my abilities as a presenter, I was onto a winner with my fifteen- and sixteen-year-olds. Drugs, GBH, robbery, burglary, knife crime, the age of criminal responsibility (surprising variations depending on the country). These were enough to make even the most reluctant participants sit up.

I always left enough room for questions at the end of each session, but not so much that they started to get restless – mentally moving on to whatever they had next. Just as I got to…

'OK. We need to finish there. You can pack up and go off to your next lesson.' And just as the class started to move towards the door, a voice rang out from the back of the room.

'You put me away!' It was an angry accusation and certainly unnerved me. I had never actually trained as a youth magistrate, but maybe I had forgotten some event.

I could see who it was: a boy who had been sitting at the back – tall, spotty-faced and with lank hair and black trousers instead of the uniform grey, his shirt hanging out. He had no blazer or tie. I certainly didn't recognise him from any case I'd ever sat on.

Students who hadn't yet left stopped in their tracks and looked from me to the boy and back again – some, I had no doubt, genuinely shocked. Others were probably looking for a bit of sport and wondering what they were about to witness. I *certainly* didn't want witnesses to whatever was about to happen.

'Right, off you go.' I put on the sternest voice I could muster as the last reluctant stragglers left the room. As they disappeared, the boy approached me. I didn't think I was about to be assaulted, but I hadn't dismissed the possibility and backed off a fraction. By this time, he was standing in front of my desk. He was a good couple of inches taller than me. His whole body seemed tensed, shoulders up, fists clenched by his side – his eyes fixed on mine.

'I recognise you. You put me away.'

'What's your name?' By this time, I was pretty certain he'd got it wrong – but things still seemed on a knife edge.

'Michael,' he spat back.

I knew I had to start talking him down and that I needed to appear calm.

'OK, Michael. What court was this?'

There was a pause. 'Willesden.'

'And when was this?'

Another pause. 'Last year.' The fact that I was engaging with him seemed to be – ever so slightly – defusing the situation. He was now more sullen than angry. His shoulders had dropped a little, and his fists were not quite so knuckle white.

By this time, I realised, to my relief, that whatever Michael had done and wherever he'd been, I'd had nothing to do with it.

'Michael, I can promise you I've never even been to Willesden Magistrates Court. Also, I've never dealt with young offenders. You must be confusing me with someone else.'

I was curious to find out what he had done and somehow engage him in conversation as much as anything to see where he'd got to with his life. However, before I could start questioning him, he'd marched off – his body still tense. I guessed his manner towards me was characteristic of his behaviour in general and that his fellow students would be inclined to give him a wide berth.

Although I never discovered what he'd been found guilty of, I wouldn't have been surprised if violence had been involved.

When I finally tracked Neil down and relayed the incident, his reply was, 'Oh, yes. Sorry, I should have warned you about him. It's rare he appears.' Thanks, Neil!

I carried on with the sessions for a further five years. From time to time, there were students who already seemed to know so much about the law that they made me suspicious about what they might have been up to. However, I never had a repeat of the Michael situation.

The experience with Michael made me regret I hadn't had the opportunity of sitting in the Youth Court (the training would have taken me beyond the five years I was able to sit). Staff in schools dealing with 'naughty' children get frustrated that they don't have time to follow them up once they've disappeared. Sometimes, word comes back, e.g., they've been arrested and are awaiting trial, they're inside, or they've left home. Sometimes, and best of all, they've settled down.

If they have been accused of a crime and are between the ages of ten and seventeen, they appear in front of magistrates in a Youth Court. These magistrates are specially trained to deal with young people. Proceedings are much less formal than in a normal court. There will always be a member of the Youth Offending Team available to talk to the youth and present sentencing options to the Bench. And, quite rightly, in the Youth Court, there is much more emphasis than in the Adult Court on supporting the welfare and rehabilitation of the young person.

NAMES ARE IMPORTANT

Although heads are increasingly seen as managers rather than ex-teachers, they're still expected to know the names of the majority of their staff. And, as I've indicated elsewhere, that can be as many as two hundred. An extremely challenging task.

At my Barnet school, we had two Asian support staff. They were friendly and engaging and always addressed me as 'Andrew'. To my enduring shame, although I knew their names, I could never remember who was who. I had absolutely no excuse – they certainly didn't look the same. Feebly defending myself, I can say I only ever encountered them in the staffroom, and interaction was limited. Five years went by without me ever addressing either of them by name. Of course, I always greeted them as though I knew. But it's a kind of bluff which you might think you're getting away with, and, if you're honest, you can imagine the conversation that might take place after you've gone.

'Have you noticed? He never calls me by my name. I don't think he knows it.'

As for students, they all know your name and, in any case,

will usually address you as 'Sir'. Unless you teach them or have regular encounters with them (as, for example, you might with prefects), they don't expect you to know their names.

I have recounted my chastening experience with the two support staff. I had a similar one with a student who I seemed to encounter quite frequently.

As with so many students, the usual exchange was:

'Hello.'

'Hello Sir?'

With David, it was not a usual exchange. We often had a chat on the lines of:

'How's the work going?'

'What are you up to today?'

I prided myself that we had a connection, although, in the back of my mind, there was a sense that if I knew his name, I would call him by it. That sense was exacerbated by the fact that David was now in his fifth year at the school, and our exchanges had been repeated many times.

This particular morning, I met him on a landing on the main staircase. He was coming up. I was going down. We both stopped – moving out of the way of staff and students passing us.

'Hello, Sir.'

'How's it going then? Are you ready for your first exam? What is it? English?'

'All good thank you.'

'Well, good luck. I'm sure you'll do well.'

By this time, I was feeling pretty pleased with yet another positive interaction with David and had started to move on up the stairs. Just as I turned to move away:

'You don't know my name, do you, Sir?'

I was stopped in my tracks. My pride deflated like a punctured balloon. I turned back to face David. I knew that 'No, I don't' was certainly not on the cards. David had a friend with him who was lingering – waiting to go downstairs. At least he wasn't someone I was familiar with, and I really couldn't imagine him piping up with, 'Nor mine, Sir.'

For some reason, I had 'D' in my, by now, rather scrambled mind.

'It's Daniel.'

David shook his head.

Foolishly I abandoned 'D' and, in my panic, just guessed. 'Trevor.'

David smiled. He clearly sensed my discomfort – although I felt there was more sympathy there than derision. Nevertheless, I couldn't go on flailing around – working my way randomly through the alphabet. I just wanted what had started as a pleasant encounter but had turned into a stomach-churner to end.

'It's David, Sir.' There was still a 'Sir' but probably with rather diminished respect behind it.

We went our separate ways, with me inwardly repeating 'David' over and over again.

On a different tack, throughout my time in schools I noticed a gender difference regarding names. An article in the *Daily Express* (November 1978) supported the impression: 'In some schools, the boys are called by surnames and the girls by Christian (sic) names.' As recently as 2018, a team of psychologists at Cornell University found that people were twice as likely to call male professionals by their surname than they were women (*Independent* – July 2018).

My own name has always been good to play with – whether accidentally or on purpose. Over the years, there have been many variations – some on notes or pieces of work. Occasionally some were verbalised:

Malcalpine

McCroupain

McAffine

Callpin

McCowpine

McKalpin

Mack Calpine

McKatpin

I often wished I'd been named 'Smith' or 'Brown'!

OBSESSIONS – LITTER AND GRAFFITI

'Tell us, Mr Macalpine, what's your attitude towards litter?'

That could well be the first question at an interview for prospective heads.

Headteachers are obsessed with litter. My daughter, Zoe, at her large secondary school in north London, became fascinated by what she termed 'the Mitchell swoop'. This in reference to the head's ability to pick up litter without breaking stride. If she found herself walking down the same corridor, she would retreat a respectful distance in order to witness the elegance of the dip, catch and rise – much as predatory birds will pick fish from the sea.

I like to think I had internalised something of the Mitchell swoop long before my first headship. Incomprehensibly, no interviewing panel ever asked me a question about litter.

Nevertheless, it remained an obsession – and one I clearly shared with headteacher colleagues up and down the country. There was an incident with a particularly difficult fifteen-year-old. I had just about managed to keep him in after school, much to his annoyance and frustration. I finally let him go – partly because he was about to get himself into even more trouble, partly because I was expecting a visitor – the deputy from a neighbouring school coming to discuss some class observations she wanted to set up.

Some twenty minutes later, after releasing the boy, I happened to look out of my office window, which overlooked the front of the school. Dusk was starting to settle, but I could make out patches of white all the way down the drive leading some one hundred yards to the school gates. Being somewhat puzzled, I decided to investigate. Stepping outside the front entrance, I soon encountered the first 'white patch'. It was a piece of blank A4 paper.

I had never really considered what those 480-page reams of paper separated sheet by sheet might look like. They look so neat in their packets or sitting on the printer tray. Nor, I'm sure, had my detainee – clearly the culprit. He must have found the packet on his way out and, in a final show of defiance (for that day at least), had scattered the contents.

I started to gather up the sheets – mostly one by one. No 'Mitchell swoop' here – more a crouching walk reminiscent of some ancient ancestor. All the while trying to keep fingernails intact as they inserted themselves between cheap A4 paper and asphalt.

I'd got some three-quarters of the way to the gates when I became aware of a body looming over me.

'Hi. I'm Janice. You must be the head.'

Although she'd never seen me before, she wasn't asking a question – just making an intelligent observation.

Obsessions, and mine was (and still is) an obsession, can backfire, viz., my visit to a south-London school as a prospective candidate for the headship. The head, Bernie, as he was known to all, was about to retire. It was well earned. He had worked hard to raise standards in what might have been described as a 'sink school' when he took over. He had definitely lifted it out of the mire, and I'm sure he would have been hoping for a decent field of applicants to take over. The fact that I was visiting by myself suggested otherwise.

Bernie greeted me at the school's entrance which, I felt, was a nice touch. There was no traipsing to the school office and being told, 'He'll be with you in a minute.'

He was imposingly tall and, like the majority of his students, black.

We stood chatting while looking out towards the front of the school. I had spotted, and I was sure he had, too, a piece of litter on the floor between us and the entrance doors. It was break, and just then a couple of girls walked past.

'Pick up that piece of litter can you please, girls.'

With hindsight, it was probably a risk I wouldn't have taken. Anyway, whether a reasonable or unreasonable request, the girls took no notice and just walked straight past. Mortifying for him, I'm sure, and embarrassing for me. Without saying a word, Bernie went and picked up the offending article himself, and we retreated to his office. I decided the headship would be a tough ask that I wasn't quite ready for.

A second question in that hypothetical headship interview might go as follows:

'And what about graffiti?'

Headteachers are also obsessed with graffiti. There are many ways to deface, or further deface, a pristine surface. The spray can is often the weapon of choice, although, in the hands of someone like Banksy, it can be likened to an artist's brush. He's not the only person who's established himself as graffiti 'artist'. There are now companies that hire them out, and their work can be beautiful. However, heads prefer to quote the definition of graffiti as being illegal and 'involving the unauthorised marking of public space by an individual or group' (Oxford Languages). Their view and, I have to say, my own, is that a spray can in the wrong hands can wreak havoc. Anything from the abusive 'Smithy's a wanker' to the obscene – images of dicks or tits. Occasional attempts at artistry (very nice but not on the gym wall, please) rarely work, and even if they do, they're likely to encourage lesser talents to have a go. It's usually the caretaker's job to remove graffiti. Cue more of the usual observations and complaints…

'Those bloody kids. I haven't got time to keep rubbing down walls. Can't we find out who's doing this?'

Graffiti has to be removed as soon as you find it, i.e. to ensure it doesn't encourage others. If it's after school and there's no caretaker around, it falls to muggins.

And so to an after-school, inter-school staff cricket match. I fancied playing myself, but before I had the embarrassment of not being asked, I made mention of how much work I had to do that afternoon. However, about the time the opposition was due to arrive, I was making my way across the playground towards the art block when I spotted on its wall a large jumble of hieroglyphics which I recognised as a 'tag'. As far as I was concerned, they were meaningless symbols which meant nothing except to the perpetrator and their mates. I knew there was no chance of tracking down the 'artist'. It had to be removed ASAP – certainly before the morning influx of students. Having equipped myself, I set to work with a stiff brush.

Meanwhile, the two cricket teams, mostly in whites but with a smattering of motley attire, were making their way towards the field at the back of the main building – and past the art block. They were chatting away when one of the visitors noticed this man in a white boiler suit furiously attacking graffiti on the side wall of the building. As relayed to me subsequently, the exchange went something like this:

Visiting cricketer: 'Good to see your caretaker hard at it. Ours are useless.'

Host staff member: 'Oh no. That's not our caretaker. That's the head.'

At the risk of looking ridiculous, I probably earned a few brownie points.

Obviously, I'm not serious about those interview questions, but litter, graffiti, scruffy kids, tired displays, poor signage, and unwelcome reception areas all militate against the pride that you, as head, are trying to engender in the minds of staff and students. And those parents whose children you are trying to recruit will look elsewhere.

PARTIAL SUCCESS – TOTAL FAILURE

Peckham in 1971. In my introduction to Peckham, I referred to those youngsters desperate to get out of school and start working (in the 'real world') as soon as possible – in particular, white working-class boys. They were bottom of the heap then, and it appears little has changed. A report published by the Ambition Institute in 2020 found that white pupils on free school meals had significantly worse GCSE results than black or Bangladeshi pupils – the two next lowest groups.

Darren certainly came into the 'bottom of the heap' category. Tall with a mess of long, straggly, ginger hair, he was a stereotype of the 'Can't wait to get out' brigade. He was fourteen, with a year to go until he was 'free'. Mind you, it could have been worse. In 1972, ROSLA (Raising of the School Leaving Age) came in, and Darren would have had to wait two years before he could leave. He would probably have voted with his feet, i.e., literally walked away. He never did homework, never had his books – or anything to write with. His dad was a chippy, and Darren just wanted to join him and start earning.

On this particular day, as his form tutor, I was due to go and see his parents after school. Darren had punched another boy in his maths class and had been suspended. My aim was to register a 'final warning' – of which he'd had several. The parents had become used to such visits – as had I.

Darren lived on an estate of terraced houses about half a mile from the school. As I turned a corner and the familiar red front door came into view, I saw Darren striding towards me.

He had an explosive temper, and certainly not for the first time, I felt he was up to no good. The rather worrying difference on this occasion was that he was carrying a large saw. He was angry, armed, young and strong. Despite this, and for some reason I couldn't explain, a strange sense of calm came over me. I think it was a combination of knowing Darren and, in the past, having talked to him about where his behaviour was leading. At the same time, I knew that any agitation on my part would exacerbate the situation. I turned and started walking alongside him – hoping he wouldn't just make a run for it or threaten me with his saw. I was on his left as he continued walking – the saw swinging back and forth in his right hand.

'Where you off to, Darren?'

'Billy's. He won't know what's hit him – the cunt.'

I knew Billy – another boy in the same year – who also couldn't wait to leave and whose appearances were rare.

'Why? What's this all about then?'

'He dissed my mum. He's done it before. Not going to do it again, though.'

'I can understand how angry you are, Darren. That would piss me off as well. But attacking him with a saw is just going to get you into a load of trouble and make things worse.'

'I don't give a fuck. I just want to get him.' I tried to avoid the saw as the pace quickened.

'And end up being arrested? You don't want that – and your mum definitely wouldn't. And I don't want to see you getting kicked out of school.'

That last bit was true – but I couldn't say I'd be shedding tears when he finally left.

Silence. The pace slowed just a fraction. There was a sense of steam being let out. We walked on for a while.

'He just gets on my tits – that's all.'

'Of course, he does. He's already in lots of trouble himself.' Silence. We walked on.

'Why don't you give me the saw, Darren, and we'll sort this out on Monday. He won't get away with it, and you won't end up in a police station.'

We continued walking. After a while, we stopped, and Darren handed me the saw. By now, it seemed all his aggression had ebbed away. He didn't look sheepish but certainly seemed relieved.

'Thanks, Darren. I assume you got this from your dad's stuff. I'd better look after it for you. You'll need to come and see me first thing on Monday. Meanwhile, just stay out of trouble.'

'Thanks. Sir... so what's going to happen to me?'

'We'll deal with that on Monday. Meanwhile, you need to get home.'

Darren walked off towards his house, and I went home – still carrying his saw. (Unlike Darren, I probably looked legitimate enough not to be stopped.) Of course, he wasn't the only one wondering what was going to happen next. I could understand his frustration about school. At the same time, his temper and aggression were almost certain to get him into serious trouble. A permanent exclusion (an expulsion, in other words) was likely to leave him on the scrapheap. At the time, there were – and still are – units for children who can't cope with normal school, and with whom normal schools can't cope. Places have always been at a premium, but we were eventually able to get Darren into one of the units.

In the immediate future, things might not get much better for Darren but, on this occasion at least, with a little help from me, he'd avoid the police.

I was no help at all with the next incident. Cut to a few years later – the Isle of Dogs. Morning break. Breaktimes at this school were stressful at the best of times, with disputes, extortion and, from time to time, fights. On top of all this, there had been a spate of gang-related stuff with a complaint from our nearest neighbour that boys from our school had been hanging around with the clear intention, so we were told, of paying off an old score.

I had started my day with a couple of demanding lessons – bright A-level students testing my understanding of the metaphysical and convincing me, not for the first time, that A-level teaching wasn't for me. This was followed by a drama 'cover' lesson. Although Heather, recovering from an operation, had left a lesson plan, I was not about to run through a range of drama activities which I knew she'd be brilliant at but which would leave me feeling completely out of control. Despite protests, I fell back on reading plays rather than acting them.

Staffroom coffee and a sit down were very welcome. I had bluffed my way through the lesson, almost, but not quite, implying that Heather had suggested reading rather than performing and ignoring pleas on the lines of 'But, Sir, we always do performances in this lesson.'

A knock on the staffroom door. No one moved for a moment, but I could see that Pauline, my colleague in the English department, was about to leave and had opened the door. I couldn't see who she was talking to, but after a muttered conversation, she turned back to the staffroom.

'They need help in the top playground. Apparently, there are some intruders on-site.' It was almost a command.

Despite this, there was a range of responses – some staff urgently leaping to their feet. Older, 'wiser' ones wearily easing themselves out of armchairs. I got up from my seat at a table. The staffroom emptied – patchily.

I found myself behind Cecil, head of history – white-haired and ponderous at the best of times. He was shuffling his way out alongside his friend Pat, another leftover from the grammar school days in Poplar. Pat's original six foot two was now down to about five eleven courtesy of a stoop which was probably brought on by three years of battling with what I once heard him refer to as 'oiks'.

'God knows how many times we've had these incidents,' said Pat.

Cecil echoed this. 'Yes, they certainly seem to be becoming more frequent. You know, I can't remember a single occasion when we were in Poplar when we had kids coming on-site like this. I suggest we take our time.'

At this point, I overtook them and quickened my pace,

catching up with three staff members going through the outside door to the playground. Although I felt impelled to help sort whatever fracas was taking place, I could feel my heart beating faster.

'They're probably gone by now,' said Amil, holding the door open for me. Amil was always calm and relaxed – certainly not given to panic. The exit opened out onto a passageway leading up to both playgrounds. You then either turned left at the end or went straight on. The other three disappeared left while I carried straight on, thinking I'd definitely get to the playground before them. As I reached the end of the passageway, I heard pounding feet coming towards me. Almost immediately, they came into view – five of them. They were clearly the culprits heading out of the playground, out of the school and probably, scot-free. I had been going in one direction and them in another. They looked like fifteen or sixteen-year-olds and were armed with baseball bats. There was little I could do about the group as a whole, but there was a straggler at the back – running towards me. I knew, for sure, where he'd been and what he'd probably done. He was clearly one of the intruders. All I needed to do was stick my foot out, and he would have gone flying. But… I froze. Fear took hold. I was just frightened. I might get hurt – my foot might get injured. He might get up and attack me. I just let him run past and carried on towards the playground – pretending, in my mind, that I was en route to dealing with the trouble, but, in reality, knowing that I was already too late.

That moment of cowardice has haunted me ever since. As with Darren and his saw, I usually felt calm in situations where there might be a threat of violence and generally managed to defuse them.

This was different. The situation was already out of control. I'd never had to face anything so threatening either before or since, so I don't really know whether I'd be calm and decisive on another occasion – or panicky as I was that time.

Postscript. I subsequently found out that the intruders had been targeting Dave Matthews, a fifteen-year-old. While being appalled at the attack, we were not totally surprised, given Dave's involvement with gang warfare beyond the school's gates. It would have been nice to think he'd learnt a lesson. The reality was that tensions between various local groups would only increase.

PASTY FACED

Post-headship I joined the London Challenge – a highly successful government scheme set up in 2003 to support failing or potentially failing schools in the London area. I was a frequent visitor to a Catholic boys' school in Brent – crumbling, chaotic and always on edge. The school was in total contrast to its girls' counterpart with 'convent' at the front of its name. The convent had polished wooden floors and a sense of peace and quiet which wouldn't have been out of place in a nunnery. It was ruled, with a rod of iron, by its female head. A rod of steel was needed in the boys' school.

Part of my role this particular day was to observe and assess a range of lessons in the boys' school.

My first observation and the school's first period of the day was Year 7 maths – a class of eighteen boys – sixteen of them BAME plus one probably Greek and one Portuguese. The class's full complement was nineteen. As was my custom with observations, I was sitting halfway down one side of the room in order to get the best possible view of the whole class.

After about twenty minutes, student number nineteen walks in – white, very white, pasty-faced, skinny and clearly undernourished – his hair plastered down and probably never washed. He looks as though he lives under the stairs. It's a boiling hot June day with ties loosened and blazers off. Number nineteen is dragging a grey sweater along the floor. He doesn't have a blazer or a tie – only a grey sweater. Hints of surliness and defiance – head down, a kind of shuffling gait – all probably established through having to respond to constant reprimands. He wouldn't be out of place in Fagin's gang of pickpockets.

This is Colin. He walks to a free table and slumps himself down.

From my vantage point at the side, I've got a good view of him.

Amy, an experienced teacher of long-standing, knows not to take him on when the lesson's still got ten minutes to run. She carries on with basic equations on the whiteboard, turning around from time to time to check on the class and, I'm guessing, on Colin.

The buzzer goes. 'Pack away quickly, please, 7H and stand behind your tables.' She dismisses the class row by row. It comes to Colin's row, and he makes to leave. Amy calls him back.

'Colin. Come here, please. I need a word.'

Colin stops by the classroom door. The rest of the class has sidled around him. Colin turns towards the corridor outside. He's straining on a leash – desperate to get out of the classroom but not quite able to…

'Colin. Come here.' Finally, he turns round.

'Colin, where's your bag?'

'Ain't got one.' He turns to go.

'Why were you late?' Amy's tone is direct without being confrontational. She knows it's a miracle Colin's made it to school at all.

'Just was.' Shoulder shrug.

'Have you got anything to write with?'

'No.'

'Do you want a pen or pencil?'

'Nope.' And he's gone.

I'd seen many Colins' in my time. There was always a back story – frequently sad, if not tragic.

Watching Amy's sensitive handling of him, I guess she knows much of that back story.

I have a brief chat with Amy, who's tidying up her desk as she greets the next class.

'I guess you want to know about Colin. A large family with a mum on benefits. Colin's got brothers here and sisters at the convent. All the boys are in trouble from time to time. Mum's just about coping.'

Meanwhile, the classroom has filled up – bags are being dropped, and chairs scraped back. I know I shouldn't be taking up any more of Amy's time.

As if echoing my thoughts, Amy says, 'Sorry, but I need to get this lesson going. Catch me at lunchtime if you want.'

'Of course. Understood. Yes – I'll hope to catch up with you at lunchtime.'

After lunch, and a brief session with Amy, where I learn more about Colin's family, I'm changing my usual routine and sitting at the back – of a science lesson. By 'back', I mean as far from the teacher as it would be possible to get in any of the school's classrooms. No chance for the teacher at the front to see any mischief going on there. The class is an amalgam of three different science groups – put together because the others have gone on a trip. The remainder either haven't paid, haven't brought back their permission notes – or have just been banned from going. Not an easy class to handle. It takes me a while to realise that one of the classes is Colin's – but no sign of Colin. In his case, I can't imagine either money or a permission slip would have been forthcoming.

Some ten minutes into the lesson, I think I hear a thump behind me. I can't really explain this as I'm pretty sure there's no class next door – but I ignore it. However, I notice two students at a table on my left, looking at each other. Neither of them is taking any notice of the teacher – or doing any work. There's a table of four boys in front of them (all the boys have managed to seat themselves at the back of the class – as ever), and two of them turn around giggling and mouthing something which I can't decipher. Then, out of the corner of my eye, I think I see the floor-level cupboard door behind me twitch. I sense there's someone or something in there. For a moment, I remain seated – torn between suggesting to the boys that they need to get on with their work ('probably' need to get on with their work might be more appropriate given that they don't know me from Adam) – and investigating the cupboard. I bend down to open the cupboard door – not knowing what, if anything, I'm going to see, and there's Colin crouched inside, still clutching his grey sweater. He's in this very cramped space and looking down at the floor of the cupboard. I can't ignore what I'm witnessing.

'Colin, you need to get out of there.'

He emerges holding a fistful of biros and pencils.

Still standing, he manages to snap a couple of these in half in front of the student nearest him. They clatter to the floor. He then takes a seat at the table next to me at the back of the class in the huge lab. The teacher, already struggling with a mixed, motley and restless group and far away at the other end, hasn't noticed the addition to her numbers. Nor has she noticed that no one in the two back rows is facing her. There's a chaotic scramble as she dismisses the class at the end of the lesson. Standing by the door, I relay the incident to her at the same time as watching Colin, now twenty yards down the corridor, leaving a trail of pens and pencils behind him, which he continues to throw down on the floor. Before I leave, I speak to the head, who has little to say apart from the fact that it was one of Colin's very rare appearances.

Children like Colin exist in every inner-city school. As Amy rightly pointed out, in ninety-nine cases out of a hundred, there's a sad back story with poor housing and low-paid employment adding to the challenges every parent faces bringing up teenage children. It's tempting for school staff to take on the role of social worker – and many do. However, that's really not appropriate as it means neglecting their primary function of helping children to learn. Where schools are large enough, they can actually employ someone full-time who will work with social services to help families in need. Not every school can go that far, but some contact with social services is essential for all but the most advantaged schools.

REFERENCES

In the 1980s and 1990s, heads could write more or less what they wanted in a reference. And short of libel or slander, there was unlikely to be any comeback. So, for example, a 'rave' reference could either indicate a supportive head helping a talented teacher get a promotion – or it might be an attempt to offload someone.

Around the mid-1980s on the Isle of Dogs, we were looking to fill two posts – English and physics. I received two similar references. Both extolled outstanding character and ability: 'You would be delighted to get her', and, 'We would be devastated to lose him'. We appointed both. One was an English teacher who proved to be brilliant – until, with our blessing, she went off to write poetry. The other was a physics teacher – male, as was then almost always the case. (Even now, in 2025, female physics teachers are a rarity.) His interview wowed us. His experience, his knowledge of the subject, and his ability to articulate the importance of physics were all hugely impressive. As far as the appointments panel was concerned (including myself, I'm ashamed to say), it was a case of 'act in haste, repent at leisure'. The 'outstanding' physics teacher proved to have other interests. He quickly became the school's NAS/UWT rep (National Association of Schoolmasters/Union of Women Teachers), calling regular meetings in school and attending many more outside. He was doing all he could to ferment a 'workers' revolution. At the time, I was still a member of the 'other' union

– the NUT (National Union of Teachers), but I was finding this increasingly conflicting. As acting deputy, I was helping to run the school. Taking part in union action often meant undermining that role. (There is more on this under 'Strikes' below.)

As to our physics teacher, we were left regretting our precipitate action in appointing him.

Although not as hard to find as physics teachers (especially female ones), good music teachers were, and still are, thin on the ground. Given a choice, a significant number would rather be musicians, not teachers. They may be good with individuals, but many have minimal capacity for passing on their passion to whole classes of students, with all the planning, marking and disciplining that's involved.

In Peckham, we had a head of music – his was a department of one – Mr Hughes. His only defects were class control, organisation and poor attendance (the latter stress-related, following the first two). In short, he was a disaster. To be fair, he was aware of his shortcomings and was keen to move out and on – ideally to a small private prep school where, one hoped, his stress levels would quickly drop. In this, he was supported enthusiastically by the head at the time. It was no secret that he was considered a liability.

It came as a shock when I realised the lengths our head was willing to go to in order to get rid of the lacklustre Mr Hughes. One day I found myself in his secretary's office (the head was out, and his secretary was nowhere to be seen). I was standing next to a filing tray at the top of which was a reference headed, in bold letters, 'Reference on behalf of Jason Hughes'. Hard to miss. With half an eye on the door and half an ear on the sound of footsteps, I was able to scan enough of the reference to realise my head had been prepared to perjure himself in a desperate effort to move Mr Hughes on. My eye was caught by a series of absurd phrases: 'outstanding ability to engage students', 'extraordinary musicality', 'infectious enthusiasm', 'would be a huge loss', etc. I took a step closer to the sheet of paper, squinting at the page and unable to believe my eyes. They were just bare-faced lies. Although I could certainly understand the head's wish to offload Mr Hughes, I couldn't go along with the implementation. Such behaviour might well end up in court in 2025. Forty years ago, reference writing was an art – often a dark one. How to imply that your star teacher wasn't quite ready for promotion (even though she was) and, without going as far as the reference on Mr Hughes, suggest your no-hoper had potential and might well flourish in a different setting. Now references have become little more than bland statements of fact.

'This is a person. They exist.' The fact that you can sue for damaging comments makes headteachers wary, and although there is no obligation to provide a reference, it is rare that they don't.

Quite often, where the bland statements of fact mask the truth about an applicant, there'll be an invitation on the lines of, 'Please contact me if I can be of any further help.' At this point, warning bells should sound!

SMOKING

Growing up in north London in the 1950s, it seemed everyone smoked – actually, some eighty per cent of the population. People smoked in shops, on TV, and in films. People even smoked at work. It was seen as cool, glamorous – and cheap. My parents smoked, and so did their friends. There were always ashtrays and cigarette lighters (not matches!) in our living room.

In 1953, when I was in my last year at prep school, myself and three friends decided to get together after school to smoke. We could have just stolen cigarettes from home. However, we were a little more ambitious than that and decided on pipes – not the adult ones our grandads had where they seemed to spend forever pushing tobacco into the bowl ('tamping' to the uninitiated) – rather miniature ones which we knew Woolies sold. We felt these would be easier to get hold of and suit the ambitions of us twelve-year-olds rather better. We needed pipes plus matches plus tobacco, and we divvied up the roles between us with Jemil, our fourth member, as a lookout. I got given Woolies for the pipes, and although I was no Artful Dodger, I had established some 'street cred' earlier in the month by walking out of a model train shop with a set of signals tucked under my raincoat. As if it makes it any better, they weren't for me. They were for a railway enthusiast friend of mine.

Then there was tobacco. All of us stole cigarettes – with varying degrees of risk en route. Tommy, our fourth member, carried the main responsibility and was fairly confident, given that his mum, his dad and his mum's sister all smoked, and there were packets of fags all around the house. In the end, we had enough tobacco for four large pipes – let alone miniature ones.

One day after school, we assembled and went off to the nearest Woolies – four very excitable twelve-year-olds out on a criminal enterprise.

Jemil and I walked into the store to find it fairly deserted. We wandered around until we found the pipes – halfway down one of the long counters. Jemil stayed up one end, where he had a good view of the store. At a nod from him, I grabbed four pipes and stuffed them into my pocket. There were no security cameras in those days, and we made our way to the exit, buying some sweets on the way out just to seem legitimate – all the time experiencing huge adrenaline rushes. The matches from the nearby corner shop were less of a challenge. Micky, who had been tasked with this, just waited until there was no one in the shop and the owner had left the counter and then grabbed a box. We stood out in the street – hearts pounding. This was a Tuesday, and we'd already decided that we'd execute our grand plan the following day.

Wednesday afternoon came, and the four of us, having been dismissed at the end of school, managed to sneak up one of the many staircases to a small classroom at the top that we knew was hardly ever used. We arranged some chairs around a desk so that we were facing each other and proceeded to take the cigarettes apart and stuff the tobacco into the tiny pipe bowls. Soon, us twelve-year-olds were leaning back on our chairs and puffing away like adults.

Until, that was, we heard the heavy tread of footsteps coming up the stone staircase. We froze – looking at each other and hoping that whoever it was wasn't about to appear at the open door.

No such luck.

A moment later, big burly Emlyn, the caretaker, large belly and red face, came wheezing in. There was no time to hide the evidence.

'What you lot doing here?'

If the smell, and the smoke, didn't give us away, the evidence on the table and in our hands certainly did. He looked from one to other of us – his brow furrowed. Eventually (Emlyn wasn't that bright), the penny dropped.

'Right! Clear that lot away and come with me.'

By this time, all the bravado and excitement had drained away, and the mini-adults had become little boys again. We followed Emlyn down the stairs in silence and out to the school's entrance.

Once there, there was no discussion. It was, 'Get off home now. You'll be seeing the head in the morning.'

We sloped off home, tails between our legs. The next day, one by one, our parents were called in. The other members of the gang received a variety of punishments. In my case, my father, instead of thrashing me, offered me £5 if I didn't smoke until I was twenty-one. It was a very tempting offer in the 1950s – about £100 in today's money. The bribe worked, and I never smoked again. By the time I got to twenty-one, I had forgotten about that £5.

On to boarding school, where we assumed all the 'masters'

(no women teachers of course) smoked. Their staffroom was completely out of bounds – even for the more rebellious of us – but it was easy to imagine them puffing away during their breaks. I certainly remember being hauled over the coals for some misdemeanour by my housemaster. He frequently interrupted his admonishments by playing with his pipe, pushing tobacco into the bowl (like our grandads), lighting and relighting it.

In the 1970s, when I was working in Peckham, smoking was still popular. We had a head whose catchphrase was, 'Anyone got a fag?' The request seemed quite normal in those days. During my first headship in the 1980s, smoking was still commonplace amongst staff, despite solid evidence of the link between smoking and lung cancer. Staff offices were often shared, and if you happened to be billeted with a smoker, that was just too bad. One such office, apart from the giveaway smell, had nicotine-stained walls that, over a couple of years, had gone from white to dirty yellow. The potential for mass resignations put me off from taking any action.

I fared much better with my second headship. Being the first member of staff appointed, I was in a position to lay down some ground rules – one of which was no smoking on site.

Perhaps I should have been clearer about what 'site' meant. One day, looking out of the staff kitchen window, I spotted a smoker by the school gates.

'Who's that, and why isn't he in lessons?' I demanded of a colleague.

Clearly, my eyesight was failing. 'That's not a "he" – it's Rebecca Cleverly,' was the reply. Rebecca was deputy head of science – probably gearing herself up for a lesson on lung cancer.

Rebecca anticipated the 2007 legislation which banned smoking in enclosed public places and in the workplace. The era of smokers hanging around outside buildings – be they pubs, cafes, offices, etc. – had begun.

STUDENTS: THEIR PRIVATE AND PUBLIC THOUGHTS

Students have their preoccupations – often far removed from any thoughts about a school, particularly as they get into their teens and become increasingly conscious of their bodies, their sexuality and their relationships with their peers. These are areas that most teachers don't see, hear or know about.

I found this example in a classroom waste bin. What I was doing rummaging through it, I've conveniently forgotten. It was a tear-off self-assessment slip. On the front, the student had written the following (verbatim) thoughtful reflections on her work: 'I ave had most success with making my mechanism because I'm quite good at woodwork. I have had problems with graphics because I am not a very good drawer, I will attempt to solve them by trying harder and not giving up so easy.'

I was mystified as to why she (not 'he' as I was soon to discover) had jettisoned the comments until I turned over and found the following, very different, reflections. It is hard to work out who is going out with who, but you get the gist. The point is that her thoughts are for private consumption only or, maybe, with a close friend.

'Going out with Luke 4 months 1 day
Jodie, out with Jamie 2 weeks 4 days
Lucy, who split up for 1 week 2 days
So altogether, going out with Luke for 3 months 1 week
Today I've liked Luke for 4 months 2 days
12.5.96 went out with him the next day
I (heart) Luke. S'

Amongst the anecdotes in this book, there are others which tap into what lies beneath the surface of student lives, e.g., Beverley, Carol and friend in 'Under Your Skin', Mark in 'Suicide Note', and Michael in 'Mistaken Identity'.

Quite rightly, children with special needs get extra attention.

However, there is a strong argument for providing an outlet for every child for their thoughts, their worries, their concerns and their fears. Leaving these unexplored and sometimes festering explains, in part, why so many adults end up turning to counselling, or even therapy.

I regret I never attempted to survey, directly, the students I taught. However, what follows is a very brief 2021 snapshot, from three secondary schools, of what students like and dislike about their school.

They were given the following brief:

'I'm writing a book about schools and what students think of them. Your contribution would be really helpful.' They were asked to present their thoughts under two columns – 'Likes' and 'Dislikes'.

The majority of them took this as an invitation, as you'd expect, to talk about their subjects and their teachers. In amongst these comments, however, were some expressing deeper thoughts which, you'd think, the school would want to explore further. They are presented (again verbatim), and all come under the heading 'Dislikes':

'bad grades, not having friends, loneliness, spending time alone at lunch'

'there's always ganabe to be a person you want to punch but can't.'

'Teachers refuse to admit they're wrong as it would lessen their egos and damage their God complexes'

And here are a couple of 'Likes':

'When we talk with the teacher about non-lesson subjects in class.'

'My one friend'

Nearly half the respondents put 'Friends' in the 'Likes' list.

Earlier in my school career, one of my colleagues did a survey of his form. As a newly appointed head of English trying to establish a more relevant curriculum, he thought I'd be interested in these reflections from one of his brightest students. I hasten to add she wasn't the one I was teaching!

'English – I think English is OK if we're allowed to use our own imagination to write our own thing. Essays I find boring because we are told what to write about, and school isn't a very interesting subject. I like expressing my opinions about things.........Books we are given to read are normally so boring that I can't pick up the book, let alone put it down again. We should be allowed to write what we want to write. Not all the time but some of the time at least.'

If students' emotional needs are met – as well as their educational ones – then 'naughty' boys, such as the one below, might not resort to comments like this (from my Somers Town school):

Head of Maths: 'So, what are your plans now?'

Student: 'I'll take my exams and get out of this fucking shithole as soon as possible.'

TRUMPET

Around my fortieth birthday, I decided to learn the trumpet. I'd struggled with various other instruments, including the accordion in Paris! I loved the brassiness of the trumpet's sound and felt (pretty optimistically) that I might, at last, have found something I could play. The die was cast, and a friend recommended a teacher. I sat on our sofa, reached for the phone and, plucking up my courage, made the initial phone call…

Pause at the other end. Was my voice too deep?

'And how old did you say you were?'

'Forty.'

A further pause. 'Did you say fourteen?'

'No, forty.'

I could almost hear the cogs whirring at the other end.

'OK. I normally tutor children, but that's fine.'

Sometime later, but well before I'd mastered the valves and the embouchure and had tested my teacher's patience with unrecognisable renderings of well-known songs, I was taking my Grade 3 Practical. This didn't mean I'd passed Grades 1 and 2. At that time, so I understood, Practicals started with Grade 3. This was ambition on a foolhardy scale.

I enlisted my friend Maggie as accompanist. She was, and still is, confident, reassuring and tolerant – all qualities that were essential to support me. I knew she would calm my nerves, but I tested her to the full. The examiner – sixtyish, tall, slim, goatee beard, wearing a tweed sports jacket and tie – stood to one side waiting patiently, i.e., not looking at his watch despite a schedule to get through, while I, in common with all great soloists, was making sure the position of the piano was exactly right. All this was putting off the evil moment when I'd actually have to play. But if the piano was in the right place, the notes certainly weren't. So it was Grade 3 failed. Heading towards the end of my musical career.

In the meantime, I was to take my Grade 1 Theory. I was in my Hornchurch headship. The Grade exams were taken in a local school that, in common with many, metamorphosed into an AEI (Adult Education Institute) after six p.m. As those teachers working late leave, a group of institute tutors arrive. The local school just happened to be our rival – the head and the school described elsewhere ('Havering Inspector for Secondary Education'). That particular evening the institute had been turned into an exam centre, which was why I was there. I arrived just before six, hoping I wouldn't bump into my rival but preparing myself mentally to counter what I knew would be his charming – but subtly mocking – superciliousness. I walked through the entrance doors and into the spacious foyer milling with teenagers. No forty-year-olds in sight. They probably mistook me for an examiner rather than an examinee. In the middle of a group, I spotted the deputy, Llewellyn – friendly, genial, balding, rather overweight and with a lovely Welsh lilt to his voice. He was heading for retirement – partly to escape the head. There had always been a bond between us – probably generated by a shared, but implied, antipathy to his boss.

He grinned. 'What are you doing here?'

'I've come for my Grade 1 Theory,' I said rather sheepishly, hoping none of the other students would hear.

He didn't bat an eyelid.

'OK. Get your skates on. They're just about to start. You just go up those stairs into the hall. You'll be given a desk number, and you'll be sitting in pairs opposite another candidate. Good luck. Maybe time for a chat afterwards.'

I didn't take much of this in, dreading that one of my own students would spot me, and made my way up to the hall that looked like the typical exam centre it was, except that the long lines of individual desks emanating from the front had been replaced by small tables with two chairs opposite each other. Just as you might have when meeting a friend for a coffee.

I was given a desk number and directions by what looked like a sixth former. Most of the other candidates were already seated, and it didn't take me long to find my place.

I sat down and looked at the paper. Then I looked up and did a double (not to say triple) take. My 'pair' was Shelley Thomson –

not only a Year 9 pupil at my own school, but in the French class I was teaching for one period a week. She was actually fourteen, and by this time I was beyond forty. Shelley had a distinctive fringe and an open, alert face. She was polite and conscientious. If I had to meet one of my students in these circumstances, I could have done a lot worse.

'Hello, Sir.'

Shelley was far too polite to voice what must have been her shock at facing her headteacher.

'Hello, Shelley.'

There were no further pleasantries, and I hoped any shock I felt in metamorphosing from headteacher into pupil didn't show. I wondered what must have been going through Shelley's head. Meanwhile, the scraping of chairs continued alongside the chatter of nervous voices.

Eventually, as if by magic, the noise ceased. We could see up the far end of the hall a tall, grey-haired and dark-suited man.

'You may start now.' His voice echoed through the hall.

'Well, good luck, Shelley.'

'And you, Sir,'

We worked away, although I couldn't resist looking up from time to time. Maybe she did the same, but we never coincided, and our eyes never met. Eventually, 'Put your pens down please,' signalled the end of the exam.

Papers were collected, desk by desk, while we waited to be dismissed.

'How did you find it, Shelley?'

'Yeh. Good.'

'Well, see you tomorrow. Period 5, I think.'

I would love to have said: 'I'm sure I can trust you to be discrete,' but that might have suggested I didn't trust her. I knew that I would quickly have to get back into headteacher mode, and I had to trust that Shelley would prove as flexible. A tall order for her, I felt.

'Yes. See you, Sir.' With that, Shelley was off with, I'm sure, a sigh of relief at curtailing any more polite chat.

I was prepared for some comeback the next day. Some sniggering whispers, maybe. Possibly something worse from the usual culprits.

'How are your exams going, Sir?'

'Bit old for it, aren't you, Sir?'

'Grade 1, was it?'

But whatever, if anything, Shelley said to her friends and, I guess, parents, never came back to haunt me.

I got one hundred per cent – and I found that Shelley did too. But, unlike Shelley, who was soon playing in the school orchestra, I was never able to translate theory into practice.

ELEVEN

AN A-Z OF LEADERSHIP

I never fooled myself that I was God's gift to teaching, although I certainly experienced success and satisfaction en route. Triumphs were down to student responses when we ditched irrelevant books and schemes of work and hit the spot with programmes that engaged them.

I spent seventeen years as a teacher and fifteen as a head, but I eventually discovered that I was a better leader than a teacher. However, unlike teaching, where I like to think that myself and colleagues broke new ground, my leadership skills were more based on cherry-picking the ideas of others – nuggets of wisdom culled from a range of people and books. I list some of them below. I hope they'll resonate with many of you – and no doubt you'll have your own, quite different, list.

In 2018, 1,246 paperbacks were published with 'leadership' in the title. A 2020 survey showed fifteen thousand books on leadership and management in print. Many, many thousands more have bitten the dust. On top of that, literally, millions of articles on the subject have appeared – a high proportion belonging to academia and having no relevance for those at the chalkface, as it were.

'Leadership' – as opposed to management – is, in 2025, the

term in vogue. However, it hasn't always been thus. One of the great gurus, Peter Drucker – who published his first book on the subject eighty years ago – talks about management rather than leadership. Twenty-seven of his books are still in print. The nomenclature may have changed, but his wisdom endures.

In terms of layout, what follows is borrowed from another favourite writer, Robert Townsend. His book *Up the Organization*, also first published decades ago (1970) is still a bestseller. As recently as 2007, The Wharton Centre for Leadership and Change Management ranked *Up the Organization* first among eighty books that 'every manager must read'. He laid it out as an A-Z, and I have copied the approach.

My list contains lots of models. I hope that if they don't shed light on your own leadership style, they at least shed light on those you know. And, if nothing else, provide some food for thought. Here goes:

Appointments. Try to appoint people better than yourself. Easy in my case! Dictators will appoint 'Yes' men and 'Yes' women.

Arguments. If you can't win the argument rationally – as opposed to dictatorially – then how good is the argument?

Assume. Ass U Me. Never assume. We tend to make assumptions about people, their motives and actions. They also make assumptions about us. My story about the girls in the toilets (see 'Toilets') is a great example. I made an assumption that I didn't check out before charging in. For their part, the girls assumed their head had a small area of his brain which still functioned.

Attention to detail. Around the time I was looking for my first headship, I encountered Trevor Jagger – a wise ILEA chief inspector of schools. He offered a piece of advice, culled no doubt from hundreds of others, and that was 'attention to detail'.

He didn't mean moving a comma here, starting a paragraph there – rather making sure budget reconciliations actually add up, ensuring letters to staff or parents don't contain glaring errors or get school dates wrong. At my Barnet school, a field trip letter was sent out that included an equipment list. Halfway down, given it was likely to be cold, was the instruction to bring 'thick socks'. Unfortunately, the first 's' had been replaced with a 'c'.

Trevor Jagger also offered a question – 'Would you send your child to the school you're head of?' There are plenty of heads who would wriggle their way out of that one.

Break rules. General MacArthur, an outstanding leader in both World Wars, is quoted as saying, 'Rules are mostly made to be broken but too often they're for the lazy to hide behind.' However, great military leaders have a lot to teach us.

Blame your predecessor. 'He has a lot to live up to' is heard much less often than, for example, 'Given the circumstances, he did well' or 'Impressive – bearing in mind it wasn't really his forte'. Builders are the masters at the blame game. 'Who put this together then?' 'Was he qualified?' 'I hope you didn't pay much for that' etc. There is an old joke about the three envelopes. It can apply to any walk of life but let's put our own heads in the firing line.

The incoming head is replacing his failed predecessor. The predecessor leaves behind three envelopes. His parting advice…

'When things get tough, open these one at a time.'

Three months go by, and the honeymoon period hasn't been quite as smooth as our head would have liked. She opens the drawer containing the three envelopes. She tears open the first. It reads, 'Blame your predecessor.' She does, and things start to improve.

Another three months go by, and the school is sliding

backwards again. Our head opens the second envelope. It reads, 'Reorganise.' This seems to work.

Finally, however, nine months in, and hardly anything is working anymore. She opens the drawer one last time and pulls out the note. It reads, 'Prepare three envelopes.'

Gordon Brown – to his credit – often tells a version of this story.

The offices of football managers are littered with such envelopes.

Climate. Litwin and Stringer's 'Organizational Climate Questionnaire' (1968) was an attempt to identify elements of the work environment that influence the actions and performance of employees. It was trailblazing work and, as with so many good theories, it has survived, revised over fifty years on in different forms for different audiences. On the 'Leadership Programme for Serving Headteachers' (a government-funded training programme started in 1997), we used the following:

Flexibility
Responsibility
Standards
Rewards
Clarity
Team Commitment

Which of these is given prominence at any given moment depends on where the organisation is at. Obviously, in our case, the organisation was the school. The ideal is that if you are successful, you'll tick all of the boxes all of the time. The reality is that often, for example, Team Commitment may be high, but Standards are not. Or that there is too much Flexibility and not enough Responsibility.

Compromising. Townsend's *Up the Organization* suggests that compromise leads nowhere. 'If two sides can't agree, listen to them both and then pick one of them.' I can see how a compromise leaves neither side happy. However, as a natural compromiser, I find his suggestion challenging. King Solomon would agree with Townsend. He didn't cut the baby in half. Rather he came down on the side of the mother – once he'd worked out who the mother was!

Decisions. Stephen Covey's *The 7 Habits of Highly Effective People* has a brilliant decision-making matrix:

1. Urgent and Important, e.g., Meeting a bidding deadline for much-needed funds. Dealing with a fire.
2. Not Urgent but Important, e.g., Preparing a farewell speech for a departing colleague.
3. Urgent but Not Important, e.g., Waving goodbye to the football team as they head off for a match.
4. Not Urgent and Not Important, e.g., Changing the pictures around in your office.

An easy-to-remember and simpler variation on the decision-making matrix is, 'Do, Delay, Delegate, Dump.'

Under 'Not Urgent but Important', I found 'Sleep on It' useful as a way of avoiding kneejerk reactions – risking, of course, accusations of procrastination. Amazing how you can wake up in the morning and realise that, although the 'crisis' needs to be dealt with, it's no longer as urgent as you thought.

Delegation. And reflecting on delegation: Are you holding on to too much? Are you empowering others? How much responsibility are you giving your team? How much can they take? Are you micromanaging? Conversely, if you've established a shared culture where staff understand the big picture, your absence for a week might almost pass unnoticed.

Distributed leadership. This helps reduce the 'us and them' culture. At the school on the Isle of Dogs, all the senior staff's offices were ranged in a line down one corridor. Some wag christened it 'Hierarchy Boulevard', implying its remoteness from the 'real' world of the classroom. Try bringing middle leaders and younger staff onto your senior team on a rolling programme for a period of time. This way, you can start to make links between the top brass and the foot soldiers.

Eighty percent thinking, twenty percent doing. One of my colleagues attributed her success as a head – and she was hugely successful over a long period – to this 80/20 formula. I have to confess that I was never very good at thinking – unless I was doing it. It was probably 20/80 for me.

Failure. The classic mantra is that you learn from failure. It might be better to say that you can learn from failure, but you won't always.

The actor Will Smith's grandmother once told him, 'Don't let failure go to your heart and don't let success go to your head.'

James Dyson spent fifteen years creating 5,126 versions of his Dual Cyclone vacuum cleaner before he made one that worked.

On a tiny, tiny scale, I was a bit like Dyson in that I applied for nine headships before I landed at Hornchurch, information which may make you wonder why on earth you're reading this – or have read this far. The point is I didn't let failure get to my heart. Rather I combined bloody-mindedness with bit-by-bit analysis of where I was going wrong.

Flattery. I love Adlai Stevenson's words, 'Flattery's fine as long as you don't inhale.' Sadly I didn't take much notice of them when invited to apply for the post of Havering's secondary inspector (see above)!

Good practice. Share it!

Hard conversations. Don't duck them. Be clear but not cruel. Like all heads, I had to have hard conversations with staff when I felt they had been out of order by word or action. I tried to make sure I was clear, although I often imagined a subsequent conversation going something like this:

Friend of offender: 'So what did he say?'

Offender: 'You know... I'm not quite sure.'

Importance. Meaning your own. Never forget your own importance to your staff. Conversations with the head are likely to merit an evening debrief with friends or family. The conversations you have with staff should take this into account.

Instincts. Should you trust them or not? I certainly distrusted colleagues who 'knew' straight away who to appoint. Having said this, there are many who think that 'gut reaction' should be the only test. The truth probably lies nearer the middle. If you do have a gut reaction, be prepared to justify it.

Jobs. Does your personal spec include delving into a candidate's private life? It probably shouldn't, but it's easy to fool yourself into thinking you've got the right candidate when they tick all the 'academic' boxes. I have a dear friend who set up and ran a hugely successful IT company in the States. He cut his teeth at another company that included, in its appointments' process, inviting shortlisted candidates out to dinner – with their spouses. Of course, that was just wives in the early days! I used to suggest to colleagues that camping outside a candidate's house could help with assessments of character. One deputy I appointed actually wondered whether she had been subjected to this level of scrutiny!

Kids. 'Those bloody kids.' I can hear most caretakers I have known giving vent to their frustrations. And yet 'kids' don't have to be pejorative as in, 'I'm taking the kids' football training this afternoon.' What about 'pupils'? That's in pretty common usage in UK secondary schools. 'Students' is also often used, although it's also a way of referring to those at university. And 'children'? Are these younger? In the course of writing this book, I've struggled with the terminology – as have many writers – starting pieces with 'kids' and moving on to 'children'.

Kate Clanchy in the first fifty pages of her brilliant book *Some Kids I Taught and What They Taught Me*, refers to children, adolescents, students, kids, boys and girls. I'm not the only one struggling. As head, there is also a dilemma. Do you have a free-for-all, or do you try to standardise the nomenclature? For my money, that's overly prescriptive.

Keep your eye on the goal. Hard to do unless you know what the goal is!

Leadership styles. Daniel Goleman, Richard Boyatzis, and Annie McKee describe six distinct leadership styles in their 2002 book *Primal Leadership*. They suggest that no one style should be used all the time. Instead, the six styles should be used interchangeably, depending on the situation and the people that you're dealing with. Apart from 'Authoritative', which every leader should aspire to, can you identify any styles that you, or those around you, overuse – or underuse?

Affiliative: Useful when there are tensions amongst staff. However, although there may be a place for social events which bring people together and which are non-work related, wanting everyone to get on with each other and be friends can be seen as too touchy-feely and lacking in rigour.

Authoritative: This is seen as the most positive style, and the one which will characterise effective leaders. They inspire and move staff towards an agreed goal. The approach generates commitment.

Coaching: This is about developing your staff. It might include regular in-depth conversations focusing on long-term life goals or regular in-service training sessions. The style should be part of a leader's armoury but can be seen as external to the school's main mission: student learning.

Coercive: In 'Headteachers of All Sorts' (see above), there are numerous examples of leaders who only use this style. It's the 'telling style'. Do this, or else! However, it will be needed in crisis situations, e.g., to the caretaker, 'You need to get that lock changed straight away,' or to a child, 'Get to your lesson – now!'

Democratic: This style focuses on collaboration. Leaders actively seek input from their teams, and they rely more on listening than directing. It should develop, amongst staff, a sense of involvement. Overused, it leads to lengthy meetings perceived by many as time-wasting. It can also make assumptions about the readiness of staff for such an approach.

Pacesetting: The typical pacesetting leader will aim to 'pull a school up by its bootstraps'. Effective when they're drafted in to sort out one that is failing. Quick results are needed, but it's likely that long-term sustainability will be lacking. Such heads will often move on before their quick fixes are rumbled! Over a long period, it can lead to burnout, exhaustion and high staff turnover.

Leadership. 'To lead people, walk behind them.' – Lao Tzu

Loudest voices. Don't listen to them. They're rarely representative was a lesson I learnt from the early days of my first headship. (See above Hornchurch – 'Going Forward')

Mistakes. They're not the same as failures. Everyone makes mistakes – getting a name wrong, forgetting an appointment, punishing the wrong child. Admit your mistakes openly. Denis Waitley, an American motivational speaker, claimed, 'There are no mistakes or failures, only lessons.'

Never walk past mediocrity. The most successful heads are the most demanding in terms of standards. Michael Wilshaw, head of Mossbourne Community School between 2003 and 2011, was as demanding on staff as he was on students. Under his leadership, the school became one of the most successful in the country. He subsequently became Ofsted's chief inspector.

Optimists and pessimists. I love Albert Schweitzer's quote: 'To the question whether I am a pessimist or an optimist, I answer that my knowledge is pessimistic, but my willing and hope are optimistic.'

Open door. During the day, heads and senior managers need to be as accessible as possible to their staff. They certainly won't feel that way if doors are always closed. Paperwork can be done at home.

Peer group pressure. Teenage children experience considerable peer group pressure. So many of them will hide their ability for fear of being called a boffin or a swot. Just being a teenager itself is stressful enough. Gay and lesbian students will feel an extra layer of stress. Do they hide it or 'come out'? If they decide on the latter, how will their peers react? Our job as teachers is to give all children the strength to be themselves.

Pregnancy. Is it something in the air? The time of year? Something to do with the six-week summer break?

There's a knock on the open door.

'Andrew, can I have a word?'

'Course, Gill. What is it?'

'I've just told my family, and I also wanted you to know that I'm expecting a baby.'

'That's fantastic news, Gill! (Genuine delight – felt and shown). When's it due?' We discuss the staffing and timetable implications. I reassure Gill that we can sort things out.

Two days later. Another knock on the open door.

'Come in, Soulla. What is it?'

'Well, I wanted you…' The words are the same – just in a different order. My enthusiasm wanes just a fraction.

The following week Amanda knocks. Don't get me wrong, I am happy for her, but I'm starting to have nightmares about timetable gaps.

Three weeks after Amanda, it's Kruti who knocks on the open door – a door which, on occasions, I now wish was closed. It's the same story. I'm just hoping Kruti can't see inside my head, which is now full of Hieronymus Bosch nightmare scenes. Can I afford another session with my shrink? I'm desperately hoping the smile I'm still managing won't be seen as a rictus grin.

Pressure up, not down. Heads are in a unique position to exert pressure down, as we saw in 'Headteachers of All Sorts'. And it's so tempting to take aim at those under you. Football managers are brilliant at this. Jose Mourinho, for example, has always blamed his players for poor results and taken credit for good ones. When he was Prime Minister, one of Boris Johnson's inner coterie was described as a 'Kiss Up – Kick Down' boss. 2022 saw a shocking example of 'Kick Down' when, without warning, eight hundred P&O Ferries workers were sacked – by pre-recorded message!

Priorities and posteriorities. Most of us have 'to-do' lists. We might call them 'priorities' or put them in priority order. Items at the bottom of these lists often get carried from one list to the next. Peter Drucker termed these items 'posteriorities'. They're the ones we should decide not to tackle. Every time I write – or rewrite – a list, I have his phrase ringing in my ears. I try to follow it – with varying degrees of success.

Procrastination. Do you put off difficult tasks until the last possible minute – or even beyond. Going back to those lists above, I tried to tackle the hardest tasks first. Many would disagree and go for the easier ones. For me, if I do that, I've still got that knotty one hanging over my head.

Quick wins. My introduction of McDonald's vouchers at Hornchurch and my exclusion, at Barnet, of a boy before he'd even started worked in my favour. In those instances, I didn't hang about 'getting the feel'. If you go too far down that road, staff will think: a) Nothing's changed, and b) Who is this person? The other thing I did early on at Hornchurch was to meet with every member of staff individually. It took time but was well worth it in terms of me getting to know them and them feeling, quite rightly, that they were important in my eyes.

Radiators and Drains. I think it was Professor Tim Brighouse (ex-Schools' Commissioner for London) who coined this phrase. Of course, not all staff fall neatly into categories, but this one helped me focus on individuals – those whose dispositions were unremittingly sunny and those whose presence always cast a dark shadow. I worked with one head of a department whose sentences were always punctuated with sighs. I wanted to point this out to her but, probably wisely, ducked the confrontation. I tended to duck any encounter with her – unless I was feeling so positive that I could cope with some cold water thrown over me.

Resignations. These can seem even worse than pregnancies. And it's much more likely to be the staff you least want to lose. With someone who's been a pain in the arse for eighteen months, you can afford to use the 'I'm really happy for you' line, but when it's one of your star performers getting a promotion, you shouldn't just show your delight – you should feel it. If you're begrudging and being a dog in the manger about it, it will not, understandably, go down well with your staff.

'So. Did you tell him?'

'I did.'

'What was his reaction?'

'Bedrudging, I'd say.'

'Mean bugger, isn't he?' Or some such phrase.

Think about the various responses you got when you gave notice you were moving on.

Round Tables v. Square Tables. Round tables – good. Square tables – bad. Oblong tables – worse. Cabinet meetings continue to be chaired from an oblong table – as they have since the time of Gladstone, who commissioned it. It means that many of those on either side of him can't see him, and he can't see them. The ones at each end will inevitably feel marginalised – as they probably are. Vladimir Putin has been happy to inherit a table some twenty feet long. Visiting dignitaries are seated down one end. Putin seats himself at the other – thus projecting an image of power. By contrast, a round table sends out the message that all have an equal voice. The shape of the table and how you use it conveys a message. As head, you have to decide what message you want to convey.

Seating plans. There were no seating plans – as in telling students where to sit – when I started teaching. The nearest we got was, 'Jamal, you need to come and sit at the front', as you see him heading for the back of the class and managing to swipe Sarah's books onto the floor on the way. Most schools in 2025 now use seating plans them so as to mix girls and boys, separate the naughty ones and put different abilities together. Apart from anything else, they are a powerful classroom behaviour management tool. Most effective when changed regularly.

Sigmoid Curve. The Sigmoid Curve arose from the work of two French academics in the middle of the nineteenth century. It suggests that those who are successful in running organisations are self-reflective and will constantly be looking to refresh and reinvent their organisations and, by implication, themselves. The model suggests a way of looking at this process. In its original form, it posits:

1. An initial dip in the development of an organisation – the start of the purple curve (bottom left).
2. What happens next in successful organisations is that there is a period of growth (purple line curves up).
3. The growth cannot continue indefinitely, and eventually, there will be a dip (purple line starts to drop down).
4. Assessing when this dip is on the horizon can be tricky. However, it is better that changes are made sooner rather than later while the organisation still has the energy to reinvent itself, i.e., at A.
5. The cycle then repeats itself. The blue line has an initial dip followed by growth. At the point at which the initial growth (the purple line at A) would be declining, the blue line is still rising.

The theory obviously can't apply to every organisation in the same way, but it is potentially a useful way of looking at an organisation's development.

My successor at the Barnet school modelled the Sigmoid Curve brilliantly. She increased the school's size and established it as the centre of excellence for teacher training. This development went alongside establishing links with other schools as part of a multi-academy trust, of which she became CEO. At the same time, she started working as an adviser to the Department for Education. Thus she reinvented both the school and herself.

Stern love. The phrase 'stern love' is one I picked up from a colleague decades ago. I didn't realise at the time that it came from this quote by C.S. Lewis – 'Love is something more stern and splendid than mere kindness.' In the context of the school, you love your students, but you have to set boundaries. They may not like it, but it's what they need, and although you may not get the love, you'll get respect.

As head, you're often faced with staff, students and parents who are upset. How tempting to offer comforting words. What they really need is a way out of their distress.

Theory X and Theory Y. Douglas McGregor's *The Human Side of the Enterprise*, first published in 1960 and voted the fourth most important book on management of the twentieth century, is still, in the twenty-first, seen as a seminal work. In it, McGregor divides management into two styles: Theory X and Theory Y. Theory X is authoritarian, and Theory Y is participative. In the first, managers hold a negative view of employee motivations, and in the second, they make positive assumptions. According to McGregor, Theory Y managers who trust people to take ownership of their work produce much better results. Theory X managers believe employees must be commanded and controlled.

It's a crude distinction between the two but a useful way of looking at your leadership – and your staff! Some of them may want to be controlled and told what to do because being left to their own devices unnerves them. Others are itching to be let off the leash.

Thank you. Two terrific words. They must be sincere – but never neglected.

Traits. In 2008, Taibi Kahler published *The Process Therapy Model: The Six Personality Types with Adaptations*.

Scores of writers have written about personality traits – or types. Depending on the writer, anything from four to sixteen. Kahler's model is accessible without being simplistic. He is not alone in suggesting that there are behaviours which are established early in life in response to prompts and rewards by significant adults. We feel good when we demonstrate them and feel like failures when we don't.

Once we are aware of our traits, we can begin to make choices about what we want to change.

Which of these are you? And how many of these can you recognise in others? What do you think are the downsides of each one?

Be perfect: I need to get everything right and not make mistakes.

Please people: This has echoes of the Affiliative leadership style (see above). I want everyone to get on and like each other – and to like me!

Hurry up: I'm motivated by pressure and having a lot to do; I'm quick thinking and want to get on with things.

Be strong: I stay calm under pressure. I can make difficult decisions without worrying about their impact on colleagues. Overused, this might be termed the 'macho' style.

Try hard: There are links here with 'Be Perfect'. 'Try Hards' look at a problem from a variety of angles and never give up.

Uniform. My track record on school uniform is suspect (see 'Uniform and Hypocrisy').

The subject of uniforms – not just school uniforms – can generate robust debate, particularly amongst some sections of the liberal intelligentsia, for many of whom it smacks of authoritarianism.

As far as school uniforms are concerned, the 'pro' camp is in the ascendancy. The vast majority of countries worldwide insist on uniforms for their secondary school students. And this is increasing. In England in 2025, it's a brave head who resists the momentum. The cost argument has more or less disappeared, given that kitting out a child for their first day at secondary generally costs no more than £100. Put this against the designer wear that parents can be asked to fork out for when liberalism holds sway!

Contrast the above with Harrow (Eton is similar), where the cost of fitting out that same (well, not quite the same) Year 7 student will be about £1,000. This includes the Harrow Hat (boaters to us) at £39.50, plus a varnishing kit to preserve its blue silk band!

There is a famous picture of a couple of Harrovians taken in 1937 outside Lords Cricket Ground. They're wearing top hats and sporting canes. They're wearing top hats and sporting canes and are being gawped at by a group of kids, reflecting the class divisions that existed at the time.

It's now 2025 and, on top of Harrow's day uniform, there is a 'best' uniform. This is worn by school monitors before lunch on Sundays and includes top hats (£260) and canes £39.50

Apart from cost, uniform cuts countless hours off those frantic early morning conversations which take place where the choice is unlimited:

'Mum (sadly more likely than 'Dad'), I don't know what to wear.'

Will it be Converse, Doc Martens, trainers? If it's a skirt, which one? Jogging bottoms? Jeans? Trousers? Which top?

Nightmare for parents. Stressful for students.

Whereas no thinking is required for a standard school blazer, stick on badges, black trousers or skirt, white shirt, school tie, plain socks, and black shoes. The only challenge is 'Have they been washed?' and 'Where are they?'

Another factor is behaviour before and after school. If

miscreants are wearing uniforms they can at least be identified as school students. And if you can see the badge on their blazers, you can identify the school.

So, despite my own schoolboy reluctance – not to say defiance where the uniform was concerned – as head, I came down firmly on the side of 'one size fits all'.

V for versatile language. This means the ability to adapt to different situations, e.g., your use of language – especially important for students who must learn that talking to friends, family, teachers and lovers (assuming they're old enough!) all require different 'registers'. If a football has gone from one playground to another, 'Oi, Janet, give us the ball back' might do. But when it's gone in someone's garden, and you've knocked on the door, more appropriate would be, 'Sorry to trouble you, Mister, but our ball's gone into your garden. Can we have it back, please?'

Walking pace. Even if you have that 'Hurry Up' trait I refer to above, and your natural walking pace is fast, it's not good for staff to see you scurrying around the school. They may well think something's wrong somewhere and that you're on your way to dealing with it. A measured pace exudes a sense of calm and control, which you hope transfers to both staff and students.

X-rated. There's a Peter Cook and Dudley Moore sketch, 'This Bloke Came Up to Me'. It consists mostly of the C word. It's still available on YouTube. I include it as a question. What would you do if…?

In my case, I was covering a lesson as the head (a rare event, thankfully, in case you're wondering why I wasn't busy running the school). It was maths, and, for once, not only had work been set by the absent teacher, it was mostly engaging them. However, some twenty minutes in, I became aware of two boys sitting one behind the other, talking quietly. I was about to issue a 'You need to get on with your work', when I realised they were re-enacting the 'This Bloke Came Up to Me' sketch. I managed to contain a smile and let it run for a while. Eventually, I did resort to the 'You two need to get on with your work'. I sensed they were, misguidedly, relieved to think that they had not been overheard.

What would you have done?

- Nipped it in the bud?
- Sent them out?
- Punished them?
- Got them to repeat the sketch in front of the class? (A big risk that one.)
- Other?

Yes. A member of staff comes to you with an idea. Whenever you can, use 'Yes'. And if, as is often the case, the proposal being put to you is just too complex, demanding and expensive, try to avoid 'No'. Let them down lightly. Maybe a 'That'd be great, but...' Even, provided you mean it, 'We might well revisit that.' Or some such formulation.

Zoom. Remote learning has increased post-COVID, but schools are not able to follow the lead of the majority of organisations – coming in one day and working from home the next. Also, contact between students and teachers is more positive face-to-face. And students certainly don't want to be deprived of school as a social area where friendships are made.